HOSPITALITY, TOURISM AND MARKETING STUDIES

NEW TRENDS TOWARDS MEDITERRANEAN TOURISM SUSTAINABILITY

HOSPITALITY, TOURISM AND MARKETING STUDIES

Additional books in this series can be found on Nova's website under the Series tab.

Additional e-books in this series can be found on Nova's website under the e-book tab.

NEW TRENDS TOWARDS MEDITERRANEAN TOURISM SUSTAINABILITY

LUÍS M. ROSALINO,
ALEXANDRA SILVA
AND
ANTÓNIO ABREU
EDITORS

nova
publishers
New York

NOTICE TO THE READER

The Publisher has taken reasonable care in the preparation of this book, but makes no expressed or implied warranty of any kind and assumes no responsibility for any errors or omissions. No liability is assumed for incidental or consequential damages in connection with or arising out of information contained in this book. The Publisher shall not be liable for any special, consequential, or exemplary damages resulting, in whole or in part, from the readers' use of, or reliance upon, this material. Any parts of this book based on government reports are so indicated and copyright is claimed for those parts to the extent applicable to compilations of such works.

Independent verification should be sought for any data, advice or recommendations contained in this book. In addition, no responsibility is assumed by the publisher for any injury and/or damage to persons or property arising from any methods, products, instructions, ideas or otherwise contained in this publication.

This publication is designed to provide accurate and authoritative information with regard to the subject matter covered herein. It is sold with the clear understanding that the Publisher is not engaged in rendering legal or any other professional services. If legal or any other expert assistance is required, the services of a competent person should be sought. FROM A DECLARATION OF PARTICIPANTS JOINTLY ADOPTED BY A COMMITTEE OF THE AMERICAN BAR ASSOCIATION AND A COMMITTEE OF PUBLISHERS.

Additional color graphics may be available in the e-book version of this book.

LIBRARY OF CONGRESS CATALOGING-IN-PUBLICATION DATA

New trends towards Mediterranean tourism sustainability / Luis Miguel Rosalino, Alexandra Silva, Antonio Abreu, editors.
    p. cm.
  Includes index.
  ISBN 978-1-62257-627-2 (hardcover)
  1. Sustainable tourism--Mediterranean Region. I. Rosalino, Luis M. II. Silva, Alexandra. III. Abreu, Toqo.
  G156.5.S87N48 2012
  338.4'791091822--dc23
                      2012028160

Published by Nova Science Publishers, Inc. † New York

CONTENTS

PREFACE

Since the last half of the XX century the tourism sector represents a significant part of many countries' economies, as a major source of income and employment. Tourism provides entrepreneurial opportunities and today´s increasing demand for new products and destinations requires meaningful involvement and more responsible and sustainable tourism practices. The Mediterranean Basin has been identified by the WWF as one of the most important regions in the world, for its outstanding biodiversity, topographic and climatic features, east to west from Portugal to the shores of Lebanon and north to south, from Italy to Morocco and Libya. This environmentally fragile region is a leading touristic destination. Historically this region has been shaped by human influences creating the Mediterranean landscape we experience today. This constant human presence over several centuries is perhaps one of the main forces driving ecological loss and destruction in the region both in terrestrial and coastal marine areas. If sustainably managed, however, tourism can be an important tool for the ecosystems' conservation, by redirecting revenue towards for the preservation of the natural and cultural heritage and the implementation of research and education programs.

This book presents and discusses examples of contemporary and traditional sustainable nature based tourism practices within the Mediterranean Region, which can become effective pathways for regional economic development. Nature based activities in marine reserves or other protected areas, are examples on how the European Mediterranean Region natural heritage can be sustainably used as a touristic resource. Examples from whale watching in the Strait of Gibraltar's area (Chapters I) shows that among tourist industries based on wildlife-encounter, whale watching is a successful example on how the natural heritage can be sustainably used as a touristic resource, assuring a high socioeconomic yield to the local community and promoting the conservation of cetaceans.

The book also includes chapters on other present-day touristic approaches in the Mediterranean landscape, such as geotourism (Chapter II) and golf (Chapters III). Geotourism in Portugal focus on the establishment of nature itineraries to explore the geology (natural material and immaterial heritage) and its associated landscape. In chapter II, authors present examples of geotouristic activities anchored on western Portuguese geo-landscape characteristics. Golf represents the largest sports-related travel market and it is a growing worldwide industry. Chapter III reveals the Spanish reality, as it is the European country with the highest ratio of golf courses per inhabitants. Golf courses in Spain have a high performance regarding their sustainability, with few serious environmental and socioeconomic impacts, if management incorporates measures focused on hydrology and socio-economic profitability.

Portrayed in this book are also case-studies of the adaptation of traditional approaches to the contemporary management of available natural resources. These include modifications of hunting and nautical activities to the needs of present day touristic markets (Chapters IV and V). Hunting is one of the oldest human activities that directly tie to the exploitation of natural resources, first for survival and then related to social status, and recreational goals. Nowadays, hunting is a consumptive form of nature tourism and a growing business worldwide. Since it is based on the direct exploitation of game species, this touristic activity may rapidly become unsustainable. Chapter IV focus on the sustainability of recreational hunting tourism in Greece. The chapter assesses whether how hunters' requests and game management affects the persistence of this growing activity and may become an important economic activity. Nautical activities constitute a dynamic industry sector that has a key role in promoting environmental protection and awareness. It is clear that any deterioration in the marine ecosystem will have a negative impact on tourism in general and water-based activities in particular. The coastal characteristics of Croatian' Mediterranean coast make this region the perfect study area to evaluate the sustainability of nautical tourism. Chapter V shows how Croatian nautical tourist can be further developed to offer qualitatively better options. The greatest threat to its sustainability, however, is the "unchecked construction of new nautical facilities under the mounting pressure of the interests of equity capital". Authors point out the need to quantify the region's carrying capacity (i.e. available space) for determining the growth of new nautical accommodation infrastructure and simultaneously protect the aquatic environment. The authors conclude that management based on solid data and considering social and environmental factors as top priorities is the only route to sustainability.

Finally, the application of a Group of Tourism Sustainability Indicators (GTSI) to assess the state of the touristic sector is illustrated, using Portugal as a case study (Chapter VI). These indicators covered different areas that include Qualification, Diversification, Economic Relevance, Seasonality, Environment and Impact in the Community, and revealed that Portuguese tourism sector may be classified as generally sustainable.

We honestly expect that the various forms of alternative or sustainable tourism, such as 'nature-based tourism', presented in this book, can be a starting point to a broader discussion regarding the sustainability of the touristic offer within the Mediterranean region. We believe that what we call 'alternative' will become 'mainstream' within a decade. The examples presented, anchored on the cultural landscape (natural and man-made) of the Mediterranean region, intent to develop critical awareness of the ways in which tourism can enhance the welfare of people and protect the natural and cultural heritage sustainably.

Luís M. Rosalino[1,2] *and Alexandra Silva*[1,3,4]

[1]Isla Campus Lisboa, Laureate International Universities
[2]Universidade de Lisboa, Centro de Biologia Ambiental,
Faculdade de Ciências da Universidade de Lisboa, Portugal
[3]Universidade de Lisboa, Centro de Oceanografia,
Faculdade de Ciências da Universidade de Lisboa, Portugal
[4]Instituto Nacional dos Recursos Biológicos (INRB-IPIMAR), Portugal

In: New Trends Towards Mediterranean Tourism Sustainability   ISBN: 978-1-62257-627-2
Editors: L. M. Rosalino, A. Silva and A. Abreu   © 2012 Nova Science Publishers, Inc.

Chapter 1

TOWARDS A SUSTAINABLE WHALE-WATCHING INDUSTRY IN THE MEDITERRANEAN SEA

C. Elejabeitia[1], E. Urquiola[2], P. Verborgh[3] and R. de Stephanis[4]

[1]Calle Fernando Barajas Vílchez, Santa Cruz de Tenerife,
Canary Islands, Spain
[2]El Pinito, La Orotava, Canary Islands, Spain
[3]CIRCE, Conservation Information and Research on Cetaceans,
Algeciras Spain
[4]Department of Conservation Biology,
Estación Biológica de Doñana (CSIC), Américo Vespuccio, Sevilla, Spain

ABSTRACT

In the growing diversity of wildlife-encounter tourist industries, whale-watching stands out for its market success as well as for its contribution to the conservation of cetaceans and its significance to sustainable tourism. In the Mediterranean Sea, the area around the Strait of Gibraltar has become the most relevant whale-watching destination. Here, participating agents have been able to take advantage of the rich cetacean diversity, and the industry shows a growing trend towards a fairly balanced mix of quantity- and quality-driven operations. The Mediterranean offers a unique potential to develop a sustainable high-quality whale-watching industry. Along with the advances made to protect the rich cetacean fauna and its natural habitats in Europe, the resources and expertise necessary to develop this potential are widely available. However, it must be planned and managed in accordance with precautionary principles and sustainability measures that have been widely recognized by specialists and proven effective in ensuring minimum impact on natural resources and, at the same time, high socioeconomic benefits for the local community.

Keywords: sustainable tourism, whale-watching, Mediterranean

1. INTRODUCTION

Wildlife watching activities have proliferated and diversified exponentially in recent years (Higham et al., 2008). Among them, birdwatching has probably been a trailblazing industry, with the UK at the head of the list of traditional and popular destinations for this type of tourism (Sekercioglu, 2002). Other wildlife tours are currently offered in many regions, including remote areas (e.g. photo safaris in African savannahs) (Akama, 1996), trekking and hiking tours in tropical rainforests (Brockelman and Dearden, 1990; Valentine, 1992), or trips to view polar mega-fauna (Lemelin and Wiersma, 2007; Lemelin and Maher, 2009). More recently, but no less importantly, the development of marine nature tourism has opened up the possibility for the general public to experience close encounters with marine wildlife and enjoy unique landscapes and environments not commonly met with in everyday life. Snorkeling and scuba diving, for instance, are increasingly common tourist activities worldwide which, according to the figures provided by the Professional Association of Diving Instructors (PADI), recruits more than 900,000 new certified divers each year (PADI, 2009). Tours to observe sharks and rays have also become common and are even regarded as an important conservation and economic stimulus in places that develop this activity (Vianna et al., 2010). Finally, whale-watching tourism has expanded internationally at an exponential rate with increasing economic impact. Whale-watching has been defined as *"air, boat, or land tours, with some commercial aspect, to see or listen to any of the 84 species of whale, dolphin, or porpoise"* (Hoyt, 2007) and includes nature tours and cruises in which cetaceans are the main attraction. The origin of whale-watching dates back to the 1950's, when commercial tours began running off the San Diego coasts(Hoyt, 1995). By 1998, whale-watching operations had already been established in 87 countries with over 9 million whale-watchers and estimated total revenue of nearly one billion dollars. A decade later, in 2008, the numbers had risen to 119 countries, 13 million whalewatchers, 2.1 billion dollars in revenue (41.4% of which was tour ticket selling direct revenue), 13,200 employees and 3,000 related businesses (O'Connor et al., 2009).

Whale-watching is associated with a high degree of engagement with scientific research and high-quality operations. Much current cetacean research is conducted using both biological and ecological approaches, with a strong focus set on conservation issues (Rose et al., 2011). Over recent years, part of this research work has yielded an extensive body of literature dealing with, among other topics, the impact of whale-watching on cetaceans and their habitat (Scarpaci et al., 2010).

Furthermore, international workgroups and action programmes have been established in an attempt to build a common management framework for low impact, high-quality whale-watching, in which the International Whaling Commission (IWC) has played an important role. Notwithstanding such advances, the lack of information relating to nature tourism (Higgins, 1996) is no exception here.

In addition, other key socioeconomic issues for the development of a sustainable whale-watching industry (e.g. quality tourist supply chain and demand, marketing strategies, market leverage, and socioeconomic impact at destination) have not yet been addressed in sufficient depth. Despite these drawbacks, the whale-watching industry has experienced continued expansion with significant growth rates worldwide in the last 20 years (O'Connor et al., 2009).

The United States, Canada and Australia are pioneering countries and leading destinations in terms of numbers of whale-watchers, followed by South Africa, the Canary Islands, and New Zealand. Other renowned destinations include Argentina, Scotland, Brazil and Chile, while other regions in Asia, Central America and the Caribbean show signs of development (O'Connor et al., 2009). In comparison, the Mediterranean region does not attract outstanding numbers of whale-watchers even though several traditional locations are located here.

The Mediterranean Sea covers an area of 2.5 million Km^2 bordered by 21 countries. It is a dynamic tourist region with a unique mix of ancient and modern cultures and boasts valuable marine and coastal natural environments. It offers significant potential to develop a whale-watching industry that could serve as a role model for the development of sustainable tourism.

In this chapter, we will address the values of whale-watching and its typology (Section 2). We will also describe the possible stages in the evolution of a whale-watching industry, with special focus on the case of the Strait of Gibraltar as an example for the rest of the Mediterranean Sea (Section 3), and will look into the potential of whale-watching in other Mediterranean areas (Section 4). The limitations and requirements for the sustainable development and management of whale-watching will also be addressed (Section 5 and 6). Lastly, final considerations, management measures and actions necessary to integrate sustainability standards in the Mediterranean whale-watching industry will be included (Section 7).

2. VALUES AND TYPES OF WHALE-WATCHING

2.1. Values Provided by Whale-Watching

The mere existence of cetaceans provides a diversity of potential values and services, among which whale-watching is just one (IFAW, 1997). With the development of a whale-watching industry, a similar wide range of values and services can be materialized: recreational, scientific, educational, financial, cultural, social, aesthetic, spiritual/psychological, political, environmental, ecological etc. (IFAW, 1997). In combination, such values and services can provide an overall impact that is worth far more than the sum of each one considered independently. The reason behind this is that the perceived benefits are amplified and additional services crucial to sustainability are provided: continuity is supported, synergies are created, and resistance to change is minimized. For example, a whale-watching site can have greater appeal if it offers attractive landscapes combined with other environmental or cultural values. The potential contribution of a whale-watching industry to local development will be more significant if it also provides scientific research and educational services to the community; or a whale-watching industry with low environmental impact is likely to get greater support from the local community. The range of values and services mentioned means that whale-watching can be carried out with a variety of purposes, e.g. recreational, commercial, educational, or scientific. The choice of whale-watching operations possible and their role in the promotion of sustainable tourism will be addressed further on.

2.2. Whale-Watching Platform Types

Depending on the platform type used, whale-watching can be carried out from the air, sea or land (Hoyt, 1995). Sea-based whale-watching is by far the most extended type worldwide. Several types of vessels are used for this purpose: canoes, kayaks and different types of motorboats (rigid-hull power boats, inflatable, with submarine vision), refurbished fishing boats, antique sailing boats, modern multi-hull catamarans, and large passenger ships (Hoyt, 1995, 2001; O'Connor et al., 2009) (Figure 1).

Sea-based platforms facilitate a more direct encounter with the animals and also offer added values that can enhance the thrill of an encounter with free ranging cetaceans. They provide an experience of travelling by sea; they can be used as a means of transport between locations and to facilitate access to environments and landscapes which would be hardly accessible otherwise. Besides, the appeal or cultural interest that a vessel itself may have can add quality to the experience. The type used will depend on the characteristics of the target cetacean species and population, and on the materials and human resources required. Other factors can play a role, such as business strategy, market conditions, limitations imposed by regulations, or the climate and weather conditions in the area. For example, areas with favorable conditions for navigation, such as the Alboran Sea (S.E. Spain), offer the possibility of running whale-watching tours on a full-day basis using small powerboats, such as semi-rigid speedboats (zodiac-type) - a possibility that is of particular interest given the fairly long distance at which the animals are found off the coast (Cañadas et al., 2005). This type of boat would be less suited for areas like the Strait of Gibraltar, where adverse weather conditions (mainly ocean swell and strong winds) are frequent, making the choice of larger and safer vessels the most appropriate option.

Figure 1. Type of whale-watching boat used in the Mediterranean Sea.

In other areas like the Ligurian Sea, off France, Monaco and Italy, where cetaceans are frequently found at even greater distances from the coast (Gannier, 2005; Gannier and Epinat, 2008; Praca and Gannier, 2008; Laran and Gannier, 2008; Praca et al., 2009; Panigada et al., 2011), multi-day whale-watching trips are more likely to be successfully offered. In such cases, vessels must be properly equipped for long cruises. Land-based whale-watching can be carried out either with or without the use of optical equipment, ideally from platforms with a high probability of sightings. Lookout points should be easily and regularly accessible, and should offer a direct view of cetacean residence areas or migratory routes. They should also be sited in areas of natural beauty and enjoy frequent favorable weather conditions. Many coastal lookout points on the Strait of Gibraltar are suitable for watching fin whales passing during their migration, since the degree of predictability in this area is very high (Gauffier et al,. 2009; Bentaleb et al., 2011). In contrast, land-based whale-watching is barely viable in the Ligurian Sea, where cetaceans are mostly found in deep offshore waters (Gannier, 2005; Gannier and Epinat, 2008; Praca and Gannier, 2008; Laran and Gannier, 2008; Panigada et al., 2011). Like sea platforms, land platforms can also offer additional appeals. For example, the lookout points ("*miradouros*") originally used by traditional whale hunters to spot their prey in the Azores and Madeira islands (Portugal) (www.ecomuseu-azores.org; www.museudabaleia.org) now support whale-watching activities and are marketed as an historic-cultural tourist attraction (Gauffier et al., 2009).

Air-based whale-watching can be carried out from helicopters, planes or other types of vehicle used for aerial navigation. It allows a unique zenithal vision of the cetaceans and a broad view of the marine scenery. The thrill that the experience of flying can provide will intensify the impact of a whale-watching trip on the participant. Whale-watching air tours are offered at several destinations in Argentina, the United States, Canada, Australia, New Zealand (O'Connor et al., 2009) and France (Mayol et al., 2009), amongst others.

3. DEVELOPMENT OF A WHALE-WATCHING INDUSTRY. THE CASE OF THE STRAIT OF GIBRALTAR

The values and services provided by cetacean-watching activities are basic motors in the evolution of economic activity at a destination or in a region. Included among them are the values which directly affect the participating agents - whale-watchers, researchers, tour-operators and nature guides - as described for ecotourism (Wells, 1997). However the flow-on effects on the local economy and social perceptions must also be considered since these can be decisive for local growth and extend far beyond the local economic structure. Tourism is a dynamic, globalized, and multidimensional industry that may directly or indirectly cause significant impact on the local socioeconomic structure (e.g. conditions in the labor market, restrictions in the use of natural resources and limited access). The success of a given strategy designed to develop a tourist business or destination may cause a "copycat" effect on other local businesses and other destinations, which in turn may accelerate the emergence of desired or undesired effects. These may erode the image perceived by local people, visitors and potential travelers, as we will see further on, and the reputation of a given destination and tourist activity may suffer. A shift in the demand from, and social acceptance of, tourism could affect many businesses at the destination but also other non-local businesses (tour operators, other product and service suppliers that depend on tourist flows) and agents participating in the tourism industry. The worldwide iconic image of cetaceans has contributed to the reputation of whale-watching as a tourist industry deeply concerned with the conservation of the environment. Along with the success of whale-watching in the tourism market, the substantial values provided by the activity have become relevant in other areas such as environmental education, awareness-raising, conservation management, and scientific research, as well as a source of income and employment. Whale-watching tours should ideally be projected as an ecotourist experience, or at least incorporate a strong educational component by including, for instance, other marine fauna, *"in order to appeal to more people as well as to give a well-rounded ecological interpretation"* (Hoyt, 2002), or other socio-cultural resources and attractions related to the whale-watching experience. Ecotourism has been defined as *"responsible travel to natural areas that conserves the environment and improves the well-being of local people"* (TIES, 2010), and must therefore be regarded as a role model for sustainable tourism. The benefits that ecotourism can provide have been widely emphasized (e.g. protecting the local culture, stimulating the development of local facilities, improving governmental support, and promoting intercultural exchange and a better understanding of other cultures). Nonetheless, ecotourism also has its drawbacks: its implantation may lead to weakened personal relations and loss of cultural authenticity and sustainable lifestyles, which in turn can result in social conflict, increased levels of pollution and noise, overcrowding, socioeconomic unbalance, cultural alienation and finally, dependence on industrialized countries (Dogan, 1989; Mansfeld and Ginosar, 1994; Brohman, 1996).

Butler's Tourism Area Lifecycle Model (1980) argues that tourist destinations pass through different stages as they become more popular, thereby following a "birth- growth-maturity" pattern. A similar trend has been observed in traditional whale-watching regions (Forestell and Kaufman, 1996). In this respect, Doxey (1975) proposed a model that reflects different stages in the local community's reaction to the development of tourism at the destination which range from initial euphoria, passing through antagonism when confronting the negative effects of the development of tourism and, eventually, adaptation and acceptance of the new situation (Figure 2).

Based on Butler's model, Forestell and Kaufman (1993) suggested that the businesses involved in whale-watching operations experience similar phases, starting from discovery and competition as the industry develops, through confrontation when regulatory entities get involved, to eventual stability when the industry reaches maturity (Figure 2). Moreover, Duffus and Dearden (1990) argued that even the whale-watching public follows a similar pattern: during the early stages, when the destination is underdeveloped in terms of infrastructure and the flow of visitors is limited, participants are predominantly "expert-specialists"; i.e. experienced visitors with specific expectations and a special interest in whale-watching who do not require extensive facilities. As the number of visitors grows and new infrastructures are developed, a "novice-generalist" type of visitor becomes more common. These visitors tend to have little or no prior experience or knowledge of the activity, no specific expectations, and generally demand more developed facilities. If, eventually, the limits of acceptable change are exceeded, "expert-specialists" will no longer be attracted to the site due to its excessive degree of development and will move to other destinations. While infrastructure generally develops at a rapid pace to cover the increasing demand, the management of whale-watching activities tends to evolve at a slower pace.

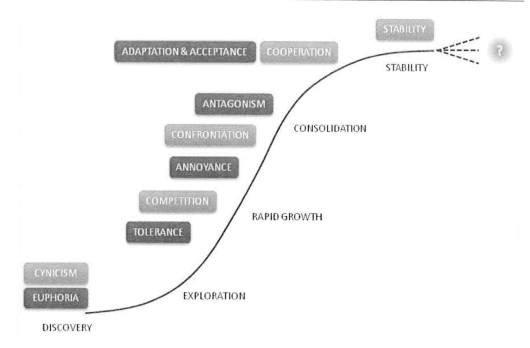

Figure 2. Stages in the development of a whale-watching industry and relations and reactions associated with operators (in grey, adapted from Forestell and Kaufman, 1996), and with the local community (in black, adapted from Doxey, 1975).

The experience enjoyed by the visitor at the destination site will determine whether the conservation message is coming through or not. Clearly, the need for a strong educational component will grow as the destination becomes dominated by "generalists" as these tend to adopt preconceived perceptions, have unrealistic expectations, and show demands and anthropomorphic behaviors clearly dissociated from nature e.g. feeding the animals or expecting excessively close encounters or even direct contact (Higham, 1998)). A phase of stability does not necessarily represent the culmination of the whale-watching industry at a destination. Much to the contrary, it can actually serve as a turning point for further future development. Whether the industry continues, renovates or declines will largely depend on the strategy followed after reaching this stage.

The development of a whale-watching industry requires three basic inputs: 1) a cetacean population, 2) visitors and 3) funding for infrastructure development. In turn, the industry must generate three main outputs: 1) economic development through sustainable operations, 2) social values based on education and low environmental impact, and 3) improved cetacean conservation through research in order to support sustainability (IFAW, 1997). Several researchers have contributed with models and guidelines to steer the development of a balanced industry. Orams (1999), for instance, proposed four different approaches for the management of marine tourism (physical, regulatory, economic, and educational). Hoyt (2007) presented a set of lines of action for achieving high-quality and sustainable whale-watching operations, whereas Higham et al. (2009) defined four types of key agents (social research, tourist operations, planning and management, and research of the natural resources and the environment) and proposed an integral adaptive management model composed of "micro-", "meso-" and "macro-" levels, which stressed the importance of natural resource planning and management. However, despite their generalized acceptance, theoretical models cannot completely mirror the real evolution of a tourist (whale-watching) destination. Intense social research work is therefore required to produce reliable data which can help guide managers through the different stages of the facility's life-cycle and monitor their impact (Johnson and Snepenger, 1993).

Whale-watching in the Strait of Gibraltar: an example of rapid evolution in the Mediterranean Sea.

While understanding that the implications and impact of developing a whale-watching industry depend on previously existing conditions, we will focus on the case of the area of the Strait of Gibraltar to provide an example of how whale-watching can contribute towards sustainable (tourism) development. The Strait of Gibraltar is probably one of the most important areas in the Mediterranean in terms of the development of whale-watching activities (Carbó Penche et al., 2007). The industry was established in 1982, when the first tours started to operate in the Bay of Algeciras (Figure 3). Nowadays, three types of whale-watching tours are offered in the region. The first type consists of two-hour trips departing from the ports of Algeciras, La Línea and Gibraltar to watch common and striped dolphins (*Delphinus delphis and Stenella coeruleoalba*) in the Bay of Algeciras (Bay of Gibraltar) (Area 1 in Figure 3). Secondly, 2-hour tours depart from the port of Tarifa. These trips search mainly for long-finned pilot whales (*Globicephala melas*), but other species are also sighted, such as bottlenose dolphin (*Tursiops truncatus*), sperm whale (*Physeter macrocephalus*), and common and striped dolphin (Carbó Penche et al., 2007; de Stephanis et al., 2008).

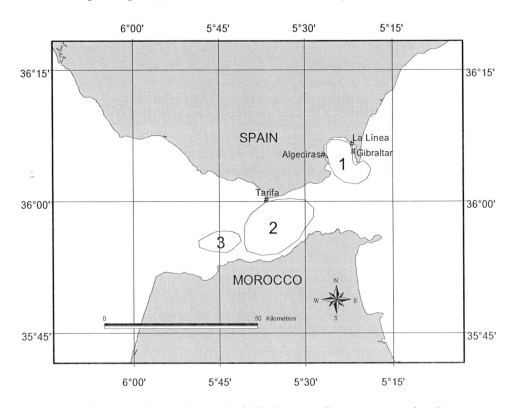

Figure 3. Types of whale-watching in the Strait of Gibraltar according to target species: Common dolphin (1): long finned pilot whale (2); and killer whale (3).

Figure 4. Killer whales (*Orcinus orca*) in the Strait of Gibraltar.

They also take advantage of occasional sightings of fin whales (*Balaenoptera physalus*) during the months of May and June (Gauffier et al., 2009; Bentaleb et al., 2011) (Area 2 in Figure 3). Finally, the third type of whale-watching trip in the Strait of Gibraltar benefits from the interactions between orcas (*Orcinus orca*; Figure 4) and red tuna (*Thunnus thynnus*) fisheries occurring from mid June through to August (Guinet et al., 2007; de Stephanis et al., 2008).

This offer consists of 3-4 hour trips organized solely when interactions take place, which may not occur every year owing to current legal restrictions on tuna fisheries (Area 3 in Figure 3).

On the whole, the following factors have contributed to the rapid development of the whale-watching industry in the Strait of Gibraltar area: tourist attractions with easy and regular access, visitor volumes above the critical threshold, product diversification, entrepreneurship and available expertise. Andalusia, and more specifically Tarifa and Gibraltar, are popular tourist destinations, and whale-watching businesses have successfully adapted their offer to the conditions of the local tourist industry. Visitors travel to Tarifa not only from nearby areas but also from other locations more than 200-250 km away (Carbó Penche et al., 2007). On this basis, together with the permanent presence of cetaceans accessible within a short distance from the coast, the local whale-watching industry has matured within a short period of time (De Stephanis, 2007; de Stephanis et al., 2008). Whale-watching businesses have been able to attract visitors with two different and compatible products (short two-hour trips or longer 4-hour tours). They have also managed to counter the frequent bad weather conditions by transferring their area of operations to the bay of Algeciras when strong East winds do not allow navigation in the Strait.

The whale-watching industry in Tarifa has to a large extent developed in accordance with the models used to describe the evolution of a whale-watching destination and the typology of operator businesses and visitors participating in a growing whale-watching industry.

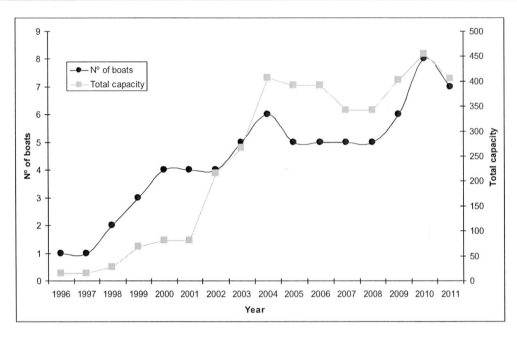

Figure 5. Evolution of the whale-watching industry in the Strait of Gibraltar area by number of boats and passenger capacity (1996- 2011).

The business started in 1998, when two foreign specialized entrepreneurs began to offer whale-watching tours from 15-passenger capacity boats in Tarifa. Between 1998 and 2001, local businessmen in the nautical sector benefited from the experience and began to set up their own whale-watching businesses, resulting in the establishment of five new businesses by the end of this short period. As the industry matured, the smaller boats that had been used during the earlier stages were progressively replaced with higher capacity motor boats (Figure 5). More recently, in 2009, a third type of business seeking to offer a differentiated product with the incorporation of new types of vessels (small rapid inflatable boats and sailing vessels) started to flourish in Tarifa. In parallel, several associations have started educational and volunteer programmes to try to conserve the various whale and dolphin populations present in the Strait. Volunteer programmes to study fin whale migrations are run during the months of May-July and November-December. At the same time, various local authorities are developing an interpretation center that will be connected with the operating whale-watching companies, thus offering a new educational product which will attempt to fill in the low season with school visits and provide formation for the whale-watching crews.

Nowadays, the whale-watching industry in Tarifa employs approximately 40 professionals during the high season (summer months). According to estimates given by the representatives of whale-watching businesses, there were nearly 39,000 whale-watching visitors during 2011. Approximately 35,000 of them (89.7%) took long-finned pilot whale tours and 4,000 (10.3%) opted for orca tours. The total direct income was estimated at around 1,000,000 €, with an estimated 39.3% "direct income/total income" ratio for whale-watching operations in the Spanish Mediterranean (O'Connor et al., 2009) (Table 1), meaning the whale-watching industry in Tarifa generates some 2,550,000 € per year (2,300,000 € corresponding to pilot whale tours and 250,000 € to orca tours).

Table 1. Whale watching economics in the Mediterranean Sea in $ (adapted from O'Connor et al, 2009 and authors observations). DI=Direct Income, TI=Total income

Country	Whalewatchers 1998	Whalewatchers 2008 (WW)	Operators 2008	Direct income 2008, in $ (DI)	Indirect income 2008, in $	Total income 2008, in $ (TI)	DI/WW	DI/TI
Spain (Mediterranean) 2011	25.000	70.000*	20*	2.968.961*	4.579.482*	7.548.443*	42*	39,3%*
Gibraltar 2008	1.875	35.371	8	834.077	1.664.551	2.498.628	24	33,4%
France (Mediterranean) 2008	712	5.258	22	739.569	811.565	1.551.134	141	47,7%
Italy 2008	53.000	14.415	6	839.426	1.836.437	2.675.863	58	31,4%
Cyprus 2008	-	<100	1	2.906	2.522	5.428	29	53,5%
Croatia 2008	21	24	1	29.090	8.093	37.183	1.212	78,2%
Greece 2008	3.678	3.283	7	297.546	407.897	705.443	91	42,2%
Slovenia 2008	-	21	1	8.866	4.431	13.297	422	66,7%
TOTAL (AVERAGE)	53.461	128.372	66	5.720.441	9.314.978	15.035.419	(44)	(38%)

* Based on own estimations for 2011.

In economic theory, the term "value" refers to the exchange value of a good. Given that money is the medium of exchange, the value of a good will be determined by its price (i.e., the amount of money for which it would be exchanged).

In reality, the price of a good is not set by its value of exchange alone, since the money that a potential buyer is willing to pay for it will also influence the final price. This concept is known as "willingness to pay" (WTP) (Just et al., 1982).

Recently, a number of studies have focused on the WTP in relation to different species. In this sense, Loomis and White (1996) conducted a review of the benefits that rare or endangered species have the potential to offer, which was later updated by Richardson and Loomis (2009). Both studies show, that in 1996 the price willing to be paid was related to the change in size of the population of a species. In 2009 however, not only the change in population size, but also the frequency of payment, the type of species or whether the species was considered as "charismatic mega-fauna" or not, affected the WTP.

Considering the characteristics of long finned pilot whale and orca populations in the area of the Strait of Gibraltar, the following reasoning can be suggested.

In the case of long finned pilot whales, the clan (Stephanis et al., 2008b) comprises approximately 213 individuals (Verborgh et al., 2009a) and resides in waters of the Strait of Gibraltar all year round (de Stephanis, 2007). The group's life expectancy is estimated at 56 years (Verborgh et al., 2009). Therefore, given that whale-watching tours targeting this group generate approximately 897,000 € annually, direct and total incomes could add up to 50,232,000 € and 127,816,793 € respectively throughout the whole life expectancy period of the animals assuming current visitor numbers. Each individual would thus be valued at 600,079 € (based on total income). Similarly, in the case of orcas, whale-watching trips target two different pods which together represent 16 individuals (Esteban Pavo, 2008). The species has a life expectancy of 60 years. Applying the same mathematics, the potential value of both pods could amount to 6,180,000 € (direct income) and 15,725,190 € (total income), meaning that each orca could be valued in 982,824 € (based on total income).

While bearing in mind that further factors need to be considered in order to obtain a more realistic assessment of the real value of cetaceans in the area of the Strait, and conscious that extrapolation of the conclusions of this example to other areas could prove risky, the resulting figures provide an idea of the potential contribution of cetaceans to economic development through sustainable tourism in the Mediterranean.

4. FROM THE RESERVE TO THE RESOURCE. THE POTENTIAL FOR WHALE-WATCHING DEVELOPMENT IN THE MEDITERRANEAN

A natural resource is any material or component ("service") provided by nature with potential economic value. When a natural resource is exploited and its potential value is realized, it then becomes a factor of production. Both terms apply in the case of cetaceans in the Mediterranean, since the animals provide a real socioeconomic value (as is the case of whale-watching in the Strait of Gibraltar), but at the same time they also offer a potential value for other regions, even if for cultural or social reasons this potential has not been made effective.

Figure 6. Bottlenose dolphins (*Tursiops truncatus*) in the Mediterranean Sea.

Mediterranean is the world's largest interior sea. Nine cetacean species are found here (Reeves and Notarbartolo-di-Sciara, 2006). Among the coastal species, only the bottlenose dolphin (Figure 6) has been included in the European Community's Habitat Directive (EEC/92/43, Annex II). Although there are no total population estimates available for this species, it is known that its distribution practically covers the entire Mediterranean. However, common dolphins are abundant only in the Alboran Sea (Cañadas, 2006) , living in its northern coastal range (Cañadas et al., 2005).

The species has practically disappeared from the rest of the Mediterranean Sea although its presence has been detected in Moroccan and Algerian waters and smaller groups have also been sighted in Greek waters and the Ligurian Sea (Reeves and Notarbartolo-di-Sciara, 2006).

The striped dolphin is by large the most common dolphin species in the Mediterranean, with an estimated population of 117,880 (95%CI=68,379-214,800) individuals in 1992 (Forcada et al., 1994). The species is mainly pelagic, and therefore less commonly found near the coast, but is nevertheless widely distributed throughout the Mediterranean (Forcada et al., 1994, 1995; Frantzis et al., 2003, Gannier et al., 2005; Cañadas, 2006; de Stephanis et al., 2008a).

Of all the cetacean species described in this area, long-finned pilot whales are probably the best studied to date. The species has been described in both the Ligurian (Gannier and Epinat, 2008) and Alboran Seas, where population estimates reach 2,000 individuals (Cañadas et al., 2005, Cañadas, pers comm), but is practically absent in the eastern basin of the Mediterranean. Pilot whales are assumed to present a matrilineal social structure (Amos et al., 1991, 1993; Schlötterer et al., 1991; Amos 1993; Heimlich-Boran, 1993; Fullard et al., 2000) and, like striped dolphins, also exhibit pelagic behavior (Cañadas and Sagarminaga, 2000; de Stephanis et al., 2008a).

Figure 7. Sperm whales (*Physeter macrocephalus*) in the Mediterranean Sea.

Their vertical distribution at sea typically ranges between 500 to 1,000 m below the surface (de Stephanis, unpublished data), where they feed primarily on squid (Stephanis et al., 2008c) . Within the Spanish Mediterranean, they are easily observable in waters off Murcia (ca. 200 individuals identified), Almeria and Granada (de Stephanis, unpublished data), as well as in the Strait of Gibraltar which harbors a resident population of around 213 individuals (De Stephanis, 2007; Verborgh et al., 2009b). Risso's dolphins (*Grampus griseus*) and Cuvier's beaked whales (*Ziphius cavirostris*) are another two species of cetaceans that can be observed (Gannier and Epinat, 2008). While the former is found throughout the Mediterranean (Reeves and Notarbartolo-di-Sciara, 2006), the latter is only present in the Alboran sea (mainly off the coast of Almeria), the Ligurian Sea (Gannier and Epinat, 2008) and in Greek waters (Frantzis et al., 2003). However, owing to the rarity of Risso's dolphins, and the outstandingly long and deep dives typical of Cuvier's beaked whales (Baird et al., 2006), sightings of these two species tend to occur on a more sporadic basis.

Another cosmopolitan cetacean in the Mediterranean is the sperm whale (Frantzis et al., 2003; Cañadas et al., 2005; Gannier and Praca, 2007; de Stephanis et al., 2008a; Praca et al., 2009; Pirotta et al., 2011) (Figure 7).

This species shows a unique social structure consisting of groups of females, calves and younger males. Adult and sub-adult males, on the other hand, live solitarily for most of their lives, although occasionally males in the reproductive phase have been observed to join groups in waters of the Balearic Islands (Pirotta et al., 2011) and Greece (Frantzis et al., 2003). The distribution of sperm whales is scattered over almost all of the Mediterranean (Reeves and Notarbartolo-di-Sciara, 2006), but the Strait of Gibraltar is a particularly good location for sightings (de Stephanis et al., 2008a). Here, the species is common and easily observable all year round (de Stephanis et al., 2008a), showing a peak presence during the months of November to July (de Stephanis, unpublished data). Sperm whales can also be sighted in the Ligurian Sea (Gannier and Praca, 2007; Praca et al., 2009), in waters off the

Balearic Islands (mainly during the summer months) (Pirotta et al., 2011), and in waters off the Greek islands (Frantzis et al. 2003). Individuals rarely migrate between the Atlantic and the Mediterranean basin, with only one case described in the literature (Frantzis et al., 2011). This behavioral isolation has lead to the genetic differentiation of the Mediterranean and the North Atlantic populations (Engelhaupt et al., 2009).

Also present in the Strait of Gibraltar are the orcas or killer whales, which have been described earlier in this chapter. The population of this species in the area is comprised of a total of 47 individuals (Esteban Pavo, 2008).

Finally, there is increasing evidence of a pronounced presence of fin whales in the western Mediterranean (Panigada et al., 2011). This species gathers in the Ligurian Sea during the summer months (Panigada et al., 2011) and disperses to other Mediterranean waters during the winter (Bentaleb et al., 2011). It has been estimated that 10% of the Mediterranean population of fin whales could be crossing the Gibraltar Strait during the winter and spring months (Cotté et al., 2009, 2011).

The importance given to the conservation of cetacean reserves in the Mediterranean is evidenced by the characteristics and large number of marine protected areas (MPA) that have been proposed and created for these animals. This includes MPAs and MPA networks established on the basis of international agreements. As such, the Protocol for Special Protection Areas and Biological Diversity of the Barcelona Convention (1976) foresees the creation of "Specially Protected Areas of Mediterranean Importance" (SPAMI). The largest, most relevant MPA in the Mediterranean is the Pelagos Sanctuary for Mediterranean Marine Mammals (formerly Ligurian Sea Sanctuary). Covering 87,492 km^2, it was designated a cetacean sanctuary in 1999 and declared SPAMI in 2001. Also relevant is Natura 2000, Europe´s most important network of natural protected areas. It builds on the European Habitat Directive, which includes the protection figure of "Special Area of Conservation" (SAC). Several SACs specifically established for the protection and conservation of bottlenose dolphins are currently part of this network. These are mainly small and coastal areas, but the creation of further SACs off-shore and the re-definition of the existing ones in accordance with the broad distribution range of this species is currently under discussion.

A total of 19 MPAs in the Mediterranean have been formally proposed or recommended within the framework of another transnational cooperation network, the Agreement on the Conservation of Cetaceans in the Black Sea, Mediterranean Sea and contiguous Atlantic Area (ACCOBAMS). Member parties have been encouraged to work on the implementation of international open sea MPAs (Alboran Sea) as part of regional networking, and to take concrete and decisive steps towards the consolidation of cetacean protected areas within national jurisdictions. Other cetacean MPAs have been established on the basis of national legislation (for instance, the "Ischia-Regno di Nettuno" reserve in Italy and the Cres-Lošinj Special Marine Reserve in Croatia). Several other small marine-coastal protected areas (e.g. RAMSAR wetlands, national parks or marine reserves) mainly found in Spain and Italy may protect at least some dolphin habitat (Hoyt, 2005). Whale-watching is already an important activity in many of all these MPAs, while other reserves show a clear potential to develop it.

According to the worldwide report of the whale-watching industry (O'Connor et al., 2009), several countries in the Mediterranean already exploit cetaceans as a tourist resource. Approximately 20 whale-watching businesses operate on the Spanish Mediterranean coast, six in the Strait of Gibraltar area, excluding the Bay of Algeciras, and the rest on the Costa del Sol and other locations further north. The latest figures for 2011 estimate a total of 70,000 whale-watchers (own data, unpublished; adapted from O' Connor et al., 2009) and a total revenue of approximately 5.6 million €. In Gibraltar alone, 8 businesses offer dolphin watching tours in waters of the Bay of Algeciras. These received 35,371 visitors in 2008. Other countries with whale-watching businesses outside Spain include France, with 22 companies that operate trips ranging from half-day to 4-7 day tours in the Ligurian Sea (mainly to the Pelagos Sanctuary), Italy, with six operators, Greece with seven, and Croatia with just one (limited to 12-day tours to the Cres-Lošinj islands). Cyprus has no whale-watching businesses as such, but it does have a vessel dedicated to research operations. The minimal activity reported in Monaco and Slovenia is probably the result of the low sighting predictability in their waters or of reduced coastlines. Data for the North African coast is practically lacking, as this area is still pretty much an "uncharted" territory as far as cetaceans and whale-watching is concerned. However, based on a recent study (Cisneros-Montemayor et al., 2010) which reveals how whale-watching development directly relates to the number of tourist visits, and on the significant cetacean reserves that may well be found in African Mediterranean waters, it is expected that whale-watching activities will gradually develop in these countries, assuming, of course, that political stability will generate a recovery of tourist flows in North Africa. In this sense the proximity to consolidated whale-watching destinations like Tarifa, Gibraltar, and the Red Sea, gives Morocco and Egypt a good chance to play a prominent role in the development of the industry. The study also suggests that whale-watching might create a substantial boosting effect and suggests the whale-watching industry may grow at a rate directly proportional to the countries' economic development.

In 2008, whale-watching generated a total revenue of approximately 15 million dollars in the Mediterranean area (O'Connor et al., 2009). It has been argued that whale-watching has been overrated and that the success of any whale-watching industry at a destination derives from other tourist developments (Moyle and Evans, 2008).

In any case, it is clear that whale-watching can stimulate the local economy thus contributing to either the development of a tourist destination or re-positioning strategies in already mature locations. Moreover, it can provide opportunities for entrepreneurship, professional and business diversification, and can promote higher visitor expenditure if properly planned and managed.

Professional skills in tourism and whale-watching expertise are important cornerstones to increase whale-watcher expenditure at the destination through specialized high-quality services. Along with whale-watching professionals, scientific groups dedicated to cetacean research and environmental education provide an additional source of expertise. Fortunately, such highly-skilled professionals are widely available in the region - at least 20 conservation-related organizations exist in the Mediterranean Spain alone, and a number of groups are active in Italy, France, Greece, and Croatia and even in Mediterranean North Africa. Volunteer-tourism, ecotourism, and up-market operations carried out in Croatia (Cres-Lošinj), Spain (Strait of Gibraltar, Vera Gulf and Alborán Sea), France (Ligurian Sea), Slovenia and Greece, among others, represent a few good examples of the types of activity that take place. In many cases, it is the organization itself that carries out the functions inherent to a specialized tour-operator. Finally, it is worth recalling the importance of pristine environments for this type of tourist operation, to underline the socioeconomic significance of cetacean MPAs as instruments to promote low-impact, high–quality sustainable whale-watching.

Table 2. Some key data and significant aspects for the development of whale-watching in the Mediterranean

➢ Approximately 46,000 km of coastline
➢ High biodiversity (cetaceans, other marine-coastal), significant natural and historical and cultural heritage related to the sea
➢ A number of natural and cultural sites have been declared "World Heritage" and "Biosphere Reserve" by UNESCO, and growing MPA network.
➢ Good infrastructure available (marine, tourist, and communications).
➢ Whale-watching offers synergy and alternative income and employment in the nautical and fishing sector.
➢ Estimated growth rate of 7% per year in Europe, twice as much as world's average (O' Connor et al., 2009)
➢ Consolidated tourist culture and intense tourist activity
➢ Four Mediterranean countries (Spain, France, Italy, and Turkey) are among the top 10 leading destinations worldwide, by visitor number and tourism receipts.
➢ The recovery of Europe's intra-regional tourist demand can favor regional travels to middle distance destinations in the Mediterranean (Dalmatian Coast, Ionian, and Aegean Seas) and strengthen Europe's leading position in this market.
➢ Israel, Malta, Turkey, Morocco and Tunisia will no doubt experience a tourist industry comeback after the recent sociopolitical changes in the area. This will favor the development of an innovative, differentiated tourist offer that may include whale-watching.
➢ Whale-watching tradition and the expertise available in many Mediterranean regions (groups engaged with cetacean research, science popularization and environmental education) facilitate specialized know-how transfer.
➢ Local, national and international initiatives for sustainable development and environmental conservation existing in the region offer an important working basis for regional cooperation (e.g., transnational initiatives such as NATURA 2000, EUROPARC, ACCOBAMS, Barcelona Convention, or UNEP MAP/RACSPA).
➢ Whale-watching is suitable for the implementation of policies and measures to boost ecological design and technologies in the nautical sector, MPA management, tourist footprint compensation programmes (GHG, water, energy), and to promote environmental responsibility, green businesses, local custody of coastal marine environments, and the study of climate change.
➢ Growing pan-European networking for the development of ecotourism and sustainable tourism (Destinet, ECOLNET, EDEN, and EUROPARCS among other).

The impact of environmental change on the sustainability of the tourism industry must also be taken into account, e.g. the impact of climate change on local climatic conditions and biodiversity (Table 2).

5. IMPACTS OF WHALE-WATCHING: TOWARDS SUSTAINABLE DEVELOMENT

Sustainable tourism derives from the concept of "sustainable development" described in the "Brundtland report" (UN United Nations Organization, 1987). Sustainability must be understood as an ongoing process that aims to reach a balanced human presence on the planet.

It implies taking actions to mitigate and compensate for negative impacts, to avoid and prevent future risks, and to maximize and promote positive effects on the environment and society. Developing and managing the whale-watching industry in a sustainable manner requires environmental, socio-economic and socio-cultural sustainability principles to be applied not only to the natural, physical, financial and human resources used, but also to processes and relations. To improve the chances of success in this endeavor, priority must be placed on decisions based on evidence and prior knowledge, involving local people and visitors, and strengthening networking and public-private cooperation. In a first approximation, the international specialized community referred to the risks and impact of integrating the whale-watching industry into the worldwide travel and recreation production system (IFAW, 1997). Owing to growing trends in the industry, intensive work has been carried out to ensure high-quality, sustainable operations, with a special focus on environmental impact. Along these lines, a number of studies have reported several negative effects that whale-watching can have on cetaceans, while others have suggested that whale-watching supposes no harm or threat to the animals.

The impact of whale-watching activities has been studied in many places around world, but, in most cases, only short term behavioural changes could be observed. There are very few places where the impact on long term demographic parameters have been investigated and the results obtained have been inconsistent, ranging from highly negative effects to no apparent effect. The best known example of a negative effect refers to the small coastal population of 56 bottlenose dolphins (Currey and Rowe, 2008) in Doubtful Sound, New Zealand. Here, population declined by around 36% between 1995 and 2007(Currey et al., 2007), mainly due to a decrease in calf survival rates, which dropped from 0.86 over the period 1994-2001 to 0.38 for the period 2002-2008 (Currey, 2008). Another report by Lusseau et al. (2006) presented an overview of the effects of boat tours on this dolphin population and concluded that dolphin-watching tourism in Fiordland, New Zealand was unsustainable. Collisions with boats were noted to have caused physical injuries to a large number of dolphins and were also responsible for the death of one calf in 2002 (Lusseau et al., 2002) which reduced the reproductive success of the population in that year by 50%, since only two calves had been born in the population. It was also observed that when the frequency of boat-dolphin interactions was too high *i.e.* during intense boat traffic, dolphins would actively move away from the boats and switch to long-term area avoidance (Lusseau et al., 2004; Lusseau, 2005). This behaviour deeply impacted their ecology, as it prevented the animals from accessing their normal feeding grounds.

Another well known example is the bottlenose dolphin population in Shark Bay, Australia. Here, an increase from one to two dolphin-watch operators resulted in a significant impact on habitat use, with 15% fewer dolphins per km^2 and reduced female reproductive success (Bejder, 2005). Despite the fact that females with the highest cumulative vessel exposure were still giving birth to calves, the majority of these calves did not survive to weaning. Bejder (2005) explains that the negative correlation between vessel exposure and reproductive success could be attributed to malnutrition, increased stress-related disease susceptibility, or increased predation by sharks. Finally, the problem of collisions between whales and whale-watching boats has been studied on a worldwide scale, totalling 32 accounts of collisions involving different species of whales (Weinrich, 2005). The author concluded that major injuries and fatalities involved vessels greater than 30m in length while transiting at high speed. On the other hand, several studies have also shown that the impact of whale-watching is not always negative. For example, Weinrich and Corbelli (2009) found no correlation between whale-watching exposure and the calving rate or calf production of humpback whales at their calving grounds off southern New England where they are under intense whale-watching pressure. From this they concluded that short term disturbance may not necessarily be indicative of more meaningful detrimental effects on individuals or populations. Within the Mediterranean Sea, the Strait of Gibraltar is the only place where the impact of whale-watching has been thoroughly studied. Long-finned pilot whales and bottlenose dolphins are the two main whale-watching target species here(Villar et al., 2007) (Figure 8). Although no data prior to the beginning of the activity in 1996 is available, both populations increased throughout the period 1999 – 2008 (between 1999 and 2008 in the case of bottlenose dolphins (Chico et al., 2011) and between 1999 to 2005 in the case of pilot whales(Verborgh et al., 2009), along with the number of whale-watching boats operating in the area. This data is consistent with the idea that different populations can respond in different ways or to different extents to whale-watching pressure. Overall, however, small coastal cetacean populations seem more prone to suffer negative impacts from whale-watching operations.

Whale-watching can cause a variety of effects on the economy of a community, many of which may relate, in turn, to other social and environmental changes. For example, strategies followed in the use of local resources may change as the economy grows, and decisions affecting the local economy can have an effect on labor specialization, employment conditions, and the distribution of wealth (IFAW, 1997). The whale-watching industry can have a stimulating effect on the local economy by improving employment, positive inter-personal relations, capacity building, the offer in education, and business and infrastructure development.

Figure 8. Long finned pilot whale (*Globicephala melas*) watching in the South of Spain (Author: Pedro García /ANSE).

It may also boost a sense of pride among the local community adopting a sustainable lifestyle (IFAW, 1997). If the industry is successful enough to be considered a role model, it can set new trends in the local economy and society.

Sustainability principles must be applied not only to ensure the long term viability of natural resources and minimize the impact of whale-watching on the environment, but also to improve socioeconomic sustainability. Thus, other aspects need to be taken into consideration such as those related to type of visitor and the quality demanded by the tourist, product innovation and quality service, networking and reputation, integration into the local community, capacity building, incentives for entrepreneurship, the contribution to local wellbeing, and sustainability awareness and the promotion of responsible attitudes. Tourism can be an important role model for the implementation of such sustainability practices (European Commission, 1993; QUEBEC-DECLARATION, 2002; World Travel and Tourism Council, 2003). Examples from destinations around the world show the diversity of the socioeconomic impacts that may derive from the development of a whale-watching industry. Some, for instance, relate to the opportunities that whale-watching can offer in the development of alternative industries in countries with a long whale hunting tradition (Iceland); others to the success of cetaceans in promoting tourism (Australia, Hawaii, USA; Pacific Coast, USA and CA.); or to the risk of development strategies based on large-scale operations (Canary Islands, Spain); or again to the difficulties that may arise once certain levels of development are reached in sustainable whale-watching destinations of worldwide recognition (Kaikoura, New Zealand); or to the benefits of community integration in local development strategies for the successful custody of natural resources (Samadai, Egypt); to the potential for a combined offer at an international level (Patagonia, Argentina and Chile); or, finally, to the importance of regulating the unbalances that are typical of a growing whale-watching industry (Machalillo, Ecuador).

Economic sustainability implies market success and competitiveness. In order to achieve a successful competitive strategy, conditions of the factors of production, demand, related and supporting industries, governance and even chance must all be considered as key factors (Porter, 2003). Counting on adequate facilities and equipment as well as skilled personnel can contribute to minimize the direct impact of whale-watching operations on cetaceans and the environment. Adequate business strategies and policies can improve socioeconomic wellbeing in the local community while minimizing the potential drawbacks of development in the following ways: 1) specialized and exclusive services can increase visitor expenditure, and diversify business and employment opportunities at the destination; 2) responsible management can lead to improved working conditions and atmosphere, thus helping to avoid abusive situations and conflicts; and 3) sustainability-oriented businesses can promote local cooperation and commercial networking, thereby improving their reputation and acceptance. These, in turn, can have an indirect positive effect on the environment and natural resources by minimizing the impact of whale-watching operations, raising conservation awareness among employees, local people and visitors, or increasing their engagement in projects for the conservation of natural resources.

From the point of view of business operations, a key element for a successful sustainability strategy is choosing the right product and addressing the right market niche. Based on the many values that cetaceans and whale-watching can provide and on the main objectives of whale-watching trips, the following whale-watching operation categories can be distinguished:

- Scientific research. Spotting and watching cetaceans is basic to the study of their biology and ecology. Increased knowledge of the surrounding natural resources and the activities and changes that affect them can provide more effective baselines for management decision processes. One of most extended synergies in the whale-watching industry is the use of whale-watching boats as opportunity platforms for research purposes, where volunteer-tourism is frequently used as a financing mechanism for research programmes.

- Tourist-commercial. Organized commercial whale-watching is the most extended approach worldwide. Here, the main aim is to offer a direct and close encounter with the animals in order to enjoy sighting them, the values they represent and other tourism-related attractions.

- Educational. The whale-watching experience can be integrated into environmental education programmes, either as the main activity or as an accessory element. These programmes can be targeted at scholars, graduates, civil associations, organizations, or other community groups.

- Professional training. Whale-watching trips can form part of professional qualification courses. A variety of issues related to cetaceans, their habitat and the whale-watching industry can be included in technical courses for operations management and marketing, group management, impact monitoring, natural resources and area management, or tourist destination management, among others. These courses can be designed for professionals (boat crews and tour guides) and entrepreneurs, but can also be aimed at management staff of protected natural areas and other technical managers working in public administration.

- Other commercial and popularisation activities. Whale-watching tours can be offered as an element in marketing and promotion campaigns, as part of activity programmes of public events and private celebrations, for documentary and film making (fiction, non-fiction) and media reports (informative, tour reviews), as "fam-trips" and "press-trips" (promotion trips for tourist operators and media agents), or as part of team-building activities, group dynamics, or "technological missions" (networking, knowledge transfer).

- Therapeutic, e.g., open sea dolphin-assisted therapies.

- Tourist-recreational. Refers to non-commercial leisure trips arranged and carried out privately (day-off, holiday or weekend excursions).

While whale-watching tours can be designed as short, half-day or full-day excursions, or as part of multi-day packages, specific niche markets other than the specialized "eco-traveler" can be addressed through additional services and product packaging. To list but a few, these may include complementary transportation, introductory talks, visits to museums and interpretation centers, provision of material and equipment for educational and informative purposes, guided tours and interpretation carried out by specialized professionals, swimming with cetaceans, bathing in remote environments or locations with tourist appeal, kayaking and other water thrills, on-site catering and entertainment, sale of promotional products, games and group dynamics, walks and hikes in natural environments or accommodation. Additionally, many activities fit the strategy of including whale-watching within a wider range of offers. Such are snorkeling and scuba-diving tours, watching other marine and coastal nature (e.g. birds, turtles and sea-lions, but also flora and landscapes), nature photo and video workshops, kayak expeditions, trekking and hiking, ship-cruises, sea transportation (regular ferry routes, coasting), other nautical offers (water jet skis and other water-thrills, nautical charters, sport-fishing and other fishing tours), visits to museums and interpretive centers related to marine nature and culture, and even visits to places of ethnographic and archeological interest, star watching, gastronomical tours and workshops, wellness programmes and adventure expeditions. Including any of the above-mentioned services and activities can increase the perceived value of the whale-watching experience and can help to ensure a differentiated product. The only limitations here are business strategy, regulations, and the state of the available resources and of the market in question.

In the light of the above mentioned aspects, it can be argued that whale-watching favors business flexibility and specialization and promotes cooperation, all of which are key requisites for any given tourist business, industry or destination to be competitive and sustainable. In addition, the offer of customer relations services, both before and after the whale-watching experience (customer assistance, customer-bonding, and networking), should be considered an opportunity to maximize the quality and success of a sustainable whale-watching business or industry.

6. THE IMPORTANCE OF REGULATION FOR SUSTAINABLE WHALE-WATCHING OPERATIONS

A further key aspect of market competitiveness is governance, i.e. the creation of effective regulations that can promote high-quality operations, and adequate policies to help ensure favorable conservation of the resources while allowing the industry to develop (Porter, 2003). Many whale-watching destinations around the world have implemented regulations for the activity with the prime objective of maintaining the viability of cetacean populations and encouraging their sustainable use - in other words, to ensure that the quality of the inherited resources essential to competitiveness are maintained for future generations. Regulations may be established either as legally-binding frameworks or as simple guidelines or codes of conduct. Either way, they should ideally be agreed upon with the participating parties (whale-watching operator businesses, research groups and other related civil organizations).

In 2010, C. Carlson published an exhaustive compilation of all the existing whale-watching regulations throughout the world. From this, it is clear that the development of an effective code of conduct should include the following set of requisites and essential attributes:

- Requisites directly affecting the natural, human and physical resources, and on-site operations (minimum distance allowed, methods of approach, specific requisites for different species and under special conditions, maximum duration and number of boats, type of operations permitted in the presence of cetaceans, human interactions, and detection methods)
- Requisites affecting the quality of acquired assets (technical characteristics of vessels, professional skills) and governance (licensing, prior submission of reports, inspections, sanctions)

- Requisites related to business management and market strategy (associations)
- Other aspects affecting the tourist business and industry (scientific advances can favor innovation and reduce impact, whereas awareness-raising programmes and actions can ensure high-quality demand and social acceptance).

As the author points out, whale-watching regulations should be flexible and capable of adapting to case-specific conditions and new scientific findings, and should complement other regulations related to the marine ecosystem and the risks affecting it. While binding regulations act as strong deterrents, there is a high chance of failure due to the ineffective application of control measures. At the same time, insufficient compliance with non-binding regulations can represent a further obstacle for the correct implementation of regulations. In the light of this, the combination of both types of measures has been considered the best approach to get around this problem (IFAW, 1997). Besides addressing aspects of environmental sustainability (e.g. direct impact minimization, sustainable use of resources, waste and risk management, education and popularization) regulations could (and should) contemplate other aspects that may have a direct impact on a destination's social and economic sustainability, such as the establishment of quality standards in customer service and business management, and cooperation among industry participants. In areas of rapid industry development, simple bureaucratic processes, monitoring and surveillance are fundamental aspects and should therefore also be included to some extent as part of the "rules of the game".

Spain's strategic policy shows that regional regulations can better reflect local sustainability issues but may also increase the risk of uncoordinated governance, meaning important sustainability issues may remain unattended. A nationwide binding regulation was established for the protection of cetaceans. The Royal Decree 1727/2007 includes a compulsory on-site code of conduct for whale-watching operations, which plays a decisive role in the improvement of environmental sustainability. However, it does not address other issues critical to the enhancement of social sustainability (e.g. the need to carry out educational programmes during tours) and economic sustainability (e.g. the need to implement a permit system and the submission of compulsory business reports prior to authorization in order to raise quality standards in the industry, or to enforce the inclusion of a specialized tour guide during operations). Such clauses have already been included in a number of regional regulations, such as the Canary Islands' whale-watching regulation, which includes these and further sustainability measures - for example, it demands a compulsory ecological impact study to minimize environmental risks. The availability of information and an effective permit system are key elements to ensure a high-quality whale-watching supply and demand. Such a system was implemented in the Canary Islands (estimated 625.000 whale-watchers per year, and ca. 5% of worldwide volume), where a seal of quality is granted to those operators complying with all legal requirements to carry out the activity. The "blue boat" flag was introduced as the most important element in the whale-watching regulation and became the most successful and effective tool for raising quality standards in the industry. A permit system can certainly contribute to minimize environmental risks and the impact of illegal operations, while promoting responsible visitor behavior and business quality.

**Table 3. Ten proposals for the development of a sustainable
whale-watching industry in the Mediterranean**

(1)	Baseline assessment of natural, material (including infrastructure and financial) and human resources available, business potential, and quantitative and qualitative impacts caused.
(2)	Construction of a whale-watching industry cluster: definition of participating agents and promotion of association.
(3)	Product design and marketing, with a special focus on niche-market business, increased visitor expenditure and visit duration, added value services, product combination and packaging, marketing and market leverage, and with the implementation of elements that contribute to sustainable tourism, e.g. interpretation programmes, eco-technologies, e-commerce and e-management, specialized supply chain, commercial and social network, or customer fidelity programmes.
(4)	Implementing a capacity building programme that includes the offer of professional qualification courses on tour guiding and interpretation, risk and impact management, financing and networking, tourist business start-up, management and marketing, eco-technologies and ICT, design and development of quality and sustainability strategies, specialized know-how for tourist agents, and introductory courses for locals.
(5)	Development of a promotion programme for locals and visitors that includes museums and interpretation centers, road signs, informative material, and cultural and scientific events as cornerstones.
(6)	Design of a business incentives programme for small and medium businesses to facilitate the implementation of eco-innovation and new technologies and the employment of specialized professionals, and to promote collaboration with local sustainability, research and conservation projects.
(7)	Design of a regulatory framework that includes a set of voluntary or binding rules elaborated with the consensus of the agents participating in the industry and adaptable to changes, in which other supporting tools are considered, e.g. code of conduct, handbook of good practice, quality charter or other types of agreement.
(8)	Assessment of the viability of implementing a certification programme specially designed for the whale-watching industry, and of its potential impact on the industry
(9)	Design of a programme for the integration of research and educational projects in the development and management strategies of the whale-watching industry.
(10)	Design of measures to improve management processes in the whale-watching industry, including measures to improve administrative processes, coordination among public organizational bodies, and to promote the integration of minorities and groups at risk, on site operations surveillance, environmental and social impact monitoring, and the development of a quality and sustainability indicator system.

While the contribution of whale-watching to environmental sustainability can be significant if carried out under the regulatory measures or frameworks that have proved efficient, any strategy developed to ensure its socioeconomic sustainability must take into account that as the market becomes more attractive, entry-barriers and competitiveness grow (Table 3).

Addressing environmental sustainability requires a systemic focus. Similarly, socioeconomic sustainability should also be addressed in a holistic manner and include issues such as high-quality product offer and tourist demand, market leverage, support of local business and culture, and support provided by the local community. These aspects and the future monitoring and assessment as the activity develops into a larger tourist industry must be considered at the planning phase. Because the theoretical models used to describe whale-watching industry development processes may not exactly represent real life, the actual potential of the industry and its impact should be assessed locally. Nonetheless, the role of the whale-watching industry at a regional and global level, and the new findings and strategies suggested for its sustainable development and management, should also be considered alongside other sociopolitical mega-trends (Table 2).

CONCLUSION

Whale-watching has grown into a solid tourist industry within a very short period of time. The many services provided highlight its importance as an alternative to other, less environmentally sustainable types of tourist operations. Cetaceans are charismatic animals, but they are also amongst the most threatened animals on earth. The development of a whale-watching industry with a strong focus on the responsible use of the resources and in compliance with existing regulations will positively affect the environment and tourism, since messages raising environmental conservation awareness are more likely to come through and generate a positive impact on tourist quality and sustainability. On the down side, whale-watching has sparked rapid economic growth in many destinations that has exceeded regulation and control efforts, leading to unbalances in terms of sustainability. Such cases have raised concern regarding the validity of whale-watching as an effective tool to exploit natural resources in a sustainable manner. The difficulty of assessing the real long-term negative impacts of the activity on cetaceans has occasionally favored uncontrolled growth of the industry, whereas the application of strict precautionary principles has restrained its development in other cases. In fact, balanced development processes have been observed at only a few whale-watching destinations owing to its short history and intense growth.

The whale-watching industry in the Mediterranean is a good example of economic development combined with a strong commitment to conservation of the environment, research and education, in which social progress has accompanied profit making. Within this context, special attention must be drawn to the case of the Strait of Gibraltar, where the absence of large scale tourism has permitted the development of a high-quality product and a high-quality service. So long as the trend continues, the potential initially shown by this area could continue to develop according to the educational and conservationist principles that sustainable whale-watching operations require.

Cetaceans are clearly an important resource in the Mediterranean. As such, whale-watching tourism offers a great potential for new and existing whale-watching destinations. However, the development of this potential must be carried out in a sensible way, in accordance with sustainability and high-quality standards, and ensuring that the results and benefits of applying sustainability measures are fully perceived by visitors, participating agents and the local community. In general, the importance of low-impact tourism grows with increasing pressure on the marine environment due to coastal areas becoming intensely populated, or to the growth of fisheries, fish farming and desalinization plants. The development of a whale-watching industry may impose further pressures on the marine environment which in turn may require the design of new policies aimed at protecting the local heritage, promoting its value as a source of income and employment, and regulating, controlling and monitoring the activities that ensue. Together, these actions may contribute to the elimination of unsustainable practices and to encourage the application of sustainability values.

Whale-watching in the Mediterranean can also contribute to the conservation of the many existing natural and cetacean reserves. MPAs are essential tools for cetacean conservation and resource management on the condition that they are backed by effective management plans or measures that include surveillance and monitoring of the cetacean populations and of the human activities that interfere with them, along with the appropriate financing mechanisms and sufficient resources to ensure an effective implementation of these measures. The intense policy-making and international cooperation work that has been carried out to protect the Mediterranean marine natural environments and biodiversity has resulted in an increase in the number of both created and proposed MPAs. It is therefore now time to implement the formulated resolutions, directives and signed agreements, by taking decisive steps to integrate all the parties involved (businesses, administrations, scientific community, other professionals and active local community members), in order to share information, promote professional expertise, adopt common policies that combine environmental conservation and high-quality tourist development, and boost a coordinated work cluster.

In all, there is still much work to be done in order to successfully integrate whale-watching into the tourism industry while maintaining all aspects that make it a singular, appealing and sustainable tourist experience. Until then, the application of precautionary principles should be mandatory for the adoption of any measure or action.

ACKNOWLEDGMENTS

This chapter is dedicated to our friend Mario Morcillo Moreno, who passed away in January 2012. Mario was the first whale-watcher in the Strait of Gibraltar, and thanks to him probably most of the research and education being carried out in the Strait continues. Thanks are also due to CEPSA, Fundación Biodiversidad, Fundación Loro Parque, and the Spanish Ministry of Research and Environment for their sponsorship. Thanks are also due to all the volunteers of CIRCE, especially to Pauline Gauffier, Ruth Esteban, Juan Manuel Salazar Sierra, Carolina Jiménez, Joan Giménez, Michelette Harris and Martin Harris.

REFERENCES

Akama, J. S. (1996). Western environmental values and nature-based tourism in Kenya. *Tourism Management*, *17*(8), 567-574.

Amos, B. (1993). Use of molecular probes to analyse pilot whale pod structure: two novel analytical approaches. In I. L. Boyd (Ed.), *Marine Mammals Advances in Behavioural and Population Biology* (Vol. 66, pp. 33-48). Oxford: Oxford University Press.

Amos, B., Barrett, J., and Dover, G. A. (1991). Breeding behaviour of pilot whales revealed by DNA fingerprinting. *Heredity*, *67 (Pt 1)*, 49-55.

Amos, B., Schlötterer, C., and Tautz, D. (1993). Social structure of pilot whales revealed by analytical DNA profiling. *Science*, *260*(5108), 670-672.

Baird, R. W., Schorr, G. S., Webster, D. L., McSweeney, D. J., and Mahaffy, S. D. (2006). *Studies of beaked whale diving behavior and odontocete stock structure in Hawai'i in March/April 2006. Fisheries Science*. Prepared for National Marine Fisheries Service,

Southwest Fisheries Science Center, La Jolla, California, by Cascadia Research Collective, Olympia, Washington.

Bejder, L. (2005). *Linking short and long-term effects of nature-based tourism on cetaceans.* Doctoral Thesis Dalhousie Univerity Canada. Dalhousie University, Canada.

Bentaleb, I., Martin, C., Vrac, M., Mate, B., Mayzaud, P., Siret, D., De Stephanis, R.,Guinet C. (2011). Foraging ecology of Mediterranean fin whales in a changing environment elucidated by satellite tracking and baleen plate stable isotopes. *Marine Ecology Progress Series, 438,* 285-302.

Brockelman, W. Y., and Dearden, P. (1990). The role of nature trekking in conservation: a case-study in Thailand. *Environmental Conservation, 17*(2), 141-148.

Brohman, J. (1996). New directions in tourism for third world development. *Annals of Tourism Research, 23*(1), 48-70.

Butler, R. W. (1980). The concept of a tourist area cycle of evolution: Implications for management of resources. *Canadian Geographer, 24*(1), 5-12.

Carbó Penche, M., Salazar Sierra, J., de Stephanis, R., and Esteban Pavo, R. (2007). Socio-economic analysis of the whale-watching industry in Andalucia, Spain. *European Research on Cetaceans Proceedings of the Annual Conference of the European Cetacean Society 21.* San Sebastian.

Cañadas, A, and Sagarminaga, R. (2000). The northeastern alboran sea, an important breeding and feeding ground for the long-finned pilot whale (*Globicephala melas*) in the mediterranean sea. *Marine mammal science, 16*(3), 513-529.

Cañadas, A, Sagarminaga, R., De Stephanis, R., Urquiola, E., and Hammond, P. S. (2005). Habitat preference modelling as a conservation tool : proposals for marine protected areas for cetaceans in southern Spanish waters. *Aquatic Conservation: Marine and Freshwater Ecosystems, 521,* 495-521.

Cañadas, A. (2006). *Towards conservation of dolphins in the Alborán Sea Hacia la conservación de los delfines en el mar de Alborán.* Madrid: Universidad Autónoma de Madrid.

Chico, C., Jiménez Torres, C., Pérez, S., Verborgh, P., Gauffier, P., Esteban-Pavo, R., Giménez, J., et al. (2011). (2011). Survival rate abundance and residency of bottlenose dolphins (*Tursiops truncatus*) in the Strait of Gibraltar. 25th Ann. Meeting European Cetacean Society, Cádiz, Spain, 21-23 Marzo 2011. *European Research on Cetaceans Proceedings of the Annual Conference of the European Cetacean Society 25.* Cádiz.

Cisneros-Montemayor, a. M., Sumaila, U. R., Kaschner, K., and Pauly, D. (2010). The global potential for whale watching. *Marine Policy, 34*(6), 1273-1278.

Cotté, C., Guinet, C., Taupier-Letage, I., Mate, B., and Petiau, E. (2009). Scale-dependent habitat use by a large free-ranging predator, the Mediterranean fin whale. *Deep Sea Research Part I: Oceanographic Research Papers, 56*(5), 801-811.

Cotté, C., d' Ovidio, F., Chaigneau, A., Lévy, M., Taupier-Letage, I., Mate, B., and Guinet, C. (2011). Scale-dependent interactions of Mediterranean whales with marine dynamics. *Limonology And Oceanography, 56*(1), 219-232.

Currey, R. J. C. (2008). Conservation biology of bottlenose dolphins in Fiordland , New Zealand. *Conservation Biology,* (October), 192.

Currey, R. J. C., Dawson, S. M., and Slooten, E. (2007). New abundance estimates suggest Doubtful Sound bottlenose dolphins are declining. *Pacific Conservation Biology, 13*(4), 265-273.

Currey, R., and Rowe, L. (2008). *Abundance and population structure of bottlenose dolphins in Doubtful and Dusky Sounds: Population monitoring in Summer 2007/2008.* Invercargill: Southland Conservancy.

de Stephanis, R. (2007). *Estrategias de alimentación de los diferentes grupos de Calderón común (*Globicephala mela*s) en el Estrecho de Gibraltar. Implicaciones para su conservación.* Cádiz: Universidad de Cádiz.

de Stephanis, R, Cornulier, T., Verborgh, P., Salazar Sierra, J., Gimeno, N., and Guinet, C. (2008a). Summer spatial distribution of cetaceans in the Strait of Gibraltar in relation to the oceanographic context. *Marine Ecology Progress Series, 353,* 275-288.

de Stephanis, R., Verborgh, P., Pérez, S., Esteban, R., Minvielle-Sebastia, L., and Guinet, C. (2008b). Long-term social structure of long-finned pilot whales (*Globicephala melas*) in the Strait of Gibraltar. *Acta Ethologica, 11*(2), 81-94.

de Stephanis, R., García-Tíscar, S., Verborgh, P., Esteban-Pavo, R., Pérez, S., Minvielle-Sebastia, L., and Guinet, C. (2008c). Diet of the social groups of long-finned pilot whales (*Globicephala melas*) in the Strait of Gibraltar. *Marine Biology, 154*(4), 603-612.

Dogan, H. Z. (1989). Forms of adjustment : Sociocultural impacts of tourism. *Annals of Tourism Research, 16*(2), 216-236.

Doxey, G. (1975). A Causation Theory of Visitor-Resident Irritants, Methodology and Research Inferences. *In Conference Proceedings: Sixth Annual Conference of Travel Research Association* (pp. 195-198). San Diego.

Duffus, D. A., and Dearden, P. (1990). Non-consumptive wildlife-oriented recreation: A conceptual framework. *Biological Conservation, 53*(3), 213-231.

Engelhaupt, D., Hoelzel, R., Nicholson, C., Frantzis, A., Mesnick, S., Gero, S., Whitehead, H., et al. (2009). Female philopatry in coastal basins and male dispersion across the North Atlantic in a highly mobile marine species, the sperm whale (Physeter macrocephalus). *Molecular ecology, 18*(20), 4193-205.

Esteban Pavo, R. (2008). *Abundancia, estructura social y parámetros de historia natural de la orca (Orcinus orca) en el Estrecho de Gibraltar.* Cádiz: Universidad de Cádiz.

European Commission. (1993). Fifth European Community Environment Programme: towards sustainability. *Official Journal, 138, 17th.*

Forcada, J., Aguilar, A., Hammond, P. S., Pastor, X., and Aguilar, R. (1994). *Steno bredanensis* in the Mediterranean Sea. *Marine Mammal Science, 10*(2), 137-150.

Forestell, P., and Kaufman, G. (1996). *The development of whalewatching in Hawaii and its application as a model for growth and development of the industry elsewhere. In: Colgan, K. (ed.) Encounters with Whales '95.* (pp. 53-65). Canberra, Australia.

Frantzis, A., Airoldi, S., Notarbartolo-di-Sciara, G., Johnson, C., and Mazzariol, S. (2011). Inter-basin movements of Mediterranean sperm whales provide insight into their population structure and conservation. *Deep Sea Research Part I: Oceanographic Research Papers.*

Frantzis, A, Alexiadou, P., Paximadis, G., Politi, E., and Gannier, A. (2003). Current knowledge of the cetacean fauna of the Greek Seas. *Distribution, 5*(3), 219-232.

Fullard, K. J., Early, G., Heide-Jorgensen, M. P., Bloch, D., Rosing-Asvid, a, and Amos, W. (2000). Population structure of long-finned pilot whales in the North Atlantic: a correlation with sea surface temperature? *Molecular ecology, 9*(7), 949-58.

Gannier, A. (2005). Summer distribution and relative abundance of delphinids in the Mediterranean Sea. *Revue D'Ecologie - La Terre et la Vie, 60*(3), 223-238.

Gannier, Alexandre, and Epinat, J. (2008). Cuvier's beaked whale distribution in the Mediterranean Sea: results from small boat surveys 1996–2007. *Journal of the Marine Biological Association of the United Kingdom, 88*(06), 1245 - 1251.

Gannier, Alexandre, and Praca, E. (2007). SST fronts and the summer sperm whale distribution in the north-west Mediterranean Sea. *Journal of the Marine Biological Association of the UK, 87*(01), 187.

Gauffier, P., Verborgh, P., Andreu, E., Esteban, R., Medina, B., Gallego, P., and de Stephanis, R. (2009). An update on fin whales (*Balaenoptera physalus*) migration, through intense maritime traffic in the Strait of Gibraltar, Paper SC61/BC6. *international whaling Commision Scientific Committee.*

Guinet, C, Domenici, P., de Stephanis, R., Barrett-Lennard, L., Ford, J., and Verborgh, P. (2007). Killer whale predation on bluefin tuna: exploring the hypothesis of the endurance-exhaustion technique. *Marine Ecology Progress Series, 347*, 111-119.

Heimlich-Boran, J. (1993). *Social organization of the short-finned pilot whale,* Globicephala macrorhynchus*, with special reference to the social ecology of delphinids.* PhD thesis. Cambridge: Cambridge University.

Higgins, B. R. (1996). The Global Structure of the Nature Tourism Industry: Ecotourists, Tour Operators, and Local Businesses. *Journal of Travel Research, 35*(2), 11-18.

Higham, J E S. (1998). Tourists and albatrosses: the dynamics of tourism at the Northern Royal Albatross Colony, Taiaroa Head, New Zealand. *Tourism Management, 19*(6), 521-531.

Higham, J E S, Lusseau, D., and Hendry, W. (2008). Wildlife Viewing: The Significance of the Viewing Platforms. *Journal of Ecotourism, 7*(2), 132-142.

Higham, J.E.S., Bejder, L., and Lusseau, D. (2009). An integrated and adaptive management model to address the long-term sustainability of tourist interactions with cetaceans. *Environmental Conservation, 35*(04), 294.

Hoyt, E. (1995). *The Worldwide Value and Extent of Whale Watching: 1995. IWC document IWC47WW2.*

Hoyt, E. (2007). *A Blueprint for Dolphin and Whale Watching Development, p* (p. 28). Humane Society International (HSI).

Hoyt, E. (2002). Whale Watching. In W. F. Perrin, B. Würsig, and J. G. M. Thewissen (Eds.), *Encyclopedia of Marine Mammals* (pp. 1305-1310). San Diego, CA: Academic Press.

Hoyt, E. (2001). Whale watching 2001: Worldwide tourism numbers, expenditures, and expanding socioeconomic benefits. *Tourism.* International Fund for Animal Welfare. Retrieved from www.ifaw.org.

Hoyt, E. (2005). Marine Protected Areas for Whales, Dolphins and Porpoises. A World Handbook for Cetacean Habitat Conservation. *Marine Ecology, 27*, 184-185).

IFAW. (1997). *Report of the workshop on the Socioeconomic Aspects of Whale Watching.* (p. 88). Kaikura, New Zeland.

Johnson, J. D., and Snepenger, D. J. (1993). Application of the tourism life cycle concept in the greater Yellowstone region. *Society and Natural Resources, 6*(2), 127-148.

Just, R., Hueth, D., and Schmitz, A. (1982). Applied Welfare Economics and Public Policy. Englewood Cliffs, NJ: Prentice-Hall.

Laran, S., and Gannier, a. (2008). Spatial and temporal prediction of fin whale distribution in the northwestern Mediterranean Sea. *ICES Journal of Marine Science, 65*(7), 1260-1269.

Lemelin, H., and Maher, P. (2009). Nanuk of the torngats: Human-polar bear interactions in the torngat mountains national park, newfoundland and labrador, Canada. *Human Dimensions of Wildlife*, *14*(2), 152-155.

Lemelin, R. H., and Wiersma, E. C. (2007). Perceptions of Polar Bear Tourists: A Qualitative Analysis. *Human Dimensions of Wildlife*, *12*(1), 45-52.

Loomis, J. B., and White, D. S. (1996). Economic benefits of rare and endangered species: summary and meta-analysis. *Ecological Economics*, *18*(3), 197-206.

Lusseau, D, Slooten, E., Dawson, S., and Higham, J. (2002). *The effects of tourism activities on bottlenose dolphins (*Tursiops *spp.) in Fiordland.* Wellington, New Zealand.

Lusseau, David. (2005). Residency pattern of bottlenose dolphins *Tursiops spp.* in Milford Sound, New Zealand, is related to boat traffic. *Marine Ecology Progress Series*, *295*(Lusseau 2004), 265-272.

Lusseau, David, Slooten, L. I. Z., and Currey, R. J. C. (2006). Research note: Unsustainable dolphin-watching tourism in Fiorland, New Zeland. *Tourism*, *3*(2), 173-178.

Lusseau, David, Slooten, L., and Currey, R. J. C. (2004). Unsustainable dolphin-watching tourism in Fiordland, New Zealand, 1-5.

Mansfeld, Y., and Ginosar, O. (1994). Evaluation of the repertory grid method in studies of locals' attitude towards tourism development processes. *Environment and Planning A*, *26*(6), 957-972.

Mayol, P., Weber, P., Bouette, N., and Gmbaiani, D. (2009). *Le whale-watching en Méditerranée française : Mise à jour de la base de données des opérateurs. Retrieved from www.souffleursdecume.com.*

Moyle, B. J., and Evans, M. (2008). Economic development options for island states: the case of whalewatching, Shima. *The International Journal of Research into Island Cultures*, *2*(1), 41-58.

Orams, M. B. (1999). *Marine tourism: Development, impacts and management.* London: Routledge Publishers.

O'Connor, S., Campbell, R., Cortez, H., and Knowles, T. (2009). *Whale Watching Worldwide: tourism numbers, expenditures and expanding economic benefits, a special report from International Fund for Animal Welfare.* Yarmouth MA (USA).

PADI. (2009). PADI statistics. Retrieved February 20, 2012, from http://www.padi.com/scuba/uploadedFiles/About_PADI/PADI_Statistics/padi statistics jun2010.pdf.

Panigada, S., Lauriano, G., Burt, L., Pierantonio, N., and Donovan, G. (2011). Monitoring Winter and Summer Abundance of Cetaceans in the Pelagos Sanctuary (Northwestern Mediterranean Sea) Through Aerial Surveys. *PLoS ONE*, *6*(7), 10.

Pirotta, E., Matthiopoulos, J., MacKenzie, M., Scott-Hayward, L., and Rendell, L. (2011). Modelling sperm whale habitat preference: a novel approach combining transect and follow data. *Marine Ecology Progress Series*, *436*, 257-272.

Porter, M. (2003). *The Competitive Advantage of Nations. Strategy* (Vol. 26). New York, NY: The Free Press.

Praca, E., and Gannier, a. (2008). Ecological niches of three teuthophageous odontocetes in the northwestern Mediterranean Sea. *Ocean Science*, *4*(1), 49-59.

Praca, Emilie, Gannier, A., Das, K., and Laran, S. (2009). Modelling the habitat suitability of cetaceans: Example of the sperm whale in the northwestern Mediterranean Sea. *Deep Sea Research Part I: Oceanographic Research Papers*, *56*(4), 648-657.

QUEBEC-DECLARATION. (2002). *Ecotourism World Summit (Quebec, CA.).* Retrieved from http://www.unep.fr/scp/tourism/events/iye/pdf/ Quebec-Declar-eng.pdf.

Reeves, R., and Notarbartolo-di-Sciara, G. (2006). *The status and distribution of cetaceans in the Black Sea and Mediterranean Sea.* (p. 137). Malaga: IUCN Centre for Mediterranean Cooperation.

Richardson, L., and Loomis, J. (2009). The total economic value of threatened, endangered and rare species: An updated meta-analysis. *Ecological Economics, 68*(5), 1535-1548.

Rose, N. a., Janiger, D., Parsons, E. C. M., and Stachowitsch, M. (2011). Shifting baselines in scientific publications: A case study using cetacean research. *Marine Policy, 35*(4), 477-482.

Scarpaci, C., Lück, M., and Parsons, E. (2010). Recent Advances in Whale-Watching Research: 2008–2009. *Tourism in Marine Environments, 6*(1), 39-50.

Schlötterer, C., Amos, B., and Tautz, D. (1991). Conservation of polymorphic simple sequence loci in cetacean species. *Nature, 354*(6348), 63-65.

Sekercioglu, C. H. (2002). Impacts of birdwatching on human and avian communities. *Environmental Conservation, 29*(3), 282-289.

TIES (The International Ecotourism Society). (2010). *Learning center-What is ecotourism?* Retrieved from www.ecotourism.org.

UN United Nations Organization. (1987). *Report of the World Commission on Environment and Development "Our Common Future", General Assembly (42, 1987, US).* Retrieved from http://www.un-documents.net/wced-ocf.htm.

Valentine, P. (1992). Review: nature-based tourism. *Special interst tourism.* (pp. 105-127). London: Belhaven Press.

Verborgh, P., de Stephanis, R., Pérez, S., Jaget, Y., Barbraud, C., and Guinet, C. (2009a). Survival rate, abundance, and residency of long-finned pilot whales in the Strait of Gibraltar. *Marine Mammal Science, 25*(3), 523-536.

Vianna, G. M. S., Meekan, M. G., Pannell, D., Marsh, S., and Meeuwig, J. J. (2010). Wanted dead or alive? The relative value of reef sharks as a fishery and an ecotourism asset in Palau. *Oceans, 5*(4), 1-41.

Villar, S., Salazar, J. M., Esteban, R., and Carbó Penche, M. (2007). Cetacean distribution in the strait of Gibraltar and analysis of the most observed species from whale watching platforms. *European Research on Cetaceans Proceedings of the Annual Conference of the European Cetacean Society 21.* San Sebastian.

Weinrich, M. (2005). A review of collisions between whales and whale watch boats. Paper SC/57/BC12. *International Whaling Commision Scientific Committee.*

Weinrich, M., and Corbelli, C. (2009). Does whale watching in Southern New England impact humpback whale (*Megaptera novaeangliae*) calf production or calf survival? *Biological Conservation, 142*(12), 2931-2940.

Wells, M. (1997). Economic Perspectives on Nature Tourism, Conservation and Development. *Environment Department Papers Environmental Economics Series World Bank.* The World Bank, Environment Department Papers, Paper No. 55.

World Travel and Tourism Council. (2003). *Blueprint for New Tourism (on line)* (p. 16). Retrieved from http://www.wttc.org/bin/pdf/ original_pdf_file/blueprintfnt03.pdf.

In: New Trends Towards Mediterranean Tourism Sustainability   ISBN: 978-1-62257-627-2
Editors: L. M. Rosalino, A. Silva and A. Abreu   © 2012 Nova Science Publishers, Inc.

Chapter 2

GEOTOURISM AND THE SLOW MOVEMENT IN PORTUGAL: A STEP TOWARDS SUSTAINABLE TOURISM

Paulo Sá Caetano[a], and Victor Lamberto[b],†*
[a](CICEGE/Faculdade de Ciências e
Tecnologia da UNL), Portugal
[b](Slow Food Alentejo,
CERENA/Instituto Superior Técnico da UTL), Portugal

ABSTRACT

Geotourism is a quite recent concept of tourism which, according to geologists, is based on the geodiversity of a place and finds support in the geological framework of a region to offer the visitor an integrated picture of the territory. However, the ownership of the "geo" part of the term is disputed when the definition is presented by non-geologists: "tourism that sustains, or even enhances, the geographical character of a place...". The debate may be somewhat reduced by the proposal of an alternative concept of tourist approach: "slow geotourism". This approach maintains the focus on the geological attributes of a region but simultaneously involves the principles of the Slow Movement.

The Slow Movement is an increasingly global movement challenging the cult of speed, in many areas as diverse as food, cities, sex, work, leisure and travel. The *slow philosophy* principles are proposed to accompany geotourism activities in order to enhance sustainability of the tourism industry. These principles together with other areas of knowledge reinforce the innovative character of geotourism and help to accomplish various objectives of sustainable development, such as the respect and value of local and regional characteristics, the enhancement of regional identity and a high level of tourist satisfaction that help maintain the destination attractive.

Examples of geotouristic itineraries are given with the primary concern focused on trying to broadcast to a wide audience, in a scientifically sound but simultaneously appealing manner, geological information and related concepts and their connection to

* pcsc@fct.unl.pt
† vlamberto@gmail.com

other areas of knowledge. Substantially different settings are considered in these examples, ranging from rural to urban and industrial areas: "the marble routes" in the region of the Estremoz anticline, a geological structure well known for the presence of vast marble beds largely exploited by the local ornamental stone industry; "the three castles region", alias Arrábida, a mountainous region in the southern part of the Setúbal Peninsula, with recognized tourist importance, already portrayed many years ago by the poet Sebastião da Gama; "ecclesiastical geology in Lisbon", where the natural stones used in the construction of many of the city's churches are the focus of a circuit through some of the most touristic areas of Lisbon; "ecclesiastical geotourism in Convento do Espinheiro" an itinerary through a luxurious hotel with an old and fascinating history. The approach with slow geotourism promotes the fruition of the visited region in a manner that is more profound, sustainable and, above all... slow.

INTRODUCTION

The first definition of geotourism, presented by the English geologist Thomas Hose in 1995 states that it is "the provision of interpretive and service facilities to enable tourists to acquire knowledge and understanding of the geology and geomorphology of a site (including its contribution to the development of the Earth sciences) beyond the level of mere aesthetic appreciation" (Hose, 1995). It is a definition that points particularly to the potential learning of Earth sciences that can be achieved by visiting sites of special interest. More recently, the definition refers doubtless to a type of tourism clearly facing the geodiversity of a region and its potential to attract tourists: "Geotourism is a form of natural area tourism that specifically focuses on geology and landscape.It promotes tourism to geosites and the conservation of geodiversity and an understanding of earth sciences through appreciation and learning. This is achieved through independent visits to geological features, use of geo-trails and view points, guided tours, geo-activities and patronage of geosite visitor centres" (Newsome and Dowling, 2010). According to the authors, this definition regards geotourism as "geologically based and can occur in either natural, rural or urban environments; it fosters geoheritage conservation through appropriate sustainability measures; advances sound geological understanding through interpretation and education and generates tourist or visitor satisfaction".

The controversy that has arisen about the definition of the type of tourism inherent to geotourism and the discussion of "who owns" the "geo" part of the term, results from another definition, created by journalist and senior editor of the National Geographic Traveler magazine Jonathan Tourtellot[1], and presented in a study carried out in 2002 by the Travel Industry Association of America, which assigns a non-exclusive geological character to the term: "geotourism is "best practice" tourism that sustains, or even enhances, the geographical character of a place, such as its culture, environment, heritage, and the well-being of its residents". The "geographical" nature referred to here seeks to highlight the sense, integrity or identity of the place (Tourtellot, 2011). In an attempt to promote "reconciliation" of the terms, the author suggested the explicit inclusion of the word "geology" and, presently, in the so-called "Arouca Declaration" (that resulted from the International Congress of Geotourism

---

[1] who had coined the term a few years before, in 1997, although publication of the definition only occurred in 2003 (Stokes et al., 2003); J. Tourtellot has admitted that, at the time, in 1997, he was unaware that, only two years earlier, an "English geologist", Thomas Hose, had proposed exactly the same term for what he considered meaning geological tourism, *sensu stricto*.

held in Arouca, Portugal, in November 2011) the following definition is proposed: "geotourism should be defined as tourism that sustains and enhances the identity of a territory, taking into consideration its geology, environment, culture, aesthetics, heritage and the well-being of its residents". However, the discussion did not end here (see Jonathan Tourtellot's post in http://newswatch.nationalgeographic.com/2011/11/16/).

This chapter presents examples of geotouristic routes, conceived for several regions in Portugal, and designed following the philosophy of the "slow itineraries" project, and is intended to contribute to the discussion on the meaning of "geotourism" by proposing the concept of "slow geotourism".

GEOTOURISM IN PORTUGAL

During the mid nineteenth century, geology became a very popular science and geological tourism became a growth industry in many areas of Europe (Macfarlane, 2003). In Portugal, geological travel for scientific or surveying reasons can be traced back to the late eighteenth and to the nineteenth centuries when the first geological studies of Portugal, including the overseas territories, were carried out. The *Academia Real de Ciências de Lisboa* (Lisbon Royal Academy of Science), founded in 1779, from the beginning followed a policy of exploiting available mineral resources in Portugal and the colonies and, from 1783 onwards, promoted several expeditions to Brazil, Goa (India), Mozambique, Angola and Cape Verde with the purpose of collecting rock and mineral samples and mapping geological aspects of these territories (Figueirôa et al., 2007). Charles Lyell and Charles Darwin visited the Atlantic Madeira and Cape Verde archipelagos in the mid nineteenth century (Wilson, 2007) and made many observations on the geology of these islands; the Azores islands were visited and geologically observed and described by Georg Hartung, a young German geologist who maintained correspondence with Charles Lyell and exchanged many views on the volcanic origin of the islands (Pinto and Bouheiry, 2007).

In continental Portugal, the first geological map was produced in 1841 by Daniel Sharpe, an English geologist who visited and mapped the "Geology of the Neighbourhood of Lisbon", which was followed, eight years later, by an identical study of the Porto region (Rebelo, 1999). Geological travel and field work carried out by the scientists Carlos Ribeiro and J. Nery Delgado around the whole country allowed them to draft the known geological boundaries which gave way to the first edition of a 1/500 000 scale geological map of Portugal in 1876 (Rebelo, *op. cit.*). Intense mapping activity by these scientists, meanwhile joined by Paul Choffat (a Swiss geologist that had been employed by Carlos Ribeiro in 1879), carried on throughout the late nineteenth and early twentieth centuries and gave an even more detailed view of the geology of Portugal. However, with the passing away of Paul Choffat in 1919, most geological field work ceased, only to be fully resumed in the 1950's by achievement of Carlos Teixeira who drove forward a new geological mapping campaign by the *Serviços Geológicos de Portugal* (Portuguese Geological Survey).

It was around this time that some geological publications began to draw attention to the importance of a "geological reading" of the territory in order to understand the phenomenon of land occupation. Zoomorphic, phytomorphic and anthropomorphic outcrops became curiosities (Figure 1) that appealed for visitation and to the notion that geological heritage sites have large tourist attraction potential. Geological travel, however, was almost exclusively made by scientists, whether during field work or in the scope of field trips organized by geological congresses.

Figure 1. Zoomorphic (tortoise - Serra da Peneda/Gerês) and phytomorphic (peduncle - Nisa) granite outcrops (photos by: C. Teixeira, left; C. Romariz, right).

Probably the first major international congress to take place in Portugal, in a Spanish-Portuguese joint organization, was the *I Congresso Hispano-Luso-Americano de Geologia Económica* (1st Hispano-Luso-American Congress on Economic Geology), in September 1971. The scientific sessions occurred in Madrid and Lisbon and the general program included 9 field trips, 3 in Spain and 6 in Portugal, with the objective of not only showing the visitors sites with geological, hydrogeological and mining interest, but also to simultaneously allow them to appreciate the "varied Portuguese and Spanish landscapes" (Macieira, 1972). Of the 6 planned excursions in Portugal, only 5 effectively took place but they covered the whole country and counted with over 100 participants (Macieira, *op. cit.*). A few years later, the 26th International Geological Congress of 1980, in Paris also included two field trips to Portugal (although only one took place) which led to the publication of the first comprehensive work on the Geology of Portugal (Ribeiro et al., 1979; 1980).

In the 1980's the concept of Nature Tourism, in which Geotourism was included, was understood as a way to promote Nature Conservation in the perception that this type of tourism is more adjusted to the natural environment and can also be socially and economically beneficial for the local populations (Costa and Oliveira, 1986). In 1987, geotouristic trails[2] were outlined for a course for Cultural Tourism Guides organized by the *Centro Nacional de Cultura* (National Centre for Culture) and by PRONATUR, a Nature Tourism Cultural Cooperative (Sousa and Costa, 1987); and in the same year, the first truly geotouristic routes were mapped for the *Serra da Estrela* Natural Park region, namely a circuit along the *Alforfa* stream, a glacial valley between *Unhais da Serra* and the *Covão do Ferro* Dam (Pedro and Costa, 1987).

In 1998, a turning point in geological travel and tourism in Portugal occurred with the creation of the *Geologia no Verão* (Summer Geology) initiative launched by the Portuguese Ministry of Science and Technology, through the *Ciência Viva* (Science Alive) program. This

---

[2] In these trail guides, the term "geotouristic" was not effectively defined, but was undoubtedly used to refer to visits to areas with particular geological interest and, therefore, to geological tourism.

program was implemented with the purpose of promoting science and technology within society and to boost the development of the general public's scientific and technical culture. With the Summer Geology project, scientists, geologists and other experts from many different institutions (universities, research centres, municipalities, cultural associations and private companies) were encouraged and financially supported to organize free field trips, visits to mines and quarries, guided visits to museums and urban geology tours. Since 2005, more than 400 events have been organized every summer (598 in 2008 alone); most recently, in 2011, 42 different institutions organized 493 events involving thousands of participants[3]. The Summer Geology initiatives have definitely widened the audience of geological travel around the whole country.

Geotourism in Portugal, nowadays, is strongly associated to geological interpretation, by visiting geological heritage sites, and to the needs, objectives and advantages of geoconservation which are put in the frontline of geotouristic activities. The creation of two UNESCO Geoparks, Naturtejo in 2006, and Arouca Geopark in 2009 broadened the approach by including not only geodiversity and geoconservation concerns, but also a "sustainable territorial development strategy" which encompasses "the economic development of its territory through enhancement of a general image linked to the geological heritage and the development of Geotourism" (www.europeangeoparks.org).

THE SLOW MOVEMENT IN PORTUGAL

Slow Food (Figure 2) is a global, grassroots organization with supporters in 150 countries around the world who are linking the pleasure of good food with a commitment to their community and the environment.

A non-profit member-supported association, Slow Food was founded in 1989 to counter(act) the rise of fast food and fast life, the disappearance of local food traditions and people's dwindling interest in the food they eat, where it comes from, how it tastes and how one's food choices affect the rest of the world.

Today, Slow Food has over 100,000 members joined in 1,300 convivia – the movement's local chapters – worldwide, as well as a network of 2,000 food communities who practice small-scale and sustainable production of quality foods. Founder and President Carlo Petrini, believes "everyone has the right to good, clean and fair food". Good, meaning a high quality product with a flavorful taste, clean meaning the naturalness in the way the product was produced and transported, and fair, meaning adequate pricing and treatment for both the consumers and producers.

Slow Food was the first established part of the broader Slow Movement which advocates a cultural shift toward slowing down life's pace. Over time, this developed into a subculture in other areas, such as Cittaslow (Slow Cities), Slow Parenting, Slow Fashion, Slow Science and Slow Travel.

---

[3] Over 16700 participants in the whole "summer science alive" program which apart from geology also includes events related to biology, astronomy, engineering and visits to castles and lighthouses.

Figure 2. The Slow Food logo.

Figure 3. The "Marble Routes" slow geotouristic itineraries.

Slow Travel, an evolving movement that has taken its inspiration from nineteenth-century European travel writers, states that all too often the potential pleasure of the journey is lost by too eager anticipation of arrival. Given this, Slow Travel, viewed as a state of mind, allows travellers to engage more fully with communities along their route, often favouring visits to spots enjoyed by local residents rather than merely following guidebooks. Slow travellers generally will look for unhurried, low-impact journeys and for a stronger engagement with communities that lie en route. As such, slow travel shares some common values with ecotourism and geotourism.

Regarding Portugal, the movement appeared in 1997 thanks to Erik and Virgínia Kristensen, and in September 1999 Convivium Évora was created (later Convivium Alentejo). From then on, this Slow Food convivium has been engaged, amongst other activities, in the creation of the so-called Slow Itineraries, a range of slow geotouristic routes, based on the geological features of the visited regions and integrating other areas of knowledge. These slow geo-itineraries, always connected to Alentejo's landscapes, culture and heritage and obeying to Slow Food and Slow Travel philosophies, started in 2000 with the Marble Routes (Figure 3).

GEOTOURISM AND THE SLOW MOVEMENT

The primary concern that has led to the creation of slow geotouristic itineraries is focused on trying to broadcast to a wide audience, in a scientifically sound and at the same time appealing manner (simple and accessible), geological information and concepts and their relation to other areas of knowledge (e.g. geography, flora and fauna, history, gastronomy), in an integrated approach where geodiversity is the starting point for the reading and understanding of the territory and many of its various spaces and landscapes, allowing the definition of new sustainable tourism products.

This approach falls largely in the scope of the Slow Itineraries project that the Slow Food Alentejo has been developing, which promotes the integration and fruition of landscapes, knowledge and savours of each region, in a manner that respects and values local communities and their territory, always bearing in mind the Slow Food Movement concepts, such as slowness, conviviality, local and seasonal products and, of course, good, clean, and fair food.

The several itineraries that have already been created have involved many people with diverse scientific backgrounds, such as geology, geological resources and geotourism and also other fields of knowledge (e.g. history, cuisine, flora and fauna, rural development), besides traditional know-how brought by the local communities. These routes present local and regional characteristics (e.g. geological context and human occupation), always united by common principles, including the promotion of Geology, the cross-over of knowledge, the respect for the local environment and culture, and the integration of traditional know-how and savours.

It must be noted that these itineraries, although mostly pedestrian, can also be followed on bicycle, motorbike, car, or even on public transport. They are often organized in a network, are always circular, developed in rural, urban or mixed areas, planned for small groups (desirably up to 15 participants) with a duration ranging from 3-4 to 6 hours, always contemplating the possibility of tasting regional specialties in traditional spaces.

These itineraries and those which are still under assessment are intended to globally contribute, among other things, to (Lamberto and Caetano, 2010; 2011):

- Increase *public awareness* of geology and geological resources and alert people to their importance;
- Consider Geology and Geodiversity as the *starting point* for reading the territory, the base layer on which all other information is based on;
- *Bringing people to Nature,* highlighting its resources, promoting its recovery for past and new uses and boosting local economy;
- Seek to *minimize negative impacts* on the territory and involve the local community in the conservation of geological heritage;
- Consider the *applications of natural stone* as geo-cultural heritage sites and resources for the teaching of geological sciences;
- Promote the study of the *provenance of geological materials* used throughout history and the protection of their extraction sites;
- *Captivate visitors* and increase the time spent in the regions involved, through the sustained fruition of a unique and often unknown heritage;
- Promote the *sustainable development* of the inland countryside, namely of rural communities which are often located in economically depressed regions;
- Foster the creation of *new sustainable tourism products* that promote the integration of various disciplines, notably through the creation of Slow Geotouristic itineraries.

SLOW GEOTOURISTIC ITINERARIES

The "Marble Routes"

The "Marble Routes" invite to enjoyment and understanding of Nature and its humanization, through a net of routes centred on the Estremoz anticline (Alentejo, South Portugal), a geological structure well-known for the presence of vast Palaeozoic (over 250 million years) marble beds largely exploited by the local ornamental stone industry (Figure 4).

Figure 4. The Estremoz anticline ornamental stone industry.

Figure 5. The Marble Routes include visits to marble quarries and historical buildings.

Figure 6. Oenogastronomy and "good, clean and fair" local products.

Located in the most important Portuguese quarrying area (nearly 400 quarries), these slow geo-itineraries assume geological and mining heritage as the regional main structuring factor, an essential tool for reading and understanding this territory and an enhancing factor for sustainable development purposes, in a humanized space where natural processes remain fully active.

A set of urban, rural and mixed circuits, geographically vast, with nodes in the Estremoz, Borba and Vila Viçosa historical municipalities, and different levels of length and difficulty in a truly web-shaped arrangement, puts together this slow geotouristic network. It comprises visits to rock outcrops, soils and hydrogeology, marble quarries, processing plants and stone applications, as well as other local features such as vineyards, orchards, taverns, historical buildings and limekilns (Figure 5); also included are various typically geological activities such as field orientation techniques, geological surveying and rock sampling (Lamberto *et al.*, 2003) besides wine and food tasting. It intends to contribute to preservation and promotion of local heritage, environmental education and discovery of Nature, and improvement of local tourism potential, centred on geology, marble products and by-products and stonemasonry, and integrating other areas such as oenogastronomy, workmanship, history, landscapes and environment, fauna and flora... (Figure 6).

Diffusion of geological and mining knowledge will also favour private initiatives on local job generation and approach to Nature, valuing local resources, improving the well-being of local communities and making possible a stronger and longer lasting connection to the territory.

The first "Marble Routes" activities started with two slow geotouristic pedestrian walks in September 2000, within the *Geologia no Verão* (Summer Geology) program. Since then, and rather regularly, both pedestrian and motorized tours have been organized, which have allowed to make known the "Marble Routes" and the multifaceted heritage of this territory located in Alentejo, the *slowest* region of Portugal, and almost always ending with a short meal and a glass of wine in a traditional and local space - the tavern.

Geotourism in the Three Castles Region of Sebastião da Gama

The region of Arrábida corresponds to the mountainous area of the southern part of the Setúbal Peninsula, located 35 km south of Lisbon, the capital of Portugal. Much of the region is designated as the Arrábida Natural Park due to its exceptional natural values, whether they be biotic (fauna and flora) or abiotic (geological). In touristic terms, this area is also referred to as the Three Castles Region due to the well known towns of Sesimbra, Setúbal and Palmela, all of which have a generally well preserved and much visited hilltop castle (Figure 7).

The recognition of the touristic importance of this simultaneously Atlantic and Mediterranean region, where ocean and land join together, very close to Lisbon, with its towns, castles and outstanding natural environment, is well documented by many travel guides, of which we highlight one called "The touristic circuit of the three castles region" (Figure 8a), written in 1949 by Sebastião da Gama (Figure 8b), a teacher, writer and poet born in Vila Nogueira de Azeitão, right in the heart of the Arrábida region.

Unfortunately, Sebastião da Gama died very early, at the age of 27, but during his short life he produced a long list of writings, many of which were much inspired by the, in his words, "beautiful and mystical" environment of the Arrábida mountains. His first book of poems is named *"Serra-Mãe"*[4], undoubtedly dedicated to Arrábida (Figure 8c); even in the above mentioned touristic guide, Sebastião da Gama always refers to Arrábida with extremely admiring words.

Finally, the area is also famous for its food and wines. The latter are known worldwide, specially the *Moscatel* sweet white wine made from Muscat grapes that grow under the very particular climatic conditions of Arrábida; as to gastronomic features, urban, rural and piscatorial flavours all mix together and one must emphasize the quality of the regional cheeses and traditional sweets (from Azeitão), the many herbs used in food confection and, of course, the wide choice of seafood (fish and shellfish) that is found all around.

Figure 7. The Three Castles of Sesimbra (a), Setúbal (b) and Palmela (c) (photos by C. Sargedas).

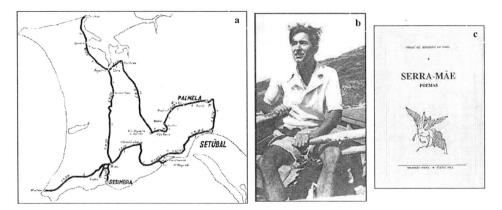

Figure 8. The Three Castles touristic circuit itinerary (a; in Gama, 1949) written by Sebastião da Gama (b; in www.azeitao.net) in 1949. Serra-Mãe (c), his first book of poems.

---

[4] Literal translation to English: "Mother-Mountain".

As has been briefly described, Arrábida presents a combination of interests that clearly point to a huge potential for *slow geotourism* activities. The first motivating combination emerges between Sebastião da Gama and geology in his "Three Castles" touristic guide, where the author describes one of the Arrábida Hills (the Risco Hill; Figure 9) as follows: "the mountain has the looks of a wave that impetuously moves forward and then, suddenly halts, cutting itself up in the air; it is a wave of rock and bush, it is the fossil of a wave[5]". This appealing description of the Risco Hill was the starting point for the production of a geotouristic route, enhanced by slow food principles: "The geology of the Three Castles Region that Sebastião da Gama wrote".

Figure 9. The Risco Hill, seen from the sea (photo by C. Sargedas).

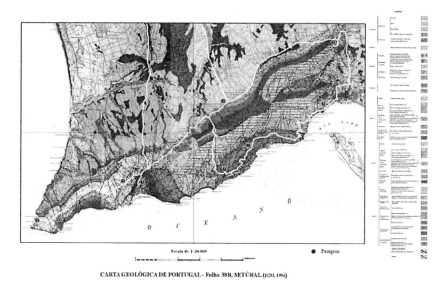

CARTA GEOLÓGICA DE PORTUGAL - Folha 38B, SETÚBAL (IGM, 1994)

Figure 10. Geological itinerary of the "The geology of the Three Castles Region that Sebastião da Gama wrote" geotouristic guide.

---

[5] In the original Portuguese version: "A serra tem o ar de uma onda que avança impetuosa e subitamente estaca e se esculpe no ar; é uma onda de pedra e mato, é o fóssil de uma onda."

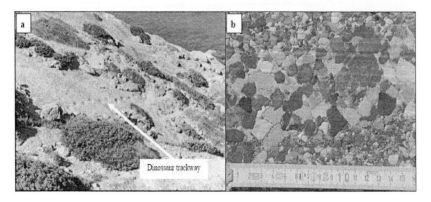

Figure 11. The Lagosteiros Lower Cretaceous dinossaur trackway site at Cabo Espichel (a); The Arrábida Breccia, a natural stone once exploited in Arrábida (b).

Figure 12. The final revelation regarding the relationship between Arrábida, Geology, Sebastião da Gama and Palmela Wines: *Serra Mãe* red wine, the title of Sebastião da Gama's first book, with Arrábida breccia in the top part of the wine label.

The itinerary that is followed (Figure 10) is very much the same as the one proposed by Sebastião da Gama in 1949 (Figure 8a), although the focus of the visit is somewhat different as it is centred mainly on the geological aspects of each of the proposed stops. In the field guide, together with the geological explanation of each stop, passages from the original guide are added in order to show diverse ways of describing the same places.

Places visited include three dinosaur trackway sites designated as Geomounuments (*Pedra da Mua*, *Lagosteiros* and *Avelino* Quarry; Figure 11a), the largest and presently inactive Arrábida Breccia (Figure 11b) quarry at *Cabeço do Jaspe*, and geological structures and stratigraphic sections in the Arrábida that explain the geological processes that gave origin to the mountains. Also included in the tour is a stop at the "Sebastião da Gama Municipal Museum" in Vila Nogueira de Azeitão, where participants are invited to become more acquainted with his life and work and where lunch can be centred on local products. The tour ends in Palmela, the major wine producing area, where a final revelation is made regarding the relationship between Sebastião da Gama, Geodiversity, Arrábida and Palmela wines (Figure 12).

Ecclesiastical Geology in the City of Lisbon

Most geotouristic activity is carried out in the Natural environment but, as we will see in this case, not exclusively. Many examples (e.g. Silva and Cachão, 1998; Cachão et al., 1999; Melen and Lamberto, 2001; Silva, 2009) prove that the urban environment also shows high potential for the development of this type of touristic activity, with the considerable advantage of allowing the establishment of relationships with cultural, historical and other characteristics of the town.

The potential for urban areas to contribute to raising awareness of geology has been widely acknowledged (Larwood and Prosser, 1996) and the nature of the "urban geological resource", or alternatively "urban cultural georesource" (Galopim de Carvalho, 1998; Caetano et al., 2003), can be outlined as follows (Bennett et al., 1996):

a) Museums, such as the Geological Museum and the Natural History National Museum (MNHN) in Lisbon, or the Marble Museum, in Vila Viçosa (Tavares and Lamberto, 2001);
b) Parks and open spaces, as they preserve natural exposures;
c) Man-made, temporary or permanent, geological exposures related to engineering works;
d) Natural stones used in building construction.

Natural stone, due to its high quality, durability, symbolism and nobleness and even to its acoustic properties, has for centuries been the most used material for the construction and ornamentation of buildings dedicated to religious ceremonies: e.g. chapels, churches, monasteries and abbeys (Hannibal, 1999). Ecclesiastical Geology is an area of geological research that should therefore be understood as the study of the rocks used as building material in these houses of worship (Sutherland, 2000; Potter, 2005; Caetano et al., 2006).

Among several purposes that a study of this kind can achieve are, for example:

a) The consideration of these occurrences as urban geological heritage sites;
b) The use of these stones as a geological science teaching resource;
c) The study of the various provenances that over time have been considered as construction material sources;
d) The study of the construction history of the city and the evolution of human occupation;
e) The creation of geo-touristic itineraries.

In the city of Lisbon, the Capital of Portugal, countless ecclesiastical buildings and other monuments have used ornamental stones in their construction and show a broad and extremely diverse variety of lithologies, from sources as near as the area surrounding Lisbon and the Estremoz Marble Zone, to places as far as Italy and Persia, and many different applications. A detailed inventory of the natural stones identified in over 70 ecclesiastical buildings throughout the city has been carried out in order to constitute a web geographical data base that may be used to achieve several of the purposes referred to above, namely the design of geo-touristic itineraries such as the one following the n° 28E tramway route between *Largo dos Prazeres* and *Anjos* (Caetano et al., 2007), one of the last Lisbon tram routes, still running, due largely to its high touristic interest (Figure 13).

Along this n° 28E tram route several sites with geological interest were identified regarding in particular the application of natural stone in ecclesiastical buildings (Caetano et al., 2007); consequently, implemented on the geological map of the city and framed by the various sites of geological interest, the tram route becomes a geological route. To start off the itinerary, in *Prazeres*, it is possible to visit an outcrop of Lower Miocene bryozoans (Figure 14) designated as "Lisbon Geomonument" under a protocol established between the Lisbon City Council and the National Museum of Natural History (Galopim de Carvalho, 2000).

Figure 13. Tram No. 28E and its route between *Prazeres* and *Anjos*.

Figure 14. Lower Miocene bryozoans Geomonument - *Rua Sampaio Bruno*.

Figure 15. The *Estrela* Basilica (left) and stone work in *S. Vicente de Fora* (right).

The route goes through some of the most touristic areas of the city, such as the *Estrela* Basilica (Figure 13), the National Assembly, *Bairro Alto*, *Baixa*, Lisbon Cathedral, St. *Luzia* Belvedere, *S. Vicente de Fora* Monastery, *Graça* and ends at the Church of *Anjos*. At these sites are some of the best-known churches of Lisbon where, in addition to issues related to religious art, history and architecture, particular attention is called to the enormous variety of natural stones (Figure 15) used in the construction and ornamentation of these buildings and to the evolution in the types of stones used over time and the constructive history of the city.

Ecclesiastical Geotourism in the Convento do Espinheiro Hotel (Évora)

The Convento do Espinheiro Heritage Hotel and Spa resulted from the rehabilitation of a XVth century convent designated as a Portuguese National Monument, and is today a luxurious hotel located on the outskirts of the historical city and UNESCO World Heritage site of Évora (in Alentejo, south Portugal). In 2009, and for the fourth consecutive year, it was considered by the World Travel Awards, the Best Spa Resort in Portugal and one of the 500 best hotels in the world by the American Travel and Leisure readers (the only Portuguese hotel in the list).

Challenged by the authors of this work to perform a commented visit to the historic stones that make up many of the spaces of the Convento do Espinheiro Hotel (Figure 16) and its immediate surroundings, the hotel unit's board responded very positively. The rapid achievement of this challenge within the "Summer Geology - 2009" (*Ciência Viva* Program) made Convento do Espinheiro Hotel, perhaps, the first hotel in Portugal to promote a geotouristic route within its premises, which in future developments should allow to promote a larger and fullest enjoyment of its superb spaces.

Based on a preliminary survey conducted on the occurrence of natural stones in the various areas of the Convento do Espinheiro Hotel, which revealed a considerable variety of lithologies, origins (e.g. Lisbon region, Alentejo Marble Zone) and diverse applications, an example is given of the cultural use of these geological resources (Bennett *et al.*, 1996) for producing innovative and captivating geotouristic itineraries.

Figure 16. The Convento do Espinheiro Heritage Hotel and Spa.

Figure 17. The Convento do Espinheiro Heritage Hotel and Spa.

Taking as a starting point the range of stones applied in both the construction and decoration of the Our Lady of Espinheiro Convent, the hotel located there, and all surrounding public areas, an itinerary was proposed through the establishment of a circular route that travels through easily accessible and nearby indoor (e.g. church, cistern) and outdoor areas (e.g. scoop wheels, chapel, orange orchard). The route follows some of the most charming areas of the Hotel (Figure 17), where several points of particular interest, namely geological interest, were identified. Special attention is given to the diversity of natural stones and their applications in the construction and decoration of buildings over time, and to other areas of interest such as the history and architecture of the buildings, the religious art, among others.

The proposed itinerary includes visits to various points of interest such as the stairs to the Diana Spa, the small and large scoop wheels, the *Campo Santo* (Holy Field), with the Mortuary Chapel of Garcia de Resende and Jorge Resende, several granite outcrops, the Orange Orchard, the Cistern, the convent cloisters, the Friar Carlos room, and the Our Lady of Espinheiro Church.

Along the itinerary, keeping in mind the principals of the Slow Food movement, many varied topics are addressed, such as the profuse use of natural stones, associated geological concepts and respective historical background, the petrogenetic cycle, local and regional geology, geochronology, the reconstruction of paleoenvironments, ornamental stones and their technological properties, the fracturing, weathering and erosion of rock materials, the magmatic processes, igneous mineralogy and petrology, hydrogeology, land occupation, the stone works and pottery, painting and related techniques (e.g. *trompe l'oeil*), the History of Portugal and religion, architecture, agricultural practices, oenogastronomic heritage and cuisine history.

During the visit, conducted in the "light of Geology", the integration of other disciplines is stressed, with special emphasis on the historical context of the implementation of certain stones. Standing out in this context are the Garcia de Resende *Campo Santo* (water and purification, marble stone and the exaltation of the poet), the cistern (water, the rule and memory of King D. *João II*), the cloisters (the granite and marble in aesthetic constructions), and the church (the foundations over granite outcrops, rock as a record of memory and power, and symbol of humility and penitence). The outlined route also involves, throughout the visit, activities such as geological map reading and geographic orientation, determination of map scales, marking the itinerary with identification and characterization of stone applications

It should be noted that the geologic information identified in the spaces covered by the Espinheiro Convent is the starting point of the route, complemented by other knowledge, allowing a deeper approach to the convent and its history (Bilou, 2006), the surrounding region and the history of Portugal. The importance of geology is often enhanced by addressing, for instance, its relationship to the particularities of land occupation, with paintings (e.g. pigments), and also with the gastronomy and wines, namely at a regional and local context.

CONCLUSION

The approach followed by these geotouristic itineraries is always multidisciplinary, using plain but scientifically sound language, focused on geological heritage, and addressing issues such as geotourism, the natural, material and immaterial heritage, promoting the mainstreaming and integration of diverse knowledge, including the connection between two sciences that deal with History, of the Earth and of Man. And, of course, they usually end with a *good, clean and fair meal,* made with the best local, traditional and seasonal products.

Therefore, the already innovative character of geotourism is, in the case of the geotouristic routes here presented, reinforced by the integration of other knowledge (e.g. history, culture, architecture, literature) and the "slow philosophy". The principles inherent to these activities formulate our conception of Geotourism more as an "approach" to tourism rather than as a "type" of tourism, similar to the suggestion made by J. Tourtellot at the recent Arouca International Congress of Geotourism (Tourtellot, 2011).

Evidently, the *slow geotourism* approach also fits well with the perception and objectives of sustainable tourism:

- it seeks to fulfil present needs of both tourists and the receptive regions while, by keeping unharmed and preserved the natural, cultural, historical and other resources essential to tourism development, it guarantees the same opportunity for the future;
- it does not bring environmental or socio-cultural stress to the receptive regions, thus preserving its overall environmental quality;
- the benefits of the tourism activity tend to reach the whole local community;
- it diversifies the touristic offer as it is based on the natural resources of the area and, at the same time, enhances the sense of place and the identity of the region;
- tourists reach a high level of satisfaction, which promotes and maintains the attractiveness of the destination.

It should be noted that the *slow geotourism* that has been promoted for a wide and diverse public (e.g. *Geologia no Verão* by the *Ciência Viva* program and the Slow Itineraries by Slow Food Alentejo), will continue in the future with other activities always framed by the *slow philosophy*. The established routes encourage not only contact with Nature but also socioeconomic development which, together with what must nowadays be considered as the fourth pillar of sustainability, i.e., culture, will contribute for an effective sustainable development of the regions involved. With *slow geotourism*, the geological framework of the visited region is always the starting point for reading and understanding the territory and its specificities (in a manner that is very similar to the oenological concept of *terroir*), and local cuisine emerges as its synthesis: "a country cuisine is its own landscape presented in a casserole" (Josep Pla).

As "a fast life is a shallow life" (Honoré, 2006), the hereby presented *slow geotourism* approach promotes the comprehension and fruition of slowness, which apparently is not a strange concept for all those who orbit the field of geology and geosciences, since it is present, for example, in the geologic time scale and in many of the known geological processes.

ACKNOWLEDGMENTS

Authors acknowledge: Paulo Hasse and Graça Brito for helpful suggestions and valuable collaboration in many slow geotouristic events; Carlos Costa for references on early geotouristic initiatives in Portugal; Rogério Rocha, for information on the first leading international congresses held in Portugal; Paula Robalo, for information and numbers concerning the Summer Geology Program; Carlos Sargedas, for the magnificent aerial photos in Arrábida; the cooperation and dedicated involvement of Dinis Pires, Director of the Convento do Espinheiro Heritage Hotel and Spa; Rita Vaz Freire and Adélia Gomes for introducing us to the natural stones in the churches of Lisbon; Daniella Pagliarello, Raquel Martinho and Mariana Quininha for help in creating the ecclesiastic database for Lisbon; Vanda Rocha, from the Sebastião da Gama Museum in Azeitão; all participants in the slow geotouristic events that have been organized over the last years.

REFERENCES

Bennett, M., Doyle, P., Larwood, J. G. and Prosser, C. D. (Eds.) (1996). *Geology on your doorstep. The role of urban geology in earth heritage conservation*. London: The Geological Society.

Bilou, F. (Coord.) (2006). *Convento do Espinheiro, memória e património*. Évora: SPPTH.

Cachão, M., Freitas, M. C. and Silva, C. M. (1999). Geologia Augusta: Património, geologia urbana e cultura. *Comunicações I Seminário Património Geológico Português*, 1-10.

Caetano, P. S., Lamberto, V. and Verdial, P. H. (2009). Ecclesiastical geology in the city of Lisbon, *ASMOSIA IX, ASMOPSIA/ICAC*, Tarragona, *poster*.

Caetano, P. S., Lamberto, V., Verdial, P. H. and Brito, M. G. (2009). *A Geologia da região dos três castelos de Sebastião da Gama. Guide book, Geologia no Verão 2009*. Évora: Associação Slow Food Alentejo.

Caetano, P. S., Verdial, P. H., Gregório, P., Heitor, A. P., Pedro, B. and Silva, I. (2003). A criação de circuitos geológicos no Almada Forum – um exemplo de divulgação da Geologia em meio urbano. *Ciências da Terra* (UNL), Lisboa, *n° esp. V*, 106-107; CD-ROM, I24-I27.

Caetano, P. S., Verdial, P. H., Lamberto, V., Gomes, A. and Freire, R. V. (2006). Geologia eclesiástica na cidade de Lisboa. O exemplo da Igreja do Convento dos Cardaes. *Livro Resumos VII Congresso Nacional de Geologia*, Vol. *III*, 933-936.

Caetano, P. S., Verdial, P. H., Lopes, M., Lamberto, V., Freire, R. V. and Gomes, A. (2007). *Geologia Eclesiástica, dos Prazeres aos Anjos. Guide-Book Geologia no Verão 2007*. Lisboa: CIGA.

Choffat, P (1908). Essai sur la tectonique de la chaine de l'Arrábida. *Mem. Com. Geol. Portugal,* 1-89.

Costa, C. N. and Oliveira, L. (1986). Conservação da natureza versus rentabilidade económica – uma falsa questão. *BIOS, Revista Liga Protecção Natureza*, 34, 10-12.

Figueirôa, S. F., Silva, C. P. and Pataca, E. M. (2007). Investigating the colonies: native geological travellers in the Portuguese empire in the late eighteenth and early nineteenth centuries. In P. N. Wyse Jackson (ed.), *Four centuries of geological travel:*

the search for knowledge on foot, bicycle, sledge and camel (pp. 297-310). London: Geological Society, special publication 287.

Galopim de Carvalho, A. M. (1998). Geomonumentos – Uma reflexão sobre a sua classificação e enquadramento num projecto alargado de defesa e valorização do Património Natural. *Actas V Cong. Nac. Geologia, Comun. Instit. Geol. Mineiro, 84*(2), G3-G5.

Galopim de Carvalho, A. M. (2000). *Geomonumentos de Lisboa - Jazida de Briozoários do Miocénico Inferior de Lisboa. Pólo Sampaio Bruno*. Lisboa: Museu Nacional História Natural (UL).

Gama, S. (1949) – A região dos três Castelos que Sebastião da Gama escreveu – Circuito turístico. *www.azeitao.net/Sebastiao/circuito_castelos*.

Hannibal, J. T. (1999). Guide to stones used for houses of worship in Northeastern Ohio. *Cleveland State University Urban Center Sacred Landmarks Monograph Series*, 1-57.

Honoré, C. (2006). *O movimento Slow*. Cruz Quebrada: Estrela Polar.

Hose, T. A. (1995). Selling the story of Britain's Stone. *Environmental Interpretation, 10*, 2, 16-17.

Lamberto, V. and Caetano, P. S. (2010). Geoturismo *Slow* e rochas ornamentais. *Rochas and Equipamentos, Comedil, 98*, 52-57.

Lamberto, V. and Caetano, P. S. (2011). Slow Geotourism: an integrated approach to attain sustainable tourism. In D. Rocha and A. Sá (Eds.), *Proceed. International Congress Geotourism - Arouca 2011* (pp. 243-245). Arouca: Arouca Geopark Association.

Lamberto, V., Melen, F., Silva, A., Tapadas, C. and Xarepe, C. (2003). Rotas do mármore - rede integrada de circuitos geoturísticos. *VI Cong. Nac. Geol., Ciênc. Terra, DCTFCTUNL, n.º esp. V*, CD-ROM, I43-I46.

Larwood, J. and Prosser, C. (1996). The nature of the urban geological resource: an overview. In M. Bennett et al. (Eds.), *Geology on your doorstep* (pp. 19-30). London: The Geological Society.

Macieira, F. G. (1972). O I congresso Hispano-Luso-Americano de Geologia Económica. Sua realização e suas conclusões. *Bol. Minas, 8*(4), 203-265.

Macfarlane, R. (2003). *Mountains of the mind*. New York: Pantheon Books.

Melen, F. and Lamberto, V. (2001). A rede integrada de percursos geoturísticos da Zona dos Mármores. *Congresso Internacional sobre Património Geológico e Mineiro*, 27.

Newsome, D. and Dowling, R. (2010). *Geotourism: The tourism of geology and landscape*. Oxford: Good Fellow Publishers.

Pedro, R. and Costa, C. N. (1987). Um percurso de natureza na Serra da Estrela. *I Encontro sobre Turismo e Ambiente*. Évora.

Pinto, M. S. and Bouheiry, A. (2007). The German geologist Georg Hartung (1821-1891) and the geology of the Azores and Madeira islands. In P. N. Wyse Jackson (ed.), *Four centuries of geological travel: The search for knowledge on foot, bicycle, sledge and camel* (pp. 229-238). London: Geological Society, special publication 287.

Potter, J. F. (2005). Ecclesiastical geology – a return to Victorian field standards. *Geoscientist, 15*(10), 4-7.

Rebelo, J. A. (1999). *As Cartas Geológicas ao serviço do desenvolvimento*. Lisboa: Instituto Geológico e Mineiro.

Ribeiro, A., Antunes, M. T., Ferreira, M. P., Rocha, R. B., Soares, A. F., Zbyszewski, G., Moitinho de Almeida, F., Carvalho, D. and Monteiro, J. H. (1979). *Introduction à la géologie generale du Portugal.* Lisboa: Serviços Geológicos de Portugal.

Ribeiro, A., Antunes, M. T., Ferreira, M. P., Rocha, R. B., Soares, A. F., Zbyszewski, G., Moitinho de Almeida, F., Carvalho, D. and Monteiro, J. H. (1980). Portugal - Introduction à la géologie generale. Excursions: 016A - 045 A. *Livret-Guide, 26e Congres Geologique International*, 1-142.

Silva, C. M. and Cachão, M. (1998). "Paleontologia Urbana": percursos citadinos de interpretação e educação (paleo)ambiental. *Actas V Cong. Nac. Geologia, Comun. Instit. Geol. Mineiro, 84*(2), H33-H37.

Silva, C. M. (2009). "Fósseis ao virar da esquina": um percurso pela paleontologia e pela geodiversidade urbana de Lisboa". *Paleolusitana, I*, 459-463.

Sousa, R. and Costa, C. N. (1987). Turismo de Natureza. *I Encontro sobre Turismo e Ambiente*, Évora.

Stokes, A. M., Cook, S. D. and Drew, D. (2003). *Geotourism: The new trend in travel.* Washington DC: Travel Industry Association of America Report.

Sutherland D. S. (2000). Ecclesiastical geology. In Hancock P. I. and Skinner B. J. (eds.), *The Oxford Companion to the Earth* (pp. 292-295). Oxford: Oxford University Press.

Tavares, S. and Lamberto, V. (2001). O museu do mármore. *Congresso Internacional sobre Património Geológico e Mineiro*, 159.

Tourtellot, J. B. (2011). Geotourism via national geographic: an approach for protecting destination quality. In D. Rocha and A. Sá (Eds.), *Proceed. International Congress Geotourism - Arouca 2011* (p. 15). Arouca: Arouca Geopark Association.

Wilson, L. G. (2007). The geological travels of Sir Charles Lyell in Madeira and the Canary Islands. In P. N. Wyse Jackson (ed.), *Four centuries of geological travel: the search for knowledge on foot, bicycle, sledge and camel* (pp. 207-228). London: Geological Society, special publication 287.

In: New Trends Towards Mediterranean Tourism Sustainability   ISBN: 978-1-62257-627-2
Editors: L. M. Rosalino, A. Silva and A. Abreu   © 2012 Nova Science Publishers, Inc.

Chapter 3

SUSTAINABILITY OF GOLF IN SPAIN

Francisco J. Del Campo Gomis,
Asunción M. Agulló Torres and David B. López Lluch
Department of Agrienvironmental Economics,
Universidad Miguel Hernández, Spain

ABSTRACT

Golf sustainability definition, both from an industry or sports organization perspective, is very similar and is supported by the four basic pillars of sustainability, grouped into two blocks: environmental sustainability (ecological) and socio-economic sustainability (economic, social and cultural). The environmental sustainability of golf courses is based on the analysis of the following aspects: climate, landscape, topography, soil type, hydrology, availability of water resources, nature reserves, and historical and cultural assets. The socioeconomic profitability, the existing infrastructure, the structure of land ownership and the capital structure are the key aspects to analyze the sustainability of golf courses from the socioeconomic point of view. In Spain, a spectacular golf development has been registered in the last 20 years, mainly due to the constant increase of golf tourism. Therefore, golf is a sport socially and economically important for Spain.

However, the rise of golf in Spain may have led to various environment impacts in the areas where it is implemented and thus created problems of sustainability. In this chapter we focus on the global analysis of the sustainability of actual golf courses in Spain. We first analyzed the development of golf in Spain; secondly, we explain succinctly the relationship between golf courses and the environment; thirdly, we analyze and assess the sustainability of golf courses in Spain; and finally, we describe the major findings of this study. The general conclusion of the chapter is that sustainability of golf courses in Spain can be defined as remarkable and does not present any serious environmental and socioeconomic problems as long as four factors are taken into account: the socio-economic profitability, the capital structure, the availability of water resources and the hydrology. However, the future economic, social and environmental impacts will determine if the managers of golf courses and the Public Administrations of Spain act correctly to assure that golf courses are and will be sustainable.

1. INTRODUCTION

In 1987, the report "Our Common Future" (or the "Brundtland Report") indicated that it is in the hands of humanity to make development sustainable, i.e. to ensure that it meets the needs of the present without compromising the ability of future generations to meet their own needs. The further development of this idea has led to an integrated approach to sustainable development as a sum of four concepts of sustainability (Aledo and Dominguez, 2002):

I. *Ecological Sustainability*: demands that the development is compatible with the maintenance of ecological processes, biodiversity and biological resources.
II. *Economic Sustainability*: demands that development is economically efficient and balanced between generations.
III. *Social sustainability* requires that development increases the control of individuals over their own lives and reduces social inequalities.
IV. *Cultural sustainability*: imposes that the development is consistent with the cultures and values of people affected by it, and to help maintain and strengthen community identity.

The first commitment to sustainability given by golf came in 1997 with the project "Committed to the Environment" funded by the Commission of the European Communities 96/C/342/3060 conducted by the Ecological Unit European Golf Association. In the report, it is noted that "golf is a sizeable industry that continues to grow in Europe and cannot operate in isolation from society so it should commit to respecting the environment, as one of the main sports that are played on land, golf is likely to have more interaction with the environment" (Stubbs, 1997).

Martins et al (2003) embody the concept and outline that for the development of the golf industry to be sustainable it must be simultaneously:

I. *Competitive.* Through its ability to stay in business, generating profit in the medium- and long -erm, offering services and products of high quality.
II. *Environmentally responsible.* Golf is an industry that consumes natural resources, primarily land and water, as well as intangible services such as landscape, biodiversity or climate. Protection of these resources is vital so golf presents irreplaceable competitive advantages.
III. *Generating positive economic and social impacts.* The balanced development of golf with the tourism and construction may contribute to significant impacts on the economy.
IV. *Integrated in the regional development.* Golf is an extensive land-consuming activity; therefore, the location of course conditions is, in turn, conditioned by the physical arrangement of the territory.

Meanwhile, the Royal and Ancient Golf of St. Andrews (RandA, 2011) has also defined sustainable development and management of golf courses as: "Optimizing the playing quality of the golf course in harmony with the conservation of its natural environment under economically sound and socially responsible management". These four parameters cannot be considered in isolation, defined as follows:

I. *Quality game.* Golf clubs cannot survive unless they maintain the quality of their playing surfaces.

II. *Conservation of the environment.* In the context of the golf course, this refers to the care of the natural environment, including landscape quality, air, water and soil conservation. The impact of the course construction, as well as maintenance should also be considered.

III. *Economy.* This refers to the economic impact of design, as well as direct and indirect costs of managing golf courses, and how to affect its economic viability.

IV. *Social responsibility.* This refers to how the golf course is related to its local environment and its contribution in the broadest sense.

Both definitions of sustainability in golf, either from the first vision as an industry or the second view as a sports organization, are very similar and affect the four basic aspects of sustainability defined and grouped into two blocks: environmental sustainability (ecological) and socio-economic sustainability (economic, social and cultural).

However, it is widely accepted throughout the world of golf that to achieve golf sustainability (both environmental and socioeconomic), and that this leads to a good social acceptance of golf, it is essential to have a good management of all sustainability aspects of golf courses from "cradle to cradle", i.e. its design, construction, management and possible reversal. Thus, obtaining a sustainable golf course, there should be a continuous goal and in which all actors must ask the following (R and A, 2011): Are we currently sustainable? Could we be more sustainable? Are we going to be sustainable in 20, 50 or 100 years?

In Spain, a spectacular golf development has been produced in the last 20 years. This is due to two causes: first, the development of golf tourism, and secondly, the increase in Spanish golfers.

The sum of these causes in Spain has almost tripled the golf courses in the last 20 years (EGA, 2010). Therefore, golf is a sport both socially and economically important for Spain, but obviously the rise of golf in Spain may have led to various influences on the environment where it is located and thus creating problems of sustainability, so the development of golf in Spain will be sustainable or not.

For a full analysis of the sustainability of golf in Spain, it is necessary, first, to establish a global analysis of the sustainability of the territory, from both socio-economic and environmentally points of view, to establish if the actual number of golf courses are sustainable or if some golf courses can be built that are sustainable. On the other hand, once such an analysis has been performed to accurately locate each golf course, local analysis of sustainability through environmental impact studies and their Environmental Impact Statements should be performed.

Finally, sustainability should be analyzed in the operational phase of the golf course for what would be advisable to evaluate environmental management systems currently applied, whether general (EMAS, ISO 14001, ...) or specific for golf courses (Audubon, Committed to the environment, ...).

In this chapter, we focus only the global analysis of the sustainability of actual golf courses in Spain. To do this, we first analyze the development of golf in Spain; second, we explain succinctly the relationship between golf courses and the environment; third, we analyze and assess the sustainability of golf courses in Spain; and finally fourth, we describe the major findings.

2. GOLF IN SPAIN

In the golf world, which is detailed in Table 1, we can see that both North America and Asia are the most important areas in the number of players worldwide, representing 52.4% and 37.3%, respectively, while Europe ranks third with 5.9% of players. Taking as reference the number of golf courses continues to lead the North American ranking with 59.2%, but Europe ranked second with 18.9% and Asia third with 10.9%.

For its part, Europe is producing a spectacular development of golf as a sport that has led it to have, in 2010, more than 4.4 million players and 6,741 golf courses. Figure 1 shows the steady growth in the number of golf courses and players for the period 1990-2010 in Europe, with an average annual growth of 4.6% and 7.2%, respectively.

Table 2 shows that around 3/4 of courses and players throughout Europe are concentrated in six countries (UK, Germany, France, Sweden, Ireland and Spain). As for golf courses, Spain is the sixth and the number of players in fifth.

Table 1. Status of golf in the World

	N° Courses	% Courses / World	N° Golfers	% Golfers / World
Africa	622	2.00	133,850	0.20
North America	18,693	59.20	31,600,000	52.40
South America	663	2.10	160,455	0.30
Asia	3,440	10.90	22,520,700	37.30
Europe	5,981	18.90	3,556,500	5.90
Oceania	2,184	6.90	2,341,800	3.90
TOTAL	31,583	100	60,313,305	100

Source: National Golf Foundation (2005).

Table 2. Status of golf in Europe (2010)

Country	N° Courses	% Courses / Europe	N° Golfers (thousands)	% Golfers / Europe
United Kingdom	2,576	38.20	1,109	25.00
Germany	700	10.40	599	13.50
France	574	8.50	410	9.20
Sweden	456	6.80	512	11.50
Ireland	417	6.20	259	5.80
Spain	345	5.10	338	7.60
EUROPE	6,741		4,438	

Source: Own elaboration from EGA (2010) and Eurostat (2009).

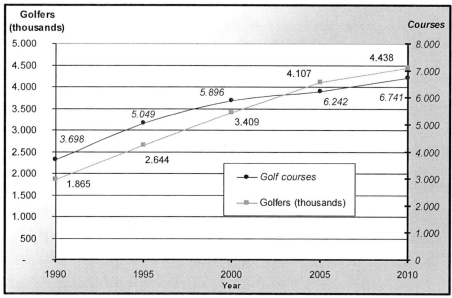

(Source: EGA, 2010).

Figure 1. Evolution of courses and golfers in Europe (1990-2010).

Table 3. Major rates in Europe golf

Country	Availability Inhabitants / course	Popularity % Golfers / Inhabitants	Capacity Golfers / course	Occupancy km² / course
United Kingdom	23,025	1.90	431	95
Germany	117,286	0.70	856	510
France	102,939	0.70	714	948
Sweden	19,428	5.80	1,123	987
Ireland	8,959	6.90	621	169
Spain	127,851	0.80	980	1463
EUROPE	86,170	0.80	658	966

Source: Own elaboration from EGA (2010) and Eurostat (2009).

Table 3 shows some rates of golf courses that will serve to analyze what is the comparative situation in golf development between Spain and the most advanced European countries concerning this sport.

Thus, the highest availability (inhabitants/golf courses) corresponds to Spain (127,851) that is 14 times than the highest of countries, Ireland (8,959), and 1.4 times than the European average; for which, according to this criterion, there is a scope to develop new golf courses.

The European country where golf is most popular (golfers/inhabitants) is Ireland where 6.9% of the population plays. The European average is 0.8%, as in Spain. However, Spain still has a chance to generate new golfers to have a value 8.6 times lower than Ireland, 4.7 lower than Sweden and 2.4 lower than the UK.

The European average for the capacity of golf courses (golfers/course) is 658 and Sweden is the country where the highest value is almost doubled (1,123). For its part, Spain has the second highest value with 980 (48% higher than the European average) mainly due to the shortage of courses and as a part of golf players are tourists from other countries, which keeps its profitability and, in turn, indicates that there is room for more golf courses.

Finally, the occupancy (km^2/golf course) in Spain is one course for every 1,463 km^2, being 51% higher than the European average and 15.3 times higher than the country with the greatest density which is the United Kingdom (95 km^2/golf course), indicating that there is still ample land to build new golf courses. As seen above, Spain is a country whose development of golfing, both golfers and courses, has potential for growth relative to other more golf-developed European countries.

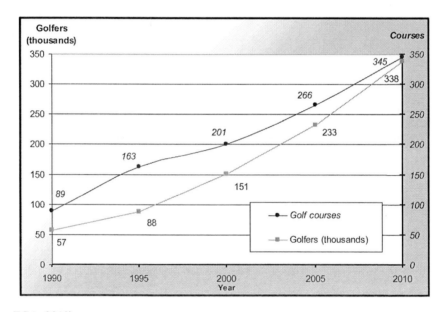

(Source: EGA, 2010).

Figure 2. Evolution of courses and golfers in Spain (1990-2010).

To better understand the development of golf in Spain, we analyze Figure 2 which shows the evolution between 1990 and 2010 of the number of players and golf courses. Players in the period 1990-2010 were multiplied by 4.9 to an annual rate of 24.6% to 333,818, while the golf courses have been multiplied by 2.8, but at a slower annual rate of 14.4% (13 courses/year) to get to 345 in 2010.

The most developed provinces in golf courses in Spain (those with more than 15 golf courses) are representing in Table 4, and show a higher concentration of this sport in the Mediterranean coastal provinces, with good weather and a large influx of golf tourists (Malaga, Cadiz, Balearic Islands, Murcia, Alicante and Girona) or in the provinces with large populations (Madrid and Barcelona). These 8 provinces represent 16% of the provinces of Spain, but at 54.6% of golf courses and 59.6% of golfers.

Table 4. Status of golf in Spain by province (2010)

Province	Nº Courses	% Courses / Spain	Nº Golfers	% Golfers / Spain
Malaga	44	13.10	22,426	6.70
Madrid	26	7.70	97,275	28.90
Cadiz	24.5	7.30	12,026	3.60
Baleares	23	6.80	8,147	2.40
Murcia	18	5.30	6,905	2.00
Alicante	17.5	5.20	10,820	3.20
Barcelona	16	4.70	38,797	11.50
Girona	15	4.50	4,490	1.30
SPAIN	337		336,986	

* January 1. Only provinces with more than 10 courses.
** 18-hole equivalent course without Pitch and Putt. 1 equivalent course = 18 holes; 0.5 equivalent course = 9 holes.
Source: Own elaboration from RFEG (2010).

Golf tourism has become the motor of development of golf in Spain, mainly in the provinces of the Mediterranean coast. Spain is the second most important country in world tourism, both in terms of number of visitors and revenue generated by them. Within tourism, in recent years, golf tourism has emerged as a product that tends to satisfy a demand generated by tourists whose main motivation is to play golf; but also in Spain, the residential tourism associated with golf, i.e. is people with second homes who spend long periods in Spain, mainly in winter, of which 11.7% play golf regularly is very important (Diario Información, 2007).

European countries that host the largest number of courses and most players are in central and northern Europe. In general, these countries have enough golf courses to satisfy their demand and, in some cases in the UK, more golf courses are being offered today that demand exists for them (EGU, 2004). However, the main problem facing the players in these countries is the climate, causing a strong seasonality in the use and enjoyment of their courses. Therefore, countries like Spain that have characteristics of ideal weather for playing golf, mainly in the Mediterranean coastal areas, currently have an excellent opportunity to meet this demand (Del Campo et al., 2006). Consequently, the high season of golf tourism in Spain is March, April and October which is very different from the product's traditional high season 'sun and beach', so the golf tourism in Spain promotes low season tourism (Turespaña, 2004).

Finally, KPMG (2008), 90% of European tour operators expected golf tourism to grow, 9% that it would stagnate and only 1% said it would suffer a gradual decline. Furthermore, these European tour operators ranked Spain as the second largest market for golf tourism in the coming years, behind Portugal.

3. GOLF AND THE ENVIRONMENT

A golf course properly planned, designed, constructed and maintained, is potentially environmentally friendly, and can contribute to improve their landscape value. The environmental benefits in Spain according to golf advocates are: restoration and landscape conservation, recovery of degraded landscapes, the positive effects on flora and fauna, the use of wastewater, and the positive effects on the socioeconomic environment (Borrego, 2002).

However, there are also some disadvantages that surround the golf courses. The controversy surrounding them relies on causes that are not inherent to the course itself, but mainly from: i) a poor performance and management of its promoters, ii) the lack of rigor in the media and procedures employed or even iii) ignorance of their managers and detractors (Borrego, 2002).

The most common criticisms are: the use of space, alteration and destruction of the environment, water consumption, pollution from the use of fertilizers and pesticides and their use as an excuse to build houses outside the urban environment. A golf course must function properly as a sports facility where golf is practiced (because this is its reason for being) and, consequently, any environmental program should be complemented with the specific requirements of the sport. This does not imply that environmental considerations must take second place, but must be balanced. Consequently, the environmental benefits will be sustainable only if the course is working properly (Stubbs, 1997).

According to the ME (2001), one of the main objectives to be achieved by any golf course is to adopt a perspective that conceives it as a space that, far from overcoming its environment, is inserted into it, forming together a harmonious and functional system. Therefore, it is necessary to adopt an environmental integration approach and to incorporate environmental sensitivity and commitment in each and every one of their decisions. Finally, the key to achieving the objectives of environmental integration requires addressing three major questions: i) Is golf a reasonable activity from the viewpoint of the environment where it is located?; ii) Is the golf course located correctly in the environment?; iii) Is the golf course properly designed, regulated and managed?

4. GLOBAL ANALYSIS AND ASSESSMENT OF SUSTAINABILITY OF GOLF COURSES IN SPAIN

Global assessment of the sustainability of golf courses in Spain for their current and future development should affect both socioeconomic sustainability (economic, social and cultural) and environmental sustainability (ecological).

To achieve this, a good management of all aspects of sustainability of a golf course from "cradle to cradle" is necessary and without ever losing sight that it must have quality facilities to enable a sustainable game.

4.1. Analysis of Socioeconomic Sustainability

The socioeconomic profitability, the existing infrastructure, the structure of land ownership and the capital structure are the key aspects to analyze the sustainability of golf courses in Spain from the socioeconomic point of view.

4.1.1. Socioeconomic Profitability

For the golf courses in the Public Sector (which is the one with the initiative), the interest of promoting a course and the main reason for its construction, is to promote the sport among all citizens (ME, 2001).

In the non-public courses, it is a necessary condition to obtain an economic return, since the golf owes its existence solely to the possibility of maintaining a return on investment (Del Campo, 2006). To make a golf course profitable you must, among others, perform a market study to explore the possibility of business, type of installation, marketing and operating model.

To analyze the socio-economic return, the following aspects should be atken into account (ME, 2001):

I. The Importance of Combining Social Benefit with Economic Profitability of the Golf Course

There is a desired balance to be achieved by the operators of a golf course, set between the interests of providing services to potential golfers, both locals and visitors (with a good price/quality ratio) and of obtaining benefits, derived from the business facility's promoter.

II. The Economic Viability of Operating a Golf Course

In Spain, it was difficult to have a golf course that was not located in a leading tourist area, which could cover the costs of building and maintaining profitability through proper exploitation (ME, 2001). The reality of the past 10 years has given this validity, as most golf courses (65%) that have been made since then, are in tourist areas. In Spain, given the nature of the club: social, commercial or mixed operating account may show some differences in items of income and expenses, with these annual benefits: € 298,980 social, € 613,350 mixed and 967,800 € commercial (Aymerich, 2005). However, the managers of Spanish golf courses have noted the current economic crisis with significant reductions of benefits. This is because golf is among the leisure services and these are the first expenses that families tend to reduce to adjust their family economies.

III. Competitors

This is discussed through the development and status of other golfing areas, distinguishing the areas where demand depends on tourism to those based solely on local players. We make a comparison of the development of golf courses in Spain, which in 2010 totaled 345, with the major golfing countries of Europe and the European average. For this, Table 5 shows the results of what would be the number of golf courses in Spain if the availability and capacity of the golf courses would be identical to the five major European golfing countries (which are over Spain in terms of number of golf courses) and the European average.

With regard to the two parameters analyzed (availability and capacity), Spain is, in all cases, below the five countries and even below the European average, which indicates a potential margin for the existence of more golf courses.

It should be noted that, according to KPMG (2008), golf courses in Spain are among the best in terms of number of rounds played in the countries of the EMA (Europe, Middle East and Africa). The 20% of Spanish courses reach average values of 54,000 rounds/year which means that they are 35% greater than the threshold of profitability of 40,000 rounds/year reported by Martins (2003).

Consequently, all of the analyses performed in this section clearly indicated that the existing golf courses in Spain may have some socioeconomic sustainable problems due to lack of profitability caused by the current crisis; but when Spain recovers from it, it will have a potential gap to make its golf courses profitable and, consequently, to build more.

Table 5. Number of golf course in Spain if the Availability and Capacity are equal to the main golfing countries of Europe

Country	Equal Availability	Equal Capacity
United Kingdom	1,916	785
Germany	376	395
France	428	473
Sweden	2,270	301
Ireland	4,923	544
EUROPE	512	513

Source: Own elaboration from EGA (2010) and Eurostat (2009).

4.1.2. Existing Infrastructure

The correct location of the golf courses will greatly determine its sustainability, mainly due to the need for certain infrastructure in the vicinity. It is necessary to emphasize the importance of the golf courses are located next to the items listed below:

I. *Accessibility:* The study of the roads to a golf course is very important because it will mark its quality and its demand. It makes no sense to locate the golf course in an inaccessible area, because a golf course cannot and should not be connected by roads in poor condition (Hawtree, 1983).

II. *Urban Infrastructure: i.e. water, electricity, sewerage etc:* As with any other work or project, planning a golf course must echo the urban infrastructure in the area: power lines, both to the clubhouse to the different machines of the course, drinking water supply (not for use of irrigation) and the sewerage to facilitate the disposal of wastewater (Urban Land Institute, 1981).

III. *Resorts:* To focus on tourism courses, the nearby presence of hotels is very important to study the housing for the tourist that is intended to attract.

Spain is known for being one of the best countries in the world for infrastructure and over the past 20 years it has undertaken a major modernization that included a key renovation of its facilities.

The network of motorways will allow all Spanish cities in 2020 to have direct access and have located more than 94% of the population within 30 km around. In regard to transport by rail (where Spain has a network of over 15,000 km), the lines of high-speed train planned that, by 2020, 90% of the population is within 50 km of a station of this network.

In relation to air transport, there are approximately 250 airlines operating 49 airports in Spain which connected the country with the major cities worldwide. Spain also has excellent sea ports with more than 53 international ports in the Mediterranean and Atlantic coasts (MF, 2010).

Infrastructure both in terms of communication and urban nature (water, electricity, sewerage ...) are generally well-developed in Spain and are not a constraint to sustainable development of golf courses. Thus, the golf courses whose target audience is Spanish players are usually located near farms with easy access and all services necessary to provide a quality service. For its part, the golf courses that are located in tourist areas on the Spanish coast, aimed primarily at attracting golf tourists, have a basic tourism infrastructure (airports, hotels, roads...) with sufficient capacity to absorb the flow of golfers; mainly because the high tourist season of golf does not match the high season of "sun and beach" tourism.

Therefore, the existing infrastructures in Spain currently contribute in a positive manner to the socioeconomic sustainability of golf courses.

4.1.3. Structure of Land Ownership

The structure of land ownership is a very important factor in locating a golf course and being able to make it sustainable, since it is a sport that requires a large amount of land for its construction (a 18 hole golf course requires approximately 50 hectares) that is often difficult or expensive to obtain. The specific aspects to take into account, to obtain land for a golf course, are the structure of farms, current uses, legal classification and ownership of land.

The influence of the structure of land ownership should be analyzed by the following items:

I. *Comparable occupancy*: Table 6 shows the number of golf courses that Spain would have if the occupancy were the same as in the leading golfing European countries. It shows that the 345 existing golf courses in Spain are very small in comparison with the level of occupancy of these countries and therefore is sustainable.

II. *Land use:* Currently 34% of the total area of Spain is intended for crops, 13% is devoted to meadows and pastures, 36% to forest and 13% to other uses, where the golf courses are included statistically (Table 7).

In Spain, there are currently 337 golf courses of 18 holes equivalent mean a total of 16.850 hectares for golf courses (considering an average of 50 hectares per course), representing 0.2% of "other areas" and 0.03 % of the total area. As a requirement of land for new golf courses in Spain, there is enough surface for implementation without affecting the development of agriculture, and that, considering that the new golf courses are set up on farmland or grassland, the surface of existing golf courses occupy only 0.08% of that surface.

It should also be noted that a possible change in land use from agricultural land into a sport activity, like golf, is well-regarded by Spanish society, as Garcia-Ferrando (2002) indicates that 84% of Spanish population are happy to convert rural land with low productivity in public areas for sports and recreation, being golf's fifth major activity on the population (21%) to use those areas.

Table 6. Number of golf course in Spain if the Occupancy is equal to the main golfing countries of Europe

Country	Equal Occupancy
United Kingdom	5,327
Germany	990
France	533
Sweden	512
Ireland	2,995
EUROPE	523

Source: Own elaboration from EGA (2010) and Eurostat (2009).

Table 7. General distribution of land in Spain (2009)

Land type	Thousands of ha	%
Crop land (total)	17,216	34.00
Dry	3,677	7.00
Irrigation	13,539	27.00
Meadows and grassland	6,745	13.00
Forest land	18,291	36.00
Other surfaces	8,284	13.00
TOTAL	50,537	100

Source: Own elaboration from MMARM (2011).

The majority of golf courses being built in Spanish tourist areas are linked to the development of a housing joined to the same ground that also holds, not taking into account the quantifying surface occupied independently of the course itself. Urbanization can be made whether or not the golf course and this one is include by housing developers in order to give added value to the urbanization (in Spain, the views to a golf course are considered to replace the views of the sea and in some cases, can mean up to an increase of 40% of its normal value independently of the course).

III. *Surface structure of farms*: Table 8 shows the structure of the agricultural area of farms in Spain, according to the Agricultural Census (INE, 2009b). Globally, there are plenty of other farms over 50 hectares (103.653) that can accommodate almost on their own a golf course and have a total of 16 million hectares (70% of all agricultural land). Obviously, any combination of any size farm can add the 50 hectares required for a golf course and therefore this should not be a constraint to sustainability.

However, in the Spanish Mediterranean coastal areas, the average size of the farms is one of the lowest, so the difficulty to find farms can be a condition for the sustainable development of golf courses. This is because it is considered that the price of land, together with the possible cascading effect of prices if they should buy various farms may not allow its economic sustainability. This problem is already reflected in the actual search, by tourism promoters for inlands for investment due to the scarcity of land and high prices of coastal areas (Diario Información, 2006).

After this analysis we can say that from the standpoint of the structure of land ownership in Spain, golf courses today are quite sustainable and future development will tend to be located further away from the coast.

Table 8. Agriculture land* ownership structure in Spain (2009)

Size	Farms		Surface	
(ha)	Nº	%	ha	%
< 1	81,630	8.40	39,655	0.17
1 a < 2	188,642	19.42	257,553	1.08
2 a < 5	232,800	23.96	736,785	3.10
5 a < 10	141,862	14.60	995,478	4.19
10 a < 20	110,966	11.42	1,558,957	6.56
20 a < 30	53,008	5.46	1,289,298	5.43
30 a < 50	54,732	5.63	2,101,808	8.85
50 a < 100	52,465	5.40	3,683,587	15.51
>= 100	51,188	5.27	13,089,671	55.10
TOTAL	967,293	100	23,752,793	100

* Agriculture = crop land plus meadows and grasslands.
Source: Own elaboration from Spanish Agricultural Census (2009b).

4.1.4. Capital Structure

To achieve economic sustainability in a private golf course, it is necessary to integrate all of the possible elements in the project that may provide capital to help finance the course. It is necessary to analyze all possible agents that are benefited by the existence of a golf course (local users, the surrounding real estate and hotels) to determine how much capital each can contribute. In the case of public golf courses, they are facing the same problem, with the exception of cases in which the public sector funds the construction.

Capital can come from several sources: public funds, private financial partners, bank financing, sale of shares, beneficiaries financially associated with the golf course (for example, capital gains from home sales associates) and funds of the Royal Spanish Golf Federation and foundations.

A very important aspect to consider is the development of an appropriate timing of investment. In general, as indicated by the ME (2001) and Fanjul (2006), it is usually not easy to find sufficient funds to fully develop the golf facilities. When this happens, coupled with some uncertainty in the acceptance of the course in the area, the project is usually developed in phases.

Golf courses in Spain have been promoted in the last 20 years primarily by real estate companies and not by the owners of the land on which they are constructed, which are usually pleased with the high prices paid for their land compared to the market value they would receive by farming.

Currently, the capital structure may become a constraint to the sustainable development of golf courses. Bank financing usually only give a coverage of 50% unless the golf course is adjacent to a residential area (Fanjul, 2006), but in the current housing crisis, bank financing for this can be almost impossible to get. Therefore, there is the need to search for other sources of funding such as partners, public funds, foundations or involve potential beneficiaries associated with it (near housing developments, service companies, hotels, ...), which currently have their investment capacity very limited.

4.2. Analysis of Environmental Sustainability

The environmental sustainability of golf courses in Spain will be analyzed based on the following aspects: 4.2.1) climate, 4.2.2) landscape, 4.2.3) topography, 4.2.4) soil type, 4.2.5) hydrology, 4.2.6) availability of water resources, 4.2.7) nature reserves and 4.2.8) historical and cultural assets.

4.2.1. Climate

The study of climatic factors is important for the sustainability of a golf course, as they will determine the time periods when golf can be played (directly affecting the profitability of the course), the irrigation requirements and the vegetation that best suits the climate. In turn, a good climate is a competitive advantage that cannot be modified by competitors. The climatic aspects to be taken into account are: sunlight, rainfall, temperatures, wind and humidity (CMAJA, 1997).

The climate is an uncontrolled determining factor, but it is the factor that is currently promoting the development of golf courses in Spain; because it is most pleasant to play golf on the Mediterranean coast from October to May than in the central and northern Europe.

Traditionally, we have classified four climates in Spain: Atlantic, Mediterranean (with three differences: typical, continental and dry), Subtropical and High mountainous (Martin and Olcina, 2001). The prevailing climate is the Mediterranean and the most important golf courses are concentrated mainly in the typical and dry subzones. This is due to the development of golf tourism which has sought for areas that allow play golf all year round and mainly in the high season for golf tourism. However, the golf courses in these areas tend to seek closeness to the sea (where we have seen that there are problems of availability of land for development) because the average temperatures are milder in winter, but rainfall is usually sparse implying that it will require the availability of water resources.

The numbers of days per year that a course is available to play has a direct impact on the playability of the course, which income depends primarily on two aspects of climate: hours of light and rain. Spain has a maximum of 80,000 rounds/year. Given that, the average annual number of rounds in a busy golf course, according to KPMG (2009), is 52,000 rounds/year, meaning that it is only being used for 65% of its theoretical maximum capacity.

Therefore, climate is one of the pillars on which the environmental sustainability of golf courses in Spain sits.

4.2.2. Landscape

The landscape quality of the territory is very important for environmental sustainability, so it is necessary that the course has a good landscape both inside and outside. Players like to play in an area as natural as possible; however, golf cannot be considered as a recreation area by itself, but as an element of the landscape integrated in the open space system within the regional ecosystem. Thus, in the vicinity of urban centers, golf can be considered as a green belt (Muirhead and Rando, 1994).

According to Otero et al. (2007) the average quality of the landscape in Spain is 4.94 on a scale of 10. The Spanish Mediterranean area evaluation fluctuates between 5 and 7 where are located most of the golf courses. The highest ratings of 8 to 10 are recorded in areas from the northern Spain, usually mountainous, where there are hardly any golf courses.

On the other hand, it could be an improvement for the landscape and the environment if the golf courses are located on previously degraded lands or where the landscape changes too much or where only native species are planted. Therefore, it is considered that the landscape is not a limiting factor in environmental sustainability for the development of golf courses in Spain.

4.2.3. Topography

An ideal design for the construction of a golf course will present a gently undulating topography that allows the integration of the course in natural terrain (CMAJA, 1997) and thus promote sustainability. The landform and its slope is very important, because poor planning of these two aspects of the golf course can make it very unattractive and unnatural to the game, so that cannot be sustainable.

Steep slopes and mountainous terrain should be avoided as much as possible as expensive construction and maintenance of the course itself, due to the large earthworks, and fatigue the players' movements (Urban Land Institute, 1981). According to the CMAJA (1997) to optimize the movement of land and to build a golf course that is attractive and comfortable to play, longitudinal slopes should not exceed 12% and 4% across. Completely flat surfaces are not also best suited for the designer of the course in shaping the landscape (Tandy, 1976). According to Martin (2008), if the slope is 5% to 10% the cost of a golf range between 4 and 7 million €, if its 10% to 20% the cost is between 7 and 10 million €, and if the slope is greater than 20% the cost rises between 10 and 15 million €.

In Spain, according to altimetry analysis of MMAMRM (2011), the topography is quite hilly (surpassed only by Switzerland and Austria) and the average altitude is 660 m. The places where most golf courses are located today and more likely to be developed, are the Mediterranean coast areas of low altitude that allow good growing conditions for the development of grass and for high use for playing, and in consequence, for environmental sustainable development of golf courses.

Another aspect to consider is the slope. According to the MMAMRM (2009), Spain has 32% of its territory in slope, considering that the ground was sloping if it had a slope greater than 20%. It is considered that when the slope is greater than 20%, the cost of construction is so high that the place is not sustainable. However, in Spain, there is still a high percentage of land (69%) that does have adequate slope and, therefore, allows for environmentally sustainable development of golf courses.

4.2.4. Soil Type

The RandA (2011) considers the quality of its playing surfaces critical to the sustainability of golf. For its part, the CMAJA (1997) indicates that the target agronomic for all golf courses is to get a good lawn. This can be achieved in any soil as long as good irrigation, drainage, fertilization and aeration is provided; but in any case, the suitability of soils for the establishment of a golf course varies depending if it is sandy, clay or rocky . Recommended soils are well structured, sandy which has good drainage conditions, and a high percentage of organic matter. The lack of some or all of the features on the ground of the property chosen hinders the growth of grass and/or increases the cost of construction of the course (Tandy, 1976).

Following Soil Taxonomy classification established by the USDA Soil Survey Staff, shows that in Spain there are four major soil types that occupy 95% of the territory (MMAMRM (2011):

- Inceptisols: they occupy 60% of the territory and a productive agriculture is developed unless they lack moisture.
- Entisols: they occupy about 20% of the territory and preferred seating at high levels (recreational or forest). These soils are in flat areas of the Mediterranean coast where a high productive agriculture is developed with frequent irrigation in river valleys.
- Ardisols: they occupy 9.5% of the territory. They range in areas where evapotranspiration exceeds the sweat most of the year, limiting agricultural production unless irrigation.
- Alfisols: they take up about 5% of the territory. They are productive upland soils. They are located in river terraces, where the presence of gravel provides drainage, making them suitable for irrigation.

In view of previous findings, it is considered that the type of soil will not affect the sustainability of golf courses in Spain, as the high use of it for agricultural activities allows a large amount of good soil that can affordably be used for golf courses.

4.2.5. Hydrology

It is important for the environmental sustainability of golf to evaluate the hydrology of the area at the time of its construction. Please note that the choice of properties in low areas as the beds of dry streams or other sump areas will require significant work to remove drainage water.

Therefore, good design of the course will consider molding the surface of the ground to drive rapidly most of the rainwater collector channels, either to take water out of the property or for storage in the lakes for later use in irrigation. In this sense, a property with a slight slope and several well-defined alternative channels would be best for a golf course (CMAJA, 1997).

The permeability of the ground represents the speed at which a fluid can penetrate. It is very important that a golf course is maintained in good condition because they must have a good drainage to avoid flooding. If the degree of permeability of a soil is high, the rainwater easily penetrates the pores. However, if the permeability is low, the rainwater will tend to accumulate on the surface or move through it, if the course is tilted. A related aspect of the excessive soil permeability is the possible contamination of groundwater with chemicals used for fertilization (e.g., nitrates) or the control of pests and lawn diseases. Most Spanish golf courses are trying to water the lawn with a slight water stress in order not to flood the golf course, which would make it impossible to play, and to use as little water as possible for irrigation.

The permeability of soils in Spain (MMAMRM (2011) shows a great diversity and the presence of a large number of areas with medium to high permeability which are valid for golf courses. Therefore, the hydrology is one factor that can be restrictive for the environmental sustainability of a golf course if, by the time of the location and construction, the corrective measures are not taken, primarily in the design of irrigation and drainage systems. However, most golf courses in Spain have resolved this factor, so this is not a threat to environmental sustainability.

4.2.6. Availability of Water Resources

The sustainable evaluation of this factor is to be performed by estimating the water needs and analyzing potential sources of water. Currently in Spain, especially in the Mediterranean coastal areas where are concentrated the most important golf courses, this resource is the most important aspect that determines the implementation and management of a course, whose location should provide a continuous supply of usable water for lawn maintenance (CMAJA, 1997).

The various water resources that can be used to obtain water for irrigation of golf courses are as follows (RFEG, 2003):

(1) Conventional resources: surface water (running water and standing water), groundwater and supply networks.
(2) Unconventional Resources: purified wastewater and desalinated water.

Rodriguez et al. (2007) used the variable "maximum potential soil moisture deficit" (PSMDmax) as an agroclimatic indicator to assess the impacts of climate variability on the irrigation needs of a golf course and the areas where most of the Spanish golf courses are settled have high PSMD and, therefore, with high irrigation requirements.

The water demand in Spain is approximately 22,200 hm3, which is distributed in agriculture (75%), households (12%), industry (10%) and services (3%). The annual water consumption of a golf course, in Spain, varies between 2,000 and 17,000 m3 (this value in the Canary Islands) being the most common value in the Peninsula of 8,200 m3, considering that half of the irrigated area of a golf course is 34.2 hectares, this implies an annual consumption of 280,440 m3.

In comparison, the average consumption in agriculture in Spain is 5,400 m3, but reaches values of 9,000 m3 for irrigation by gravity. Most courses (41%) reuse wastewater for their irrigation, while surface water and groundwater each account for approximately 26%. (Rodriguez et al., 2007). In contrast, 78% of water used in agriculture is surface water, followed by groundwater (20.7%), with only 1.2% being abstracted from non-conventional sources such as wastewater or desalination. As irrigation techniques, sprinkler irrigation accounts for golf courses near 100% (small areas of shrubs and trees can be irrigated by drip), while agriculture accounts for 25.6%, with the drip irrigation 31.8% and 42.6% of gravity (INE, 2009a).

Table 9 examines the demand for water for golf and it appears to be insignificant when compared both with the global demand (0.4%) and the agricultural demand (0.5%). With regard to water dedicated to services, where in the Spanish law is included the water consumption of golf courses (although a golf course is a farm growing grass), the importance is greater because it means 13.4%.

It is important at this point to note that a course has a very similar consumption of citrus fruit, but well short of needs in urbanized land, as shown in Table 10.

Table 9. Water demand for golf courses in Spain (2009)

Water demand	hm^3	% Golf
Total	22,000	0.40
Agricultural	18,751	0.50
Services	666	13.40
Golf courses	90	100

Source: Own elaboration from Rodriguez et al. (2007) and INE (2009a).

Table 10. Water consumption of different land uses

CROP	(m^3/ha-year)
Rice	6,000
Citrus	8,500
Lettuce	8,400
Table grapes	4,500
HOUSING	(m^3/ha-year)
Extensive detached houses (10 villas)	8,760
Extensive semi-detached houses (40 bungalows)	14,600
Intensive 4 apartment blocks (320 houses)	65,100
Intensive 2 four stars hotels (530 beds)	34,138

Source: Olcina and Amorós (2002).

Table 11. Water source and irrigation system for golf courses in Spain (2009)

	Agriculture (hm^3)	Golf (hm^3)	% Golf
Surface and groundwater	14,626	47	0.30
Wastewater	225	37	16.30
Sprinkling	4,800	90	1.90

Source: Own elaboration from Rodriguez et al. (2007) and INE (2009a).

In areas with an irregular water supply, it is recommended to provide storage of 40,000 to 60,000 m3 to ensure irrigation during the dry season. For golf courses where it is necessary to store water for irrigation, the presence of water has to respond to two objectives: to its use for irrigation and to integrate within the landscape of the course using it as an obstacle (Lynch, 1980).

Table 11 examines the sources of water for the golf courses in Spain and verified the importance of the use of wastewater as it means 16.3% of the total wastewater used in agriculture, while it is insignificant compared to agriculture, the use of surface and groundwater sources (0.3%). Finally, the sprinkler system of golf courses represents only 1.9% of water used in agriculture.

However, it is important to note that the highest demands for water for golf courses are located on the Mediterranean coast, which often has problems of water availability especially during the summer tourism campaign (Rodriguez et al., 2007). Therefore, each time it becomes more important to use reclaimed wastewater to irrigate golf courses, as evidenced by the initiatives of global management of wastewater for golf courses, for example in Madrid and Malaga.

In the province of Alicante, the Environmental Administration has placed special emphasis on water management in its environmental authorizations, because in all cases indicated that reclaimed wastewater should be used. This policy has ensured that the main source of supply of golf courses in the province of Alicante is 85% of the wastewater from the treatment plants in cities near golf courses (Del Campo, 2005b).

Finally, it should also be noted that a golf course can provide water by reusing treated water from the surrounding urbanizations, which, according to Herrero (2006), if there are around 3,422 bungalows; then the problem becomes to find the water needed to supply drinking water. Under Rodriguez et al. (2007), the cost of wastewater in Spain is between 0.06 and 0.38 €/m^3, while the conventional water is a cheaper range between 0.03 and 0.24 €/m^3, so the use of wastewater does not mean a significant increase.

Another possible source is the use of desalinated water, either from seawater or brackish groundwater, through its connection to the mains supply or building its own desalination plant. At present, according to Rodriguez et al. (2007) desalinated water represents only 7% of water used for golf, but with 80% of all golf courses in Spain located less than 10 km from the sea, increased dependence on this source is feasible, if cheaper sources are unavailable, particularly if desalination costs fall from the actual level of 0.85 €/m^3.

Therefore, the availability of water for the golf courses in Spain can clearly affect its sustainability, especially in the Mediterranean coastal areas. If measures are not taken to encourage the use of reclaimed wastewater or desalinated water, it should be noted that the high cost in some cases can endanger the financial sustainability of golf courses.

4.2.7. Nature Reserves

The criteria for an environmentally sustainable golf course regarding the natural protected areas would lead to look for places lacking any apparent natural value, giving preference to the choice of farms and other degraded sites.

In any case, choosing farms or natural areas with significant environmental constraints should be avoided, where the reduction of impacts is not a viable practice, taking into account the requirements and limitations imposed by laws and regulations relating to sensitive areas, natural protected areas and classified areas of special importance (CMAJA, 1997).

The main instrument for protecting habitat and species at European level is the "Nature 2000 network". It is a network of protected areas which includes spaces designated as SPAs (Special Protection Areas for Birds) by the Birds Directive (79/409/EEC) and areas designated for compliance with the Habitats Directive (92 / 43/CEE) in its first phase known as SCIs (Sites of Community Importance).

Its purpose is to ensure the long-term survival of species and most threatened habitats in Europe, helping to halt biodiversity loss caused by the adverse impact of human activities. It is the main instrument for nature conservation in the European Union. In Spain, 1,446 SCIs occupy 11.6 million hectares and 595 SPAs which occupy 10 million hectares, representing approximately 27% of the total Spanish surface area (MMAMRM, 2010).

Therefore, there is a 73% open area in Spain for the sustainable development of golf courses and should not be an obstacle to their sustainability, as it is not currently considered socially unfeasible to build a golf course in a protected space.

However, it should be taken into account when building a golf course nearby the existence of a protected natural area, that it may be necessary to create buffer zones or environmental corridors, as adopted by the golf course "La Sella" in Denia (Alicante). In Spain, the golf course "Dunas de Doñana" is paradigmatic, built in the largest National Park in Spain, the "Doñana" in Huelva. It was built to regenerate an existing landfill in the park and create a buffer area between the park and the building of a tourist village on the coast, all through a joint effort between the golf course, public administration and environmental groups.

4.2.8. Historical and Cultural Assets

Ruins and archaeological sites, ancient buildings of historical, archaeological fossils, geological sights, cemeteries, ruins aesthetic quality is often a cause of concern and project delays. Even the existence of ruins and archaeological remains can reconsider the economic viability of the project; the developer of the golf course may have to bear the costs of archaeological investigations and even a possible transfer of the ruins (CMAJA, 1997). Previously identified can be avoided, or consider the possibility of joining in the course helping to enhance the character of place and sustainability.

In Spain, there are many of these ruins and obviously when designing and building a golf course, their integration must be taken into account to affect them minimally (for example, preservation of Roman ruins in the hole 13 of the "Alicante Golf Club") For this it is necessary to conduct an environmental inventory and proper corrective measures in the study of environmental impact of the golf course.

Therefore, the environmental sustainability of golf courses in Spain do not have to be affected by these assets, but rather have a successful integration into the golf course coupled with good management ensuring its conservation and help its recovery.

4.3. Assessment of Sustainability

Assessing the sustainability of golf courses in Spain has been estimated by the matrix of Table 12 from the assessments given (on a scale of 1 = none sustainable to 10 = totally sustainable) to each of the factors that represent the economic and environmental sustainability. Moreover, applying the model developed by Del Campo et al. (2007), based on the AHP methodology, their relative importance was calculated for each of the items. The global sustainability of golf courses in Spain has a value of 7 (with a 6.7 for socio-economic sustainability and 7.3 for environmental sustainability), which can be regarded as remarkable and, therefore, without too many problems of sustainability. However, the socioeconomic factors of profitability and capital structure (if a new golf course is developed), and the environmental factor of availability of water resources, are the most important factors to control because may determine at any time the global sustainability of golf courses in Spain.

Table 12. Assessment of sustainability of golf courses in Spain (2011)

Sustainability	% Importance	Valuation
Global	100	7.0
Socioeconomic	60.00	6.7
Socioeconomic profitability	38.00	6
Existing infrastructure	6.00	10
Structure of land ownership	12.00	8
Capital structure	4.00	5
Environmental	40.00	7.3
Climate	6.00	10
Landscape	2.00	8
Topography.	2.00	9
Soil type	2.00	8
Hydrology	2.00	7
Water availability	22.00	6
Protected natural areas	2.00	8
Historical and cultural assets	2.00	10

Note: Scale 1 a 10 (1=not sustainable; 10= totally sustainable).

CONCLUSION

Golf is a sport that generates an important economic activity in Spain, mainly due to the constant increase of golf tourism, but it must be sustainable to be accepted by society.

The sustainability of golf courses must: i) from the golf industry vision, be: *Competitive, Environmentally responsible, Generating positive economic and social impacts,* and *Integrated in the regional development*; ii) from a sports organization vision, provide: *Quality game, Conservation of the environment, Economy and Social responsibility*. Both visions are very similar and can be joined in the idea that the global assessment of the sustainability for their current and future development should affect two blocks: socioeconomic sustainability (economic, social and cultural) and environmental sustainability (ecological). The key aspects used to analyze the sustainability of golf courses in the socioeconomic block were: 1) socioeconomic profitability, 2) existing infrastructure, 3) structure of land ownership and 4) capital structure; and in the environmental block were: 1) climate, 2) landscape, 3) topography, 4) soil type, 5) hydrology, 6) availability of water resources, 7) nature reserves, and 8) historical and cultural assets.

In the socioeconomic sustainability, Spain may have some problems caused by the current crisis: lack of profitability of the golf courses and limited capital structure for lack of bank funding. However, the existing infrastructures contribute in a positive manner and the structure of land ownership is quite sustainable if the future development will locate further away from the coast. It is important to note that when Spain recovers from the current economic crisis, it will have a potential gap to make its golf courses profitable and, consequently, to build more.

In the environmental sustainability, Spain must be alert to two aspects: i) the availability of water for the golf courses in Spain can clearly affect its sustainability, especially in the Mediterranean coastal areas if measures are not taken to encourage the use of reclaimed wastewater or desalinated water, but the high cost of these waters can endanger the economic sustainability of golf courses; ii) also the hydrology is one factor that can be restrictive if, by the time of the location and construction, the corrective measures are not taken, primarily in the design of irrigation and drainage systems. However, most golf courses in Spain have resolved this factor, so this is not a threat to environmental sustainability.

However, the rest of environmental sustainability aspects in Spain are very positive: i) the climate is the most positive pillar; ii) the landscape is not a limiting factor and conversely could be an improvement if the golf courses are located on previously degraded lands; iii) the Spanish topography allows it because the places where most golf courses are located today and more likely to be developed are the Mediterranean coast areas of low altitude and there is still a high percentage of land with adequate slope; iv) the type of soil will not affect it as the high use for agricultural activities allows a large amount of good soil that can affordably be used for golf courses; v) there is a lot of area in Spain not classified as nature reserves and should not be an obstacle to their sustainability if these areas are avoided; and vi) the historical and cultural assets can be very positive if a successful integration into the golf course, coupled with good management, ensured its conservation and its recovery.

In conclusion, the sustainability of golf courses in Spain can be assessed as remarkable and does not present any serious problems as long as four factors are taken into account: i) the socio-economic profitability, ii) the capital structure, iii) the availability of water resources and iv) the hydrology. However, the future economic, social and environmental impacts will determine if the managers of golf courses and the Public Administrations of Spain act correctly for the golf courses to be sustainable.

REFERENCES

Aledo, A., Domínguez, J. (2002). *Sociología ambiental.* Ed. Grupo Editorial Universitario. Granada.

Aymerich, F. (2005). *La industria del golf en España.* Madrid. Ed. AGM.

Borrego, S. (2002). *Campos de golf y turismo: estudio de Málaga y su provincia.* Consejería de Turismo y Deporte de la Junta de Andalucía. Sevilla.

CMAJA (Consejería de Medio Ambiente de la Junta de Andalucía) (1997). *Guía de gestión medioambiental de los campos de golf: criterios medioambientales para la planificación, diseño, construcción y mantenimiento.* Sevilla.

Del Campo, F.J., Molina, M.A., Sales, J.M. (2006). Sustainable limits for golf course development in a tourist destination. *World review of science, technology and sustainable development,* 3 (3), pp. 197-210.

Del Campo, F.J. (Editor) (2007). *Consideraciones medioambientales para el desarrollo de nuevos campos de golf en la provincia de Alicante.* Ed. Coepa.

Diario Información, 2006. Las promotoras buscan suelo barato fuera de España para aumentar su rentabilidad. *Diario Información de Alicante, April 13.*

Diario Información, 2007. El 57% de los europeos que viven en alicante rechazan el modelo urbanístico de la provincia. *Diario Información de Alicante, February 6.*

English Golf Union (2004). *Golf development strategic plan for golf in England (2004-2014).* Woodhall Spa. Ed. English Golf Union.

European Golf Association (2010). Statistics. http://www.ega-golf.ch.

Eurostat (2009). Statistics. http://www.*ec.europa.eu/eurostat.*

Fanjul, L. (2006). Financiación de campos de golf. *Conferencia Intereconomía: oportunidades de negocio en torno a la promoción de campos de golf. Madrid.*

García-Ferrando, M. (2002). Complementing tourist development with popular recreation: a challenger for the future of golf in Spain. *IV World Scientific Congress of Golf. Saint Andrews.*

Hawtree, H. (1983). *The golf course, planning, design and construction.* E. and F.F. Spon.

Herrero, A. (2006). Proyectos de urbanización sostenible en los desarrollos de golf. *III Jornadas Internacionales de Golf y Medio Ambiente. Mijas (Málaga).*

INE (Instituto Nacional de Estadística de España) (2009a). Estadísticas. http://www.ine.es.

INE (Instituto Nacional de Estadística de España) (2009b). Censo agrario. http://www.ine.es.

KPMG (2008). *Golf benchmark Survey, Rounds and Revenues Report in Europe Middle East and Africa.* http://www.golfbusinesscommunity.com/ research.

Lynch, K. (1980). *La planificación del sitio.* Barcelona. Ed. G.Gilli.

Martin, J., Olcina, J. (2001). *Climas y tiempos de España.* Madrid. Alianza editorial.

Martin, M. (2007). Aspectos ambientales en el diseño de campos de golf. *IV Jornadas Internacionales de Golf y Medio Ambiente. Almería.*

Martins, M.V. (Editor) (2003). *Estudo sobre o golfe no algarve.* Diagnóstico e áreas problema. Universidade do Algarve.

ME (Ministerio de Economía de España) (2001). *Guía para la creación de campos de golf: introducción a los aspectos jurídicos, económicos y ambientales.* Madrid.

MF (Ministerio de Fomento de España), 2011. Web: http://www.fomento.es.

MMAMRM (Ministerio de Medio Ambiente, Medio Rural y Marino de España) (2011). Web: http://www.marm.es.

Muirhead, D., Rando, G. (1994). *Golf course development and real estate.* Washington D.C.. The Urban Land Institute.

NGF (National Golf Foundation USA) (2005). Statistics.

Olcina, J., Amorós, A. (2002). Sobreexplotación de recursos de agua y conflictos de uso en el País Valenciano. *Quaderns Agroambientals. IVIFA.*

Otero, I., Mancebo, S., Ortega, Ee., Casermeiro, M.A. (2007). *Revista electrónica de Medio Ambiente.* Universidad Complutense de Madrid.

RFEG (Real Federación Española de Golf) (2003). *Gestión del agua en los campos de golf.* Ed. RFEG. Madrid.

RFEG (Real Federación Española de Golf) (2010). Estadísticas. http://www.rfegolf.es.

Rodríguez Díaz, J.A., Knox, J.W., Weatherhead, E.K. (2007). Competing demands for irrigation water: golf and agriculture in Spain. *Irrigation and Drainage.* 56(5): 541-550.

Rand, A. (Royal and Ancient Golf Club of St. Andrews) (2011). http://www.randa.org.

Stubbs, D. (1997). *Committed to green handbook for golf courses.* European Golf Association – Ecology unit.

Tandy, C. (1976). *Paisaje urbano*. Ed. H. Blume.

Turespaña (2004). *Estudio sobre la demanda extranjera de golf: la promoción y comercialización del turismo de golf en España*. Madrid.

Urban Land Institute (1981). *Recreational development handbook*. Washington.

In: New Trends Towards Mediterranean Tourism Sustainability   ISBN: 978-1-62257-627-2
Editors: L. M. Rosalino, A. Silva and A. Abreu   © 2012 Nova Science Publishers, Inc.

Chapter 4

SUSTAINABILITY OF RECREATIONAL HUNTING TOURISM: A CLUSTER ANALYSIS APPROACH FOR WOODCOCK HUNTING IN GREECE

Konstantinos G. Papaspyropoulos[1,], Christos K. Sokos[2], Nikolaos D. Hasanagas[3] and Periklis K. Birtsas[4]*

[1]Laboratory of Forest Economics, Faculty of Forestry and Natural Environment, Aristotle University of Thessaloniki, Thessaloniki, Greece
[2]Research Division, Hunting Federation of Macedonia and Thrace, Thessaloniki, Greece
[3]University Forest Administration, Aristotle University of Thessaloniki, Thessaloniki, Greece
[4]Laboratory of Wildlife, Department of Forestry and Natural Environment Management, Technological Education Institute of Larissa, Larissa, Greece

ABSTRACT

Hunting tourism is a relatively small, although developing, business sector worldwide. As with all forms of tourism, it can become a source of unsustainability, especially in terms of the economic and ecological dimension of sustainability. This chapter discusses the potential unsustainabilities of recreational hunting tourism in Greece.

It examines the cases of woodcock hunters that live in Thessaloniki, Macedonia, the second largest city in the country, with more than 1 million inhabitants. These hunters are mainly forced to travel far from home in order to hunt. By analyzing 170 questionnaires filled out by hunters, this chapter concludes that better hunting area management would prevent some environmental degradation caused by the hunters' trips, and would allow hunters to save a significant amount of money to fulfil their passion for this activity, by hunting closer to home.

---

* E-mail: kodafype@for.auth.gr.

INTRODUCTION

Hunting is one of the oldest land uses worldwide. Hunters are considered conservationists of forest and rural land since they are holders/managers of significant expanses of these environments (Graul and Miller, 1984; Stoate, 2002). However, and especially in the eastern Mediterranean, they are the land users who have been mainly prejudiced by the deterioration and fragmentation of quarry habitats, which has resulted in the degradation and reduction of hunting areas (Cassola, 1979; Sokos and Birtsas, 2005). This degradation has many impacts upon the sustainability of hunting tourism (see definition below): i) quarries and wildlife in general have less natural habitat available (ecological unsustainability), ii) hunters are forced to move to specific hunting areas, and for hunters from urban areas, this usually implies travelling far from home (economic unsustainability) (Booth, 2010), and iii) conflicts with local populations by hunting tourists may occur (social unsustainability) (CIC, 2008).

For example, in Greece the degradation and fragmentation of hunting areas is considered one of the main reasons for the development of hunting tourism (Papaspyropoulos et al., 2009b). Hunters, especially those from urban areas, may travel more than 100 km, stay overnight and eat in restaurants in order to experience this activity (Sokos et al., 2003; Matilainen, 2007).

Moreover, many hunters prefer to travel abroad for hunting, thus contributing significantly to the economies of the host countries. For example, the gross value of hunting tourism in South Africa was estimated at 68.4 million $ in 2003 (Booth, 2010), and 30 million $ in Canada in 2004 (MacKay and Campbell, 2004). Overall, in Europe and the USA hunting revenues are estimated at 16 billion €/annum and 76 billion $/annum, respectively (Booth, 2010; Grado et al., 2011). In Greece, many hunters travel abroad for hunting, mainly to Balkan countries. Travel agencies organize tours to FYROM (Former Yugoslav Republic of Macedonia), or Bulgaria, where hunting legislation is not as strict, different quarry species can be hunted, and the hunting period starts earlier. Tours are organized also to Hungary, Serbia and other neighbouring countries. On the other hand, only a few foreign hunters enter the country, and these are mainly from Italy.

An independent survey ordered by the Panhellenic Union of Hunting Material Merchants in 2010 (PEVEKE, 2010) showed that hunting contributes 1.7 billion €/annum to the country's economy. A significant part of this amount can be allocated to hunting tourism (accommodation, dining, and energy sector). However, most hunting tourism is domestic, as hunters cannot find suitable hunting areas close to their home (Sokos et al., 2003). This can be considered an important factor of unsustainability, since it may pressure quarry species due to uncontrolled concentration of hunters in one specific area (for example, an area with a previously emplaced hunting ban, which is now lifted), may be economically negative to hunters due to travel costs, and environmentally harmful due to the carbon emissions associated with the extra kilometres travelled (Sokos et al., 2003).

This chapter attempts to estimate possible recreational hunting tourism unsustainabilities in Greece, considering present management practices. In order to do so, it analyses a sample of woodcock hunters originating from a Greek urban area. Using this sampling group, we identify the percentage of domestic hunters that can be regarded as hunting tourists and discuss the problems that can occur when these hunters search for the same quarry species in specific areas far from home. To address the subject of recreational hunting tourism sustainability, in general, these results are compared with a previous inquiry (also implemented by the research team of the present chapter) that focused on hare and quail hunters. Finally, it is discussed which policies should be followed by the Greek state and hunting organizations in order to reduce unsustainabilities and contribute to the wiser use of quarry species in Greece.

BACKGROUND

Hunting Tourism

There are various definitions of hunting tourism in the literature. According to Rutanen et al. (2007) hunting tourism "can be seen as hunting in which the hunter travels outside of his own hunting area or his place of residence to hunt". Gunnarsdotter (2006, 2008) uses the definition of hunting tourist as adopted by the Swedish Tourist Authority in 2003. A hunting tourist can be "a person who temporary leaves his daily surroundings (household, working place) to hunt". Similarly, Nygard and Uthardt (2011) define the term as "an activity aiming at hunting… in a region (or country) other than one's own normal hunting territory". All these definitions imply that hunting tourism includes travelling for experiencing the activity. Willebrand (2009) on the other hand, defines hunting tourism without mentioning the need to travel; it is a commercial operation which can provide access to guide, dogs, necessary equipment, food and lodging.

For the purpose of the present chapter, hunting tourism is related mainly to the need to travel far from home to hunt. This is the factor which can cause the aforementioned unsustainabilities. Therefore, hunting tourism is defined as the activity of hunting, which is forced to take place at least 50 km from the hunter's home (100 km roundtrip). The quantitative criterion is introduced in the definition because, as explained in the next section, hunting tourism in Greece is mainly domestic, and therefore there was a need to consider a distinguishable attribute to discriminate simple hunters from hunting tourists.

Hunting in Greece

In Greece, the hunting organizations have been placed under the supervision of the Forest Service according to the Forest Law of 1969. Due to the pressure of hunting organizations, endangered species were set under conservation status, rather strict hunting regulations were institutionalized, sale of quarry species was forbidden, and hunting parks were created – these were the first protected areas. Thus, hunters were, and still are, fairly regarded by society as the first lobby interested in the protection of the environment.

Today, hunting in Greece is regulated by the Hellenic Ministry of Environment, Energy and Climate Change (2011) and is managed by hunting organizations and the Forest Service. The quarry belongs to the hunter and not to the land owner. The hunting right is acquired by issuing a hunting license, which is valid for either a prefecture, a geographical region, or the whole country, and is priced at 100-150 €. This capital is then allocated to the "Green Fund", a state-owned fund which allocates its resources to environmental policies and the private, non-profit/non-governmental hunting organizations. Both are obliged to manage the environment for the sustainable use of quarry species. However, the hunting organizations mainly employ wildlife ecologists and wardens and finance hunting management, whereas the contribution of Forest Service to hunting development is low (Birtsas et al., 2009). Hunting can be exercised on both public and private land with no additional cost; therefore, owners of private land are sometimes unfriendly to hunters, usually see no benefit from hunting tourism and show no interest in hunting management. Hunting can also be exercised in eight public and two private hunting reserves, where hunters must pay for an entrance ticket and their hunted quarries.

Approximately 220 thousand hunters in Greece (2% of the population) are issued a hunting license each year. Hunting is permitted from August 20th to March 10th. The most hunted quarries for the Greek hunters are the woodcock (*Scolopax rusticola*) and hare (*Lepus europaeus*) (Thomaides et al., 2007). The hare hunters characterize the activity as quite efficient due to the benefits they enjoy (e.g. enjoying nature, enjoying his hounds, escaping from everyday life), and do not consider replacing it with another activity (e.g. fishing, trekking, etc.). They also spend an average of 69 days and 2,000 € on hare hunting annually. Expenditure (45.8% of expenses on dogs, 43.2% to car and 11% other expenses) based on hare hunting runs into several tens of millions € at national level (Sokos et al., 2003). The same authors refer that the hare hunters believe that measures for improving the quality of hare hunting are necessary. They also declare that they would be willing to pay, as long as the effective use of their money can be assured (Sokos et al., 2003).

In the region of Macedonia and Thrace where this study is focused, hunting is practiced mainly by workers, farmers and the self-employed (Tsachalidis et al., 2003). In this region, the number of hunting licenses peaked in the hunting season of 1985-1986. However, following the season 1991-1992, the number of hunting licenses began to decrease steadily due to socioeconomic and environmental changes (Tsachalidis et al., 2003).

Since the urbanization of the Greek population in the last 30 years, many hunters presently live in large Greek cities such as Athens, Thessaloniki, Patras, and Larisa. These can be considered as the country's main domestic hunting tourists, since they need to travel far from home to experience hunting. In mountainous or rural areas, it is usual for hunters to go hunting even on foot, and thus these cannot be considered hunting tourists, as defined in the previous section. Hasanagas et al. (2008) found that a strong interest in eco-touristic values characterizes hunters who: a) are informed about environmental issues by magazines/newspapers and were initially stimulated to hunt by films, b) are of higher education level (e.g. university degree holders), c) have higher social status, and d) are sociable and do not hunt to gain social power.

Sustainability of Hunting Tourism and Research Hypothesis

In the present chapter it is considered that the sustainability of hunting tourism includes three main dimensions: i) ecological, ii) economical, and iii) social sustainability.

Ecological Dimension

The degradation and fragmentation of land, especially close to urban areas, has resulted in the reduced availability of hunting areas, and consequently the reduced availability of quarries close to big cities. In Greece, there is no spatial planning which assures that hunting areas will not be reduced. However, the Greek Forest Law restricts that hunting should take place at least 150 m from buildings. Nevertheless, there are cases where hunting areas are included within the urban design and buildings do occur within these areas. This has reduced the available hunting areas close to urban areas, and has forced a significant number of hunters, more than those who would have done it anyway, to travel far from home to hunt. This increase has caused some pressure on forest and rural hunting areas and quarry species that are not only chosen by local hunters but also by many hunting tourists.

Economical Dimension

Hunting tourism that takes place because the hunter wants to escape from his/her daily surroundings, to experience new hunting areas, or to hunt species not available in his/her local area is fully desirable. Such a hunting tourism can contribute substantially to local economies and support the fuel merchants, and the accommodation and dining sectors. However, a hunting tourism that originates because there is a lack of hunting areas and satisfactory quarry populations, rather than being influenced by a special hunting needs (e.g. specific quarry, lack of beautiful landscapes), causes economic loss, increased carbon emissions from journeys that could have been avoided, and may not bring the expected economic development to the local communities, since this type of tourist is usually reluctant to spend money.

Social Dimension

Hunting tourism and hunting tourists have to respect the local communities, their special needs and their hunting customs and traditions. However, there may be some cases when local hunters react negatively to tourist hunter behaviour and presence, or to the fact that they bag local quarries, which they believe belong to them.

All these dimensions of sustainability are tested under the next hypothesis: if statistically significant differences among clusters of hunters from urban areas are found in terms of hunting tourism behaviour (journey distance, spending), then possible unsustainabilities can occur and hunting management should be adjusted.

DATA AND DATA ANALYSIS

Study Area

Thessaloniki is the second largest city in Greece, after Athens, in terms of population. It is situated in Macedonia (Figure 1). The study was conducted in this area because Thessaloniki has many hunters: almost six thousand (Papaspyropoulos et al., 2009a). Within the rural lands of the prefecture the pressure for outdoor activities, such as trekking, hiking, and mountain climbing, forces many hunters to travel significant distances outside Thessaloniki to experience hunting (Sokos et al. 2003). This means that mostly regional (for the geographical area of Macedonia and Thrace) or general (the entire country) hunting licenses are issued for these hunters, who usually spend more money for hunting than rural hunters who travel less and usually require only local hunting licenses (Papaspyropoulos et al., 2009b).

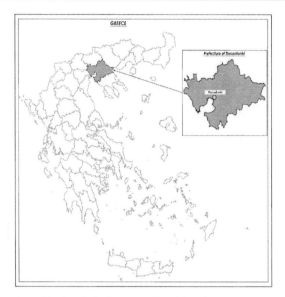

To test the working hypothesis, data were collected through questionnaires targeting hunters. This methodology is very common in socio-economic research when a study's objective is to examine citizen behaviour (Petrosillo et al., 2007; Røskaft et al., 2007; Papaspyropoulos and Pappas, 2008).

Figure 1. Study area.

Survey Development

(Source: Hunting Federation of Macedonia and Thrace).

Figure 2. Woodcock (*Scolopax rusticola*).

In the prefecture of Thessaloniki there are two hunting clubs. The questionnaires were administered to both clubs and the hunters were chosen randomly. The questionnaire consisted of 70 questions in eight (8) pages, but in the present study only eight (8) questions were used (Samuelsson and Stage, 2007), representing the eight variables of the survey. Table 1 presents the type of variables together with their levels.

The questionnaires were collected in two stages. In the first stage all completed questionnaires were collected. Of these, a small number was rejected because they presented a lack of information (e.g. lack of one answer).

In the second stage, questionnaires were selected only from woodcock (*Scolopax rusticola*) (Figure 2) hunters.

Previous research (Tsachalidis et al., 1998) revealed that hunters from urban areas prefer to hunt bird species. In Thessaloniki, most hunters prefer either quail (Order *Galliformes*) or woodcock (Papaspyropoulos et al., 2009a). Therefore there is a high possibility for increased hunting pressure on such species as a result of the consequences described previously. Moreover, woodcock is a species preferred by hunters of Mediterranean countries (Thomaides et al., 2007).

For this reason, the advanced analysis of the present survey was performed only for hunters that prefer woodcock.

Table 1. Variables used in the survey

Variable	Type	Levels
Age of hunter (in years)	Scale	-
When your first hunting license was issued? (in years)	Scale	-
Hunting quarry	Nominal, multiple response	(i) Woodcock, (ii) Duck – Goose, (iii) Woodpigeon, (iv) Turtle, (v) Roe deer, (vi) Thrush – Blackbird, (vii) Pheasant, (viii) Chukar, (ix) Quail, (x) Wild boar, (xi) Hare
Method of travelling to the hunting area (most often used)	Nominal	(i) Alone, by car, (ii) By my car with other hunters, and we share fuel expenses, (iii) By my car with other hunters, and I pay all fuel expenses, (iv) As a fellow passenger, and we share the fuel expenses, (v) As a fellow passenger, without sharing the fuel expenses, (vi) By train, (vii) By coach, (viii) Other
Travelling distance (roundtrip)	Ordinal	(i) 0-10 km, (ii) 10-50 km, (iii) 50-100 km, (ii) 100-300 km, (v) 300-500 km, (vi) 500-1000 km, (vii) >1000 km
Hunting license frequency	Ordinal	(i) rare, (ii) occasionally, (iii) annually
Hunting frequency	Ordinal	(i) less than once per month, (ii) once per month to less than once per week, (iii) 1 to 3 times per week, (iv) 4 to 7 times per week
Staying overnight frequency	Ordinal	(i) less than once per month, (ii) once per month to less than once per week, (iii) 1 to 3 times per week, (iv) 4 to 7 times per week

Sample

For the 2008-2009 hunting period, 5,662 hunting licenses were issued in the city of Thessaloniki. This number is assumed as the population of the present study. The sample consisted of 170 hunters (3% of the population) who completed the questionnaires. Of these, seven (7) questionnaires were rejected and the remaining 163 (95.9%) were analyzed in the context of "hunting quarry" variable. In a second stage, the 100 hunters that hunt woodcock were selected and analysed separately.

In a 50 km radius around the city of Thessaloniki, the total area of woodcock habitats is about 1,590 km^2 and the area of hunting prohibited areas is about 120 km^2. Thus, the approximate available hunting areas for non-touristic hunting total 1,470 km^2.

Statistical Analysis

In the first stage, a "multiple response sets" analysis was performed on the 163 questionnaires. Jann (2005) addresses the problem of multiple responses and gives examples of manipulating such variables. Nowadays, statistical packages such as SPSS (Norusis, 2007) can easily analyze such variables. As shown in Table 1, the variable hunting quarry was a multiple response one, meaning the interviewee was allowed to give more than one answer. By using multiple response analysis, the 100 questionnaires completed by woodcock hunters were extracted to continue the further analysis only using their data. Additionally, differences in preferences of quarries between woodcock hunters and non-woodcock hunters were tested using z-tests and the Bonferroni criterion (Fowler and Cohen, 1995).

The remaining 100 questionnaires were first analyzed using descriptive statistics (Bradley, 2007): means, standard deviations and boxplots were extracted for the scale variables and frequencies for the nominal and ordinal variables. A two step cluster analysis was then applied (Norusis, 2007).

The two step cluster method is a scalable cluster analysis algorithm designed to handle both continuous and categorical variables and automatically select the number of clusters. This analysis uses an agglomerative hierarchical clustering method (Norusis, 2007) and produces a range of solutions. These are then reduced to the best number of clusters on the basis of Schwarz Bayesian Information Criterion, or BIC (Okazaki, 2006). Finally, the two step cluster method estimates the relative contribution of a variable to a cluster's creation. For continuous variables it reports either the t statistic, or its significance level, and for categorical variables it reports either the chi-squared statistic (χ^2), or its significance level (Norusis, 2007).

After forming the clusters and examining the contribution of each variable in the clustering procedure, "one way analysis of variance" (ANOVA) and z-tests were used to examine how well the clusters discriminate from each other (Tseng et al., 2008).

Apart from examining the probability of Type I error (significance level α), the Power of the statistical test was also extracted. The Power (P) is the probability that the null hypothesis, if false, will be rejected. P equals $1 - \beta$, where β is the probability of making a Type II error. A value of P greater than 0.8 is desired (Murphy et al., 2008). Bonferronni's post-hoc tests were also performed. All the statistical analysis was made using the software SPSS, version 19 (IBM, New York).

RESULTS

In Table 2, the analysis of the multiple response sets shows the frequencies of Thessaloniki's hunters according to their preferred quarries, the respective frequencies of the woodcock hunters and their statistical differences.

Thus, if the detected pattern holds for the entire population, we may infer that of the 5,662 hunters, 3,474 (61.3%) are woodcock hunters and their density in the nearest hunting areas (up to 50 km from their home) is 2.36 woodcock hunters/km^2.

The main attributes of the woodcock hunters are shown in Table 3. The average woodcock hunter is 47 years old, issued his first hunting license 24 years ago (aged 23), uses his car to travel to the hunting area, also transferring other hunters, with whom they share fuel expenses, travels 50-100 km to experience hunting, issues a hunting license every year, hunts one to three days a week, and stays overnight in the hunting area less than once per month.

Results of the two step cluster analysis indicate that a three-cluster solution was the best model, as it minimizes the BIC value and the change between adjacent numbers of clusters (BIC = 1749.95, BIC change = -0.95). The resulting clusters 1, 2, and 3 contained 36, 20, and 33 woodcock hunters, which corresponded to 40.4%, 22.4%, and 37.1%, respectively. Eleven (11) woodcock hunters were not grouped. For the clustering procedure, all the variables presented in Table 3 were used.

Table 2. Frequencies and percentages of hunting quarries

	Hunters of Thessaloniki		Woodcock hunters of Thessaloniki	
Quarry	Frequency	%	Frequency	%
Woodcock (*Scolopax rusticola*)	100	61.3	100	100.0
Duck (*Anas* spp.) Goose (*Anser albifrons*)	29	17.8	17	17.0
Woodpigeon [b] (*Columba palumbus*)	47	28.8	23	23.0
Turtle dove (*Streptopelia turtur*)	55	33.7	32	32.0
Roe deer (*Capreolus capreolus*)	1	0.6	1	1.0
Thrush – Blackbird [b] (*Turdus* spp.)	29	17.8	12	12.0
Pheasant (*Phasianus colchicus*)	8	4.9	7	7.0
Partridge [a] (*Alectoris* spp.)	50	30.7	48	48.0
Quail [a] (*Coturnix coturnix*)	104	63.8	84	84.0
Wild boar [b] (*Sus scrofa*)	29	17.8	11	11.0
Hare [b] (*Lepus europaeus*)	66	40.5	29	29.0
Total	163 questionnaires		100 questionnaires	

[a] denotes difference at p<0.05 and woodcock hunters have a larger percentage.
[b] denotes difference at p<0.05 and woodcock hunters have a smaller percentage.

Table 3. Main attributes of Thessaloniki's woodcock hunters

Variable	Attribute
Age of hunter (in years)	46.7 – (SD: 11.5)
When your first hunting license was issued? (in years)	23.2 – (SD: 11.6)
Method of travelling to the hunting area	48% "By my car with other hunters, and we share fuel expenses"
Travelling distance (round trip)	47% "up to 100 km", 37% "100-300km"
Hunting license frequency	97% "annually"
Hunting frequency	79% "1 to 3 days per week"
Staying overnight frequency	71% "less than once per month"

SD: standard deviation.

Three variables were found to have a significant contribution to cluster definition (p<0.05): i) "travelling distance", ii) "method of travelling to the hunting area", and iii) "when was your first hunting license issued?". The variables iv) "staying overnight frequency" and v) "age" had a less significant contribution to the cluster separation (p= 0.730 and p=0.761, respectively). The remaining variables did not contribute significantly to the clustering procedure. Table 4 presents the attributes of each cluster in terms of variable significance.

The next step was to find out how well the three clusters differ statistically from one another. For the continuous variables "age" and "first hunting license" the one-way ANOVA tests showed that there is a difference among the clusters ("age": F=6.5, p=0.002 and Power P=0.9; "first hunting license": F=16.2, p<0.001 and Power P=1).

Table 4. Attributes of the extracted clusters (significant differences in variable values between cluster are in bold)

Variable		Cluster		
		1 (40.4%)	2 (22.4%)	3 (37.1%)
Age		**42.5**	**45.2**	**51.6**
First hunting license (in years ago)		**16.5**	**23**	**30**
Method of travelling to the hunting area (%)	Alone. by car	**50**	0	6.1
	By my car with other hunters and we share fuel expenses	8.3	**100**	**63.6**
	By my car with other hunters. and I pay all fuel expenses	16.7	0	**24.2**
	As a fellow passenger and we share fuel expenses	11.1	0	3
	As a fellow passenger without sharing fuel expenses	13.9	0	3
Travelling distance (%)	10-50 km	19.4	0	0
	50-100 km	**52.8**	**95**	6.1
	100-300 km	**22.2**	0	**81.8**
	300-500 km	0	0	12.1
	> 1000 km	5.6	5	0
Staying overnight frequency (%)	less than once per month	**83.3**	**100**	**54.5**
	once per month to once per week	8.3	0	**36.4**
	1 to 3 times per week	8.3	0	9.1

The Bonferroni post-hoc tests showed a significant "age" difference between the first and third cluster, and a significant difference between the first and third cluster, and the second and third cluster for the "first hunting license" variable.

For the categorical variables of the two-step cluster analysis, the z-tests showed which categories among the three clusters differ significantly (Table 4). An optical comparison of the three clusters is presented in Figure 2.

Our results show that cluster 2 fits the data almost perfectly. This means that the cluster is almost represented only by one category per variable for the hunters (in three of the five variables >95% of the respondents were included in one category – see Table 4). The woodcock hunters of this cluster are middle aged (45.2), experienced hunters (23 years), use their car to go hunting with others and share the fuel expenses, drive 50-100 km (round trip) and rarely stay overnight close to the hunting area, usually less than once per month. This is the typical local hunters cluster. However, they represent only 22.4% of the total sample, which is a small proportion of Thessaloniki's woodcock hunters. The remaining 73.6% seem to be obliged to hunt far from home.

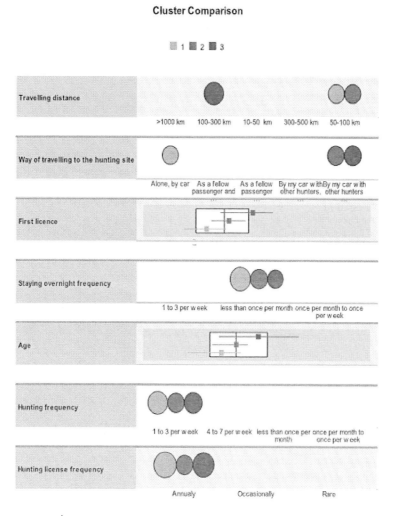

Figure 2. Cluster comparison.

Cluster 3, on the other hand, is a clear example of the "hunting tourism cluster". Here, the hunters are, on average, over 50 years old, have almost 30 years of hunting experience, go hunting with friends and may share fuel expenses or not, travel farther away from their home city to hunt, and thus are those who are the most likely to stay overnight close to the hunting area (more than once per month). This cluster contains 37.1 % of the total woodcock hunters.

Cluster 1 is quite mixed. Concerning the travelling distance variable, most of the hunters seem to be local as 70% of the hunters in this cluster drive up to 100 km (round trip) to hunt. However, 22% travel more than a 100 km in order to experience hunting. This cluster represents 40.4% of the total hunters in the sample. If the percentage of hunters in cluster 1 is divided according to the travelling distance and then added to those of clusters 2 and 3, we may hypothesize that our hunter's sample may include two groups: almost 50% of the Thessaloniki's woodcock hunters can be considered as local and another 45% can be considered as hunting tourists.

DISCUSSION

The large percentage of hunters (45%) that drive more than 100 km (round trip) indicates that woodcock hunting quality is low close to the city of Thessaloniki. Many authors refer that excessive hunting activity may lead to poor harvest success and unsatisfactory experiences for hunters (Madsen et al., 1998; Lee and Chun, 1999; Sokos et al., 2003). A similar study for hare hunters of Thessaloniki (Sokos et al., 2003) showed that 36% of these hunters often drive more than 100 km due to the high number of hunters (22.7%), the higher density of hares in the farthest area (6.7%), the knowledge of the visited area (2.5%), the hunters company (2.5%) and the beautiful landscapes of the visited area (1.6%). Whereas 64% of hare hunters do not travel more than 100 km due to the satisfactory hare populations close to home (27.5%), not knowing the physiognomy of the visited area and the risks of theft and death of their dogs (by poisoning, shepherd dogs and wolves) (16%), the limited time (12.5%), the cost (7.4%) and the absence of a car (0.6%) (Sokos et al., 2003). Similar results were found also for the quail hunters of Thessaloniki (Papaspyropoulos et al., 2009b). Around 42% is forced to drive more than 100 km (round trip) to experience quail hunting activity, while 5% of the hunters travel over 300 km (round trip).

Sometimes hunting tourists exclude local hunters and vice versa. For example, hunting tourists often go camping in the best hunting areas (starting on the previous night of the hunting trip), such as with turtle dove hunting; thus, they may exclude locals who may have previously implemented some habitat improvement actions (Sokos, 2004). According to the same author this situation prevents locals investing in actions that increase quarry population abundances, such as habitat improvements, harvest control and quarry releases.

While travelling far from home may decrease the hunting pressure on hunting areas close to the urban centre, it may put some pressure on certain distant areas that are famous among hunters. During the last 50 years many new roads have been opened in Greek forests and mountains, making new areas accessible to tourist hunters and increasing the hunting pressure on certain species, such as partridges and woodpigeons. Therefore, to minimize this process some local hunting clubs install road barriers to prevent access to cars and to permit hunter access only on foot, or have established many hunting-prohibited areas after presenting their proposals to the Forest Service.

Greek hunting tourists invest far more in car-travel expenses compared to other European hunting tourists, who have more costs related to accommodation and hunting rights (Sokos et al., 2003). The impact of increased car useage is associated to air pollution, CO_2 emissions, loss of time, and a higher cost per excursion. Moreover, the fact that there are no hunting rights costs in a certain area means that little capital is invested into hunting management and development at a local level. Thus, valuable quarry species, such as grey partridge, are not managed efficiently and their hunting is prohibited in Greece.

CONCLUSION AND MANAGEMENT IMPLICATIONS

The possibility of recreational hunting tourism development in Greece has remained untapped for various reasons. The most important is that, typically, there is no action or strategic plan by the Greek State to develop such form of tourism, and there seems to be no political will to do so. Therefore, and since hunters are reduced, especially in urban areas, unsustainability of hunting tourism in Greece is expected to decline on its own. Such a development will certainly lead to new threats, such as poaching, and the decline of rural economies.

On the other hand, recreational hunting tourism might be considered a necessary evil for many Greek urbanized hunters. A high percentage of them would have preferred to hunt close to home, instead of travelling hundreds of kilometres to do it. They are forced to spend money, time to visit areas with more quarries and less hunter congestion. This need to travel further is the result of the gathering of hunters in the urban areas of Greece, which can be a source of ecological, economical and social unsustainabilities. Hunting tourism is not organized as an industry, and it will be difficult to organize in the future due to the present Greek hunting management schemes (Birtsas et al., 2009). Under the current circumstances, it seems more appropriate that some collaborative measures should be taken by hunting organizations and the Forest Service. These should aim to control congestion, and increase the number of permitted quarry species and their populations. The development of hunting tourism will depend on the implementation of these measures.

Special attention should be devoted to the conservation and increase of hunting areas around the cities. The responsible agencies should comprehend that undocumented spatial hunting prohibitions have consequences on all three dimensions of sustainability. The list of permitted species for hunting quarry should be extended; this will result in the reduction of hunting pressure for the nowadays recognized game species, as this pressure will be shared among the new species. If larger populations of pheasants existed around Thessaloniki, for example, the pressure on woodcock would be lower. Actions such as efficient law enforcement, habitat improvement, predator control, etc. should be strengthened around urban areas. In Greece, illegal woodcock stand hunting should be restricted by wardens.

Another measure that should be implemented in the future, aiming to reduce hunting tourist pressure upon hunting areas or quarry species, should be the funding of local land owners (farmers) whose properties are used as hunting grounds. A certain percentage of the money that is allocated to the Green Fund from hunting licenses could be distributed to farmers, so that they can take measures aiming to manage and protect hunting areas and quarry species, since they are paid for the quarries hunted on their land. This is consistent with the notion of "payments for ecosystem services" (PES) (Redford and Adams, 2009), which promotes sustainability. This measure could possibly reduce the opposition to hunting tourism by locals, as described, for example, by Theodoridis (2007) on the Greek island of Tilos. Additionally, the enactment of special hunting management areas for valuable quarry species, such as roe deer and pheasant, could possibly contribute to sustainability.

All the aforementioned measures imply lowering the fuel costs, increased environmental conservation, and lowering local hunter congestion. This will result in a fully acceptable hunting tourism activity which will also include all hunters that travel far away from home, even those that decided to go on a hunting trip motivated by the possibility of experiencing something new, and escape from their daily surroundings.

REFERENCES

Birtsas, P. K., Sokos, C., Hasanagas, N., and Billinis, C. (2009). The hunting activity in Hellas. Proc. VIth International Symposium on Wild Fauna. Organized by Wild Animal Vigilance Euromediterranean Society 21-24/5/2009 Paris. *Extended abstracts* p. 52–53.

Booth, V. R. (2010). The contribution of hunting tourism: How significant is this to national Economies? in *Contribution of Wildlife to National Economies*. Joint publication of FAO and CIC. Budapest. 72 pp.

Bradley, T. (2007). *Essential statistics for economics, business and management.* Chichester, England: John Wiley and Sons.

Cassola, F. (1979). Shooting in Italy: The present situation and future perspectives. *Biological Conservation, 16(2),* 85-106.

CIC (2008). *Best practices in sustainable hunting. A guide to best practices from around the World.* CIC Technical Series Publication No. 1, Budakeszi: CIC.

Fowler, J., and Cohen, L. (1995). *Statistics for ornithologists.* Edition 2. Norwich: BTO Guide 22.

Grado, S. C., Hunt, K. M., Hutt, C. P., Santos, X. T. and Kaminski, R. M. (2011). Economic impacts of waterfowl hunting in Mississippi derived from a state-based mail survey. *Human Dimensions of Wildlife, 16(2),* 100-113.

Graul, W. D. and Miller G.C. (1984). Strengthening ecosystem management approaches. *Wildlife Society Bulletin, 12,* 282-289.

Gunnarsdotter, Y. (2006). Hunting tourism as ecotourism: conflicts and opportunities. In Gossling S. and Hultman, J. (Eds.), *Ecotourism in Scandinavia. Lessons in theory and practice* (pp. 178-192). Cambridge: CABI.

Gunnarsdotter, Y. (2008). What happens in a Swedish rural community when the local moose hunt meets hunting tourism? in Lovelock, B. (Ed.), *Tourism and the consumption of wildlife: hunting, shooting and sport fishing* (pp. 182-195). New York: Routledge.

Hasanagas N., Birtsas P., and Sokos C. (2008). Social characteristics and aesthetic ecotourism of hunters. *3rd Environmental Conference of Macedonia. Greek Chemists Union.* Thessaloniki 14-17/3/2008. http:// www.panida.gr/area/wp-content/uploads /2008_social-characteristics-and-ecotourism-of-hunters.pdf.

Hellenic Ministry of Environment, Energy, and Climate Change, (2011). *Hunting regulation for the hunting period 2011-2012* (in Greek). Athens: Hellenic Ministry of Environment, Energy, and Climate Change.

Jann, B. (2005). Tabulation of multiple responses. *The Stata Journal, 5(1),* 92-122.

Lee, H. C., and Chun, H. S. (1999). Valuing environmental quality change on recreational hunting in Korea: A contingent valuation analysis. *Journal of Environmental Management, 57,* 11-20.

MacKay, K. J., and Campbell, J. M. (2004). An examination of residents' support for hunting as a tourism product. *Tourism Management, 25(4),* 443-452.

Madsen, J., Pihl S., and Clausen P. (1998). Establishing a reserve network for waterfowl in Denmark: a biological evaluation of needs and consequences. *Biological Conservation, 85,* 241-255.

Matilainen, A. (2007). *Sustainable hunting tourism: Business opportunity in Northern areas?* Seinajoki: Ruralia Institute.

Murphy, K. R., Myors, B., and Wolach, A. (2008). *Statistical power analysis: A simple and general model for traditional and modern hypothesis tests.* Third ed. Hillsdale, NJ: Lawrence Erlbaum.

Norusis, M. J. (2007). *SPSS 16.0 Algorithms.* SPSS Inc., USA.

Nygard, M. and Uthardt, L. (2011). Opportunity or threat? Finnish hunters' attitudes to hunting tourism. *Journal of Sustainable Tourism, 19(3),* 383-401.

Okazaki, S. (2006). What do we know about mobile Internet adopters? A cluster analysis. *Information and Management, 43(2),* 127-141.

Papaspyropoulos, K. G. and Pappas, I. A. (2008). Visitors' profile and their perceptions of the aesthetic forest Kouri of Almyros, Greece. *Proceedings (in CD) of the 6th European Conference on Ecological Restoration, Ghent.*

Papaspyropoulos, K. G., Birtsas, P. K., Sokos, C. K., Skordas, K. E., and Hasanagas, N. D. (2009a). Hunters' age as an economic indicator of hunting development: the case of Prefectures of Grevena, Pella and Thessaloniki. *Scientific Annals of the Department of Forestry and Managmement of the Environment and Natural Resources of the Democritus University of Thrace. 2(II):* 336-349. (in Greek) http://www.panida.gr/site/wp-content/uploads/2009-age-of-hunters.pdf.

Papaspyropoulos, K. G., Hasanagas, N. D., and Birtsas, P. K. (2009b). Sustainable game hunting tourism: the case of Thessaloniki's hunters. *Proceedings (in CD) of the «4th International Scientific Conference 'Planning for the Future - Learning from the Past: Contemporary Developments in Tourism, Travel and Hospitality'», Rhodes.*

Petrosillo, I., Zurlini, G., Corliano, M. E., Zaccarelli, N., and Dadamo M. (2007). Tourist perception of recreational environment and management in a marine protected area. *Landscape and Urban Planning, 79(1),* 29-37.

PEVEKE, 2010. *Hunting and its contribution to Greek society and economy today.* MRB.

Redford, K. H., and Adams, W. M. (2009). Payment for ecosystem services and the challenge of saving nature: Editorial. *Conservation Biology, 23(4),* 785-787.

Rutanen, J., Matilainen, A., Muuttola,M., and Tittonen, K. (2007). Hunting and hunting tourism in Finland: Country review. In A. Matilainen (Ed.), *Sustainable hunting tourism: Business opportunity in Northern areas?* (pp. 9–30). Seinajoki: Ruralia Institute.

Røskaft, E., Handel, B., Bjerke, T. and Kaltenborn, B. P. (2007). Human attitudes towards large carnivores in Norway. *Wildlife Biology, 13,* 172-185.

Samuelsson, E. and Stage, J. (2007). The size and distribution of the economic impacts of Namibian hunting tourism. *South African Journal of Wildlife Research, 37(1),* 41-52.

Sokos, C. (2004). The Greek hunting poorness In Skordas K. and Birtsas P. (Eds), *PAN-THIRAS the everything about hunting* (pp. 86-91). Thessaloniki: Hunting Federation of Macedonia-Thrace. (in Greek).

Sokos, C. K., and Birtsas, P. K. (2005). Hunting management of pheasant (*Phasianus colchicus*) in Hellas. Proceedings of 12th Pan-Hellenic Forestry Congress. Hellenic Forestry Society, 2-5 October 2005, Drama, Hellas, p. 361-372. (in Greek) http://www.panida.gr/site/wp-content/ uploads/2005-pheasant-hunting1.pdf.

Sokos, C.K., Skordas, K.E. and Birtsas, P.K. (2003). Valuation of hunting and management of brown hare (Lepus europaeus) in rangelands. *Proceedings of 3rd Pan-Hellenic Rangelands Conference. Hellenic Rangelands and Pasture Society, 4–6 September 2002, Karpenissi, Greece.* (in Greek) http://www.panida.gr/site/wp-content/uploads /2003-harehunters.pdf.

Stoate, C. (2002). Multifunctional use of a natural resource on farmland: wild pheasant (*Phasianus colchicus*) management and the conservation of farmland passerines. *Biodiversity Conservation, 11,* 561-573.

Theodoridis, N. (2007). *Environmental and economic importance of hunting in the island of Tilos.* Master of Science Dissertation. School of Forestry and Natural Environment, AUTH. http://invenio.lib.auth.gr/record/72615/files/ gri-2007-355.pdf?version=1.

Thomaides, C., Logothetis, G., Karabatzakis, T., and Christoforidou, G. (2007). *Program "Artemis": a study on hunting harvest.* Hunting Confederation of Greece. (in Greek).

Tsachalidis E., Galatdidas S., and Tsantopoulos, G.E. (2003). Personal characteristics of the hunters in the hunting association at Macedonia and Thrace, North Greece. *Ann. Scient. Forest. Dept Vol. N.* (in Greek).

Tsachalidis, E.P., Galatsidas, S.A., and Tsantopoulos, G.E. (1998). Characteristics of hunters of Macedonia and Thrace (in Greek). *Scientific Annals of Forestry Faculty of the Aristotle University of Thessaloniki, V. MA (2),* 1345-1356.

Tseng, C. Y., Kuo, H. Y., and Chou, S. S. (2008). Configuration of innovation and performance in the service industry: evidence from the Taiwanese hotel industry. *The Service Industries Journal, 28(7),* 1015–1028.

Willebrand, T. (2009). Promoting hunting tourism in north Sweden: Opinions of local hunters. *European Journal of Wildlife Research, 5,* 209–216.

In: New Trends Towards Mediterranean Tourism Sustainability   ISBN: 978-1-62257-627-2
Editors: L. M. Rosalino, A. Silva and A. Abreu   © 2012 Nova Science Publishers, Inc.

Chapter 5

SUSTAINABLE DEVELOPMENT OF NAUTICAL TOURISM IN CROATIA

Mirjana Kovačić[*]

Primorsko-Goranska County, Faculty of Maritime Studies,
University of Rijeka, Rijeka, Croatia

ABSTRACT

This chapter analyses nautical tourism and the sustainable development of nautical tourism ports in Croatia. Croatia is a Mediterranean country with a well-indented coast and islands, which make it globally distinctive.

Its comparative advantage is a substantial archipelago comprising over a thousand islands. These natural resources contribute to the accelerated development of tourism and, in particular, nautical tourism.

Although the quality of nautical tourism has not yet reached a higher level, the elements of natural and historical heritage, together with physical capacities, allow for its further qualitative development.

The greatest threat to the further development of nautical tourism is the unchecked construction of new nautical facilities under the mounting pressure of the interests of equity capital. This chapter also examines the principles of sustainable development and the necessity of reaching a compromise between the need for environmental protection and the need for economic development.

It focuses on the implementation of new methods and techniques in determining the carrying capacity of space and the limits of growth of new nautical accommodation capacities over a specific period. The above is also important for the protection of the marine environment that involves all measures and procedures preventing pollution from ships, yachts and boats.

Preventive measures refer to all measures in compliance with regulations stipulating the safety of ships, yachts and boats, including seaworthiness of yachts, and in compliance with the requirements that nautical tourism ports have to meet in relation to preventing the pollution of the marine environment. Corrective measures primarily include procedures for minimising the damage caused by the pollution.

---

[*] E-mail: mirjana051@gmail.com.

1. INTRODUCTION

Nautical tourism is clearly a form, and a part of, tourism that takes place on water or by water. The term derives from the Greek word *naus* (Lat. *navis*) meaning ship. In broader terms, the meaning of the word is related to maritime affairs, navigation, shipping, etc. In reference books, nautical tourism is frequently identified with marine tourism, that is, only with navigation and other activities by the sea and on the sea, although nautical tourism occurs also on rivers and lakes and by their banks, both on proper or chartered yachts for recreation, sports and leisure, stationary or in navigation.

On the other hand, according to some authors (Orams, 1999; Luck, 2005), marine tourism also includes tourist activities on the beach that are not necessarily related to navigation. When other frequently used terms, such as yachting tourism, sailing tourism, leisure boating, etc. are added to the terms "nautical tourism" and "marine tourism", it becomes clear that certain issues begin to emerge when we seek to identify the scope of nautical tourism, that is, determine not only those activities on the water/sea that are considered as belonging to nautical tourism, but also those activities ashore that are complementary to navigation and to the stay of tourists/boaters on their vessels.

Differences, pertaining not only in the use of the term "nautical tourism", but also to its contents, determination and range, are present in Croatian specialised and scientific bibliography and practice.

The diversity of definitions of nautical tourism in Croatia may be illustrated by the fact that some authors include travelling on passenger, or even cargo, ships in the concept of nautical tourism (Turina, 1967), while others include sailing on small, unregistered vessels (Gvozdanović, 1969), luxury cruising (Kos and Dončević, 1970), or all types of tourism related to water, including water and underwater sports, and even marine and submarine biology and the biology of internal waters (Dulčić, 2002), etc.

Positive regulations define nautical tourism as "navigation and stay of tourists/boaters aboard vessels and in nautical tourism ports for vacation and recreation" (Tourism Industry Act of the Republic of Croatia, "Official Gazette" 8/1996, 19/1996 and 76/1998). Hence, nautical tourism is about navigation and the sojourn of tourists/boaters in nautical tourism ports and all other ports, harbours, natural coves and shelters, on their own or chartered yachts, for the purpose of leisure, sports and navigation and other, directly and indirectly, related activities.

Boat rentals are an inseparable part of nautical tourism. Nautical tourism also involves the navigation and sojourn of tourists on old, traditional ships/sailing ships. Other inseparable aspects of nautical tourism include numerous production and service activities (small shipyards, sailing organizations, the maintenance of vessels and engines, instruments and equipment, etc.).

The above also applies to boaters and vessels on rivers, lakes and channels, i.e. to nautical tourism on inland waterways. It is a fact, however, that nautical tourism on inland waterways accounts for a minor, if not undetectable, share in the performance indicators of Croatian nautical tourism today.

2. CHARACTERISTICS OF NAUTICAL TOURISM

2.1. Available Nautical Infrastructure in Croatia

A study of nautical tourism in Croatia in 2010 identified 98 nautical tourism ports on the Croatian littoral, comprising 60 marinas (10 dry-berth marinas) and 38 other nautical tourism ports, anchorages and berth places (Bureau of Statistics, Communication in 2010). These ports occupy a total water area of 3,313,110 m^2, and have 16,913 berths. On 31 December 2010, 14,431 vessels were on permanent berths, signifying a 2.5% drop relative to 31 December 2009. Sea berths were used by 87.7% of all vessels, and dry berths by 12.3%. Vessels using sea berths were motor yachts (46.7%), sailing yachts (47.9%) and other types of vessels (5.4%). Classified by flag, the greatest number of vessels was under the Croatian flag (35.5%), followed by the flags of Austria (18.2%), Germany (15.3%), the USA (6.6%), Slovenia (6.0%) and Italy (5.3%). Together, they accounted for 86.9% of all vessels on permanent berth.

Nautical tourism ports registered 206,028 transit vessels in 2010, a 0.9% increase relative to 2009. Of the transit vessels on sea berths, 32.7% were motor yachts; 64.6%, sailing yachts, and 2.7%, other types of vessels. Croatian vessels accounted for the greatest number of transit vessels (42.1%), followed by Italian (23.0%), German (10.7%), Austrian (7.6%) and Slovenian (4.9%) vessels. Together, they accounted for 88.3% of all transit vessels.

The total revenue of nautical tourism ports in 2010 amounted to HRK 547.1m (€77m), of which HRK 435.9m (€58.5m) was generated by renting berths, and accounted for 75.9% of total income. Total income in 2010 was 5.7% higher than in 2009, while berth-rental generated income was higher by 7.4%.

Croatia has over 300 ports, mostly evenly distributed along the coast and islands, which means that boaters can find safe shelter every 5 nautical miles. The period 1993-2004 saw a gradual increase in the number of marinas (from 38 to 50), but also a far larger increase in the number of other nautical tourism ports – anchorages, berth places and dry marinas, especially since 1999. Until then, there was an equal number of nautical tourism ports and marinas, but since then the number of other nautical ports has grown significantly. In 2004, there were 50 marinas and 33 ports used as anchorages, landing places and dry marinas. The number of available berths grew from 10,000 in 1993 to 15,500 in 2004, and the number of dry berths from 2,500 to 5,000.

2.2. Characteristics of Development Trends of Nautical Tourism in the Mediterranean

As most of its territory belongs to the Mediterranean, Croatia participates, to a certain extent, in all the region's activities linked to the use of the sea, as well as to activities involving nautical tourism.

Trends in nautical tourism that exist in the more-developed countries may either be expected to evolve in Croatia or are already present. The slower development of nautical tourism in Croatia in relation to Italy, France or Spain makes it possible to monitor the enabling and constraining effects that nautical tourism development had on the economies and environments of these countries. The experiences of these countries could help Croatia to conceive its own line of development. However, the specific aspects of Croatia's coast, the characteristics of its residents, the level of its economic development, including the development of communal, traffic and social infrastructure, etc. impose upon planners certain constraints that did not exist in those countries, or did not exist in the same form or in the same magnitude. In addition, conditions on the global tourist and nautical market are different today than they were during the intensive development of nautical tourism in those countries.

A review of the reference sources dealing with nautical tourism in the Mediterranean and some recent studies of Croatian authors has revealed the following trends:

- There are constraints to the construction of marinas as a result of more-efficient environmental protection, in particular with regard to the construction of marinas in naturally vulnerable areas;
- Some studies, however, show that the construction of marinas may even help to improve the environment (by transforming deserted industrial premises and areas);
- There is a growing demand for marinas that can accommodate vessels 12 to 15 metres in length or larger, as well as a demand for marinas capable of accommodating mega yachts, more than 20 metres long;
- Marinas in the Mediterranean are being expanded and their capacities increased to make them capable of accommodating mega yachts;
- The number of senior boaters is rising;
- Business operations of marinas have a seasonal character;
- The number of sailing yachts is increasing;
- The length of navigation, i.e. the time of vessels spend outside a marina is becoming shorter;
- The average number of the crew is growing;
- The number of transit arrivals in marinas is increasing;
- The average demand for charter is increasing;
- There is an upward trend in the use of repair and catering services in marinas. Especially in demand are highly specialised and sophisticated services required by technically more-advanced vessels;
- Catering and entertainment services in the marina are more frequently requested;
- Competition in the Mediterranean is steadily growing.

Nautical tourism in Croatia is a business activity subject to the international tourist market. It is an integral part of the overall tourism offering and as such cannot be studied separately from the rest of the tourism trade. To estimate the growth of demand in tourism, it is important to examine the global tourist market of the future. The average annual growth rate of international tourist arrivals in Europe by 2020 is expected to amount to about 3%. Europe will still be the most significant tourist destination in the world, but its share in the global tourist market will drop (from 70% in the 1990s to about 50% by 2020). The beginning of the twenty-first century was marked by a series of new threats to international tourism, such as terrorism, new contagious diseases, the downturn of economic growth in many countries, etc. All this has led to change in tourism trends. For example, booking is postponed until the last minute, tourists choose closer destinations, consumers are more sensitive to costs, the costs of business trips are declining, there is a growing demand for individually organised trips through the Internet and using low cost airlines, there is a decreased use of airplanes and increased use of road vehicles in international travelling, there is an increased demand for other types of accommodations rather than hotel accommodations, and destinations where a tourist has relatives or friends are becoming more popular.

There have also been great political changes in Europe that have influenced international tour travels. The transformation (both economic and political) of former East European countries and the expansion of the European Union has resulted in the reduction or elimination of customs formalities.

Consequently, the flow of people and goods is increased, while a common currency facilitates all financial transactions and comparisons. Hence, current and future trends in international tourism could be defined as follows: desirable destinations are those that are safe for visitors, easily accessed, with good medical standards, developed infrastructure and clean environment. Croatia is such a destination for some of the currently most significant tourist generating countries.

3. BASICS OF SUSTAINABLE DEVELOPMENT OF NAUTICAL TOURISM

In development plans, space has a dual role: it is seen as an inevitable factor of social and economic development, and as an object of development processes. Development processes in space evolve and are mutually coordinated. Space cannot be understood without these development processes, while development processes cannot be realised without space. To efficiently manage the coastal area, it is necessary to plan space and continually monitor its exploitation.

Despite its natural and historical conditions and advantages, the Adriatic region is suffering the consequences of poor planning and other deviations in development. These deviations were caused by the Homeland War (1990-1995), usurpation of the most valuable areas, unplanned construction, etc. Because of the mounting pressure exerted on ecological systems, the development of nautical tourism has to be systematically planned so that people can sustain their quality of life. Otherwise, development will lose its meaning. (Kovačić and Luković, 2007).

3.1. Spatial Planning Features

The spatial plans of the counties in Croatia are basic regional planning documents that determine the distribution and capacities of nautical tourism ports. The detailed communal and town plans must be harmonised with spatial plans.

The starting point for developing plans is the geographic space of the Croatian part of the Adriatic that requires the construction of adequate infrastructure for vessel accommodation.

The recommendation is that sea berths should account for two-thirds of all berths, and dry berths for one-third (Croatian Hydrographic Institute, 2006). The following advantages linked to accommodating vessels ashore support this fact:

- Preservation of natural characteristics;
- Rational exploitation of available space;
- Enhanced safety of vessels;
- Permanent access to vessels;
- Lower price of equipment for vessel accommodation.

The above mentioned facts are stipulated in legal regulations (Regulation on the Management and Protection of the Coastal Marine Area, "Official Gazette" 128/04.) according to which a standard 12-metre vessel (the equivalent of one 3-bed accommodation unit) requires an area of $112.5m^2$ for a sea berth and $90.00m^2$ for a dry berth. The result is that the sea area for a nautical port holding 400 vessels should have an area of at least $45,000m^2$ (4.5 hectares), not including piers and other constructions in the sea. For the accommodation of the same number of vessels on dry berths, an area of $36,000m^2$ is required (3.6 hectares).

3.2. Spatial Evaluation Criteria in Ensuring Environmental Protection

Considered integrally, the coastal area (sea and land) is potentially one of the most important natural resources for the development of Croatia (Environment Protection Act, "Official Gazette" 82/94, 128/99). This development has to be permanent or sustainable over a longer period, stressing the importance of the rational management of natural resources, among which space is one of the most significant. Space may be regarded as a non-renewable natural resource. Once exploited for a particular activity, it becomes largely unavailable for other activities, due to legal, social and economic reasons. This indicates the importance of criteria for determining priorities in the exploitation of space, which should be set in the early stage of planning. Within planning, a criterion may be defined as a guideline for the practical realisation of adopted planned or development goals, so that both the selection and the contents of the criteria depend upon the goals. Hence, criteria have more of a strategic value; they are global in nature and are used for defining differences between planned alternatives. The basic starting points for their determination are primarily biological and ecological values and anthropogenic impacts on the marine ecosystem.

3.2.1. General Characteristics of the Adriatic Area

The Adriatic Sea is a deeply indented bay of the Mediterranean Sea, stretching in a southeast-northeast direction for a length of 738 km and covering a total area of 138,595 km² (Riđanović, 2002). The Croatian coastline of the Adriatic Sea is 5,835 km long, of which 4,058 km belong to more than 1,000 islands (Duplančić et al., 2004). According to the latest research of the Croatian Hydrographic Institute (Duplančić et al., 2000; Croatian Hydrographic Institute, 2006), Croatia has 1,246 islands, islets and rocks, or more specifically, 79 islands (with an area greater than 1 km²), 525 islets (with an area from 100 m² to 1 km²), and 642 rocks (with an area less than 100 m²). Their total area is 3,260 km². The Croatian territorial sea occupies an area of 31,067 km². Due to mountain ranges, the basin of the eastern coast is limited and very little fresh water flows into the Adriatic (20% of Croatian rivers in terms of the quantity of water). The Adriatic is a shallow sea, with an average depth of 173 metres, and 74% of the seafloor does not exceed 200 metres. Depths of over 200 metres are located in the area of Jabučna Kotlina, while the deepest area of 1,330 metres is found in the southern Adriatic. The largest part of the Adriatic has low productivity (oligotrophic sea), while the northern Adriatic is an area of high productivity. Increased productivity in relation to the open sea is also found in coastal and channel areas, and particularly high values of primary production are present in some estuaries, such as the River Krka estuary, the River Jadro (Vranjički bazen) and the Lim Channel.

Altogether, the greatest part of the Croatian coastal sea is not polluted, and pollution occasionally occurs in some parts of the littoral close to big cities that still have inadequate systems for treating and managing waste waters of communal and industrial origin. The UN Convention on the Law of the Sea characterises the Adriatic Sea as:

- A variety of life, cleanliness, clearness and landscape to which particular attention has to be given with regard to its exploitation and conservation;
- Susceptible to threats from various types of pollution due to its size and slow exchange of water.

3.2.2. Biological and Ecological Values

Adriatic flora and fauna is extremely diverse (it is estimated that there are about 6-7 thousand plant and animal species in the Adriatic) and, since some groups of organisms, especially invertebrates, have not been fully researched, it is assumed that this number is much higher. The presence of numerous endemic species (about 12% of the species are endemic) makes Adriatic plant and animal life particularly interesting.

3.3. Potential Impacts of Marinas on the Environment

The effects that marinas have on the environment involve the immediate direct and indirect impacts of construction phases (e.g. loss of habitats, changes in sea quality and sedimentation) and permanent impacts (e.g. loss of scenery and landscapes, permanent decline of sea quality, growing noise levels, and growing local pressure resulting, for example, from traffic):

- Loss of habitats – complete disappearance of habitats due to concreted coast, change of the coastline, change of substrate, etc;
- Habitat fragmentation– interventions in the coastal area divide larger habitats into smaller parts, disrupting the activities of numerous species, decreasing the total area and size of available habitats, causing changes in migration paths, increasing edge effects and, eventually, leading to the disruption of community structures and functions and to the decline of biological diversity;
- Dredging, removal of substrate, change of the substrate type, sedimentation – all this intensifies the destruction or severe disruption of habitats, and reduces the penetration of light, which has adverse consequences for organisms, especially plant communities;
- Changes in the level of the coastline cause changes in the composition and spatial structure of communities;

- Quality of the sea – contamination/pollution of the sea;
- Noise – the increased level of noise above and under the water. Adverse consequences for the living world during periods when organisms are vulnerable (spawning, migrations, feeding);
- Competing activities – adverse effects on other activities (mariculture, beaches), mutual incompatibility;
- Cumulative effects – synergistic effects of various types of impact.

A literature-based review of research concerning the various types of marine-related contamination/pollution can be summarized as follows (Croatian Hydrographic Institute, 2006):

- When compared to other categories of dispersed sources of pollution (urban settlements and agriculture), marinas and nautical tourism cannot be characterised as main sources of dispersed pollution. Locally, however, marinas and nautical tourism may lead to a decline in the quality of sea water and to a negative impact on marine organisms and ecosystems. Most studies concerning marinas suggest a link between contaminants/pollutants (such as, heavy metals, oil carbohydrates and bacteriological pollution) and an increase in the concentration of nutritious salts (especially nitrogen and phosphorus), which leads to a drop in the concentration of dissolved oxygen;
- Some studies have detected toxic levels of heavy metals and oil carbohydrates that can have a wide range of adverse effects on marine organisms. Pollutants that affect individual organisms may result in negative consequences for the entire community;
- As sea water becomes stagnant due to poor water circulation within a marina, its quality decreases. The concentration of dissolved oxygen drops, allowing contaminants/pollutants to gather in the sediment and leading to a drop in the absorption capacity of the basin.

4. SELECTING LOCATIONS FOR NAUTICAL TOURISM PORTS IN COMPLIANCE WITH THE PRINCIPLES OF SUSTAINABLE DEVELOPMENT

The principles of sustainable development underline the need for the balanced exploitation, use and development of marine and coastal areas, taking into account the conservation of the natural characteristics of the environment.

4.1. Recommendations for the Selection of a Location in View of the Physical Characteristics of the Area

Using certain spaces for the construction of nautical tourism ports, in particular, marinas, may be considered appropriate, providing the following conditions are met (Kovačić et al., 2006):

- Adverse effects on marine ecosystems are avoided or reduced to an acceptable level;
- Adverse effects on coastal processes (water circulation, sedimentation) close to marinas, along the coast and from the coast towards the open sea are avoided or reduced to an acceptable level;
- The circulation of water is such that it ensures the basin is well aerated and that the previous quality of sea water within the marina and in the neighbouring areas is maintained or improved;
- The activities of the marina are in compliance with other neighbouring activities;
- The activities of the marina are in compliance with the social, economic, cultural and recreational values of the area.

The individual and cumulative negative impacts of marinas on the environment depend upon the location, size and design of marinas, in view of the following elements:

- Size of the marina;
- Construction solutions for breakwaters and piers (fixed, floating);
- Characteristics of the basin where the marina is located (depth, inclination, water exchange dynamics);
- Natural quality of sea water;
- Existence of fish farms or fishing areas close to the marina;
- Existence of other recreational activities close to the marina;
- Existence of vulnerable, endangered, valuable or protected habitats, communities and/or species close to the marina.

(Source: www.aci-club.hr/marina).

Figure 1. Marina Skradin.

ACI marina Skradin (Figure 1), which is situated in the Middle Adriatic, close to the Krka estuary, is a good example of a marina location adapted to the physical characteristics of the area. The location of the marina is also a good example of how to incorporate the infrastructure of a nautical tourism port into the natural environment. This marina is located in a cove northwest of the small town of Skradin (43°49.0' N 15°55.6' E; in Adriatic Croatia International Club). The marina has 153 sea berths with water and power supply, is open year-round, and has a reception office, exchange office, restaurant, toilets and showers, and parking lot. Good circulation of water in the basin allows for the aeration of the basin, prevents the water from becoming stagnant, and increases the receiving capacity of the basin. The following is important for the configuration of the basin:

- Greater depths – A greater volume of water helps to lessen the occurrence of adverse effects (stagnant water) and increase receiving capacity. Local areas that are deeper than neighbouring channels should be avoided;
- Inclination – Preference should be given to areas that have a continuous slope from berths towards greater depths, which facilitates water circulation and helps to carry off pollutants and particles;
- Deeply indented channels and bays should be avoided.

Recommendations for the design and maintenance of marinas are as follows:

- Select an open design for the breakwaters and piers (fixed or floating), which allows for good circulation and exchange of water. If necessary, structures for weakening the waves and the force of incoming water should be installed;
- Use materials that are neutral to the environment (avoid materials that emit poisonous substances and substances that are not easily degradable in the sea);
- Allow for a significant penetration of light;
- Minimise dredging (by extending breakwaters and piers in naturally deep water). Where dredging is necessary, its consequences should be minimised (do not dredge during critical periods of migrations and spawning; apply less harmful dredging methods, such as hydraulic dredging).

A good example of a well-planned and well-situated marina is Marina Vrsar (Figure 2), located on the Istria peninsula in the Municipality of Vrsar, 3 km to the north of the Lim Channel. It is connected to Poreč (9 km) and the main Buje-Pula road by a regional road. The nautical port is located at 45° 9' 12" N and 13° 36' 06" E. The distance from Vrsar to Trieste is 85 km, to Ljubljana 170 km, to Graz 350 km, and to Munich 615 km. Vrsar is 4 km away from Pula Airport and 2 km from Crljenka Sports Airport. The sea distance from Vrsar to Venice is 53 M, to the National Park Brijuni 17 M and to the National Park Krka 160 M.

Marina Vrsar has 220 sea berths and 40 dry berths. Owing to the depth of the waterway and berths between 4 and 14 metres, the marina can accommodate yachts of up to 50 metres in length. The depth of the sea at the fuel station is 4 metres. Facilities include a reception office with video surveillance, air-conditioned toilets, a premium restaurant, a café, a crane (35 t), a nautical equipment shop and sports equipment rental, a diving service, WLAN internet and a charter agency. All facilities and services in the nearby town are also available.

Figure 2. Marina Vrsar.

The building of new marinas should be avoided in areas that are of vital importance to:

- Fishing;
- The spawning, growing, feeding, shelter and migration of marine organisms and, in particular, species of commercial importance (communities of lesser Neptune grass and photophilic algae in river deltas and estuaries);
- High biodiversity;
- Species that are by law protected, rare, endangered and/or endemic;
- Areas that are exceptionally vulnerable to human influences;
- Exceptionally rare habitats of great geologic and geomorphologic value;
- Protected areas (national parks, nature parks, rigorous nature reserves etc.).

4.2. Environmental Constraints to Take into Account in the Development of Marinas

It is important to ban the construction/development of marinas in areas that are recognised as exceptionally valuable and need to be protected from adverse effects. The ban should also include marina activities that are seen as being incompatible with environmental protection programmes. Environmental protection has absolute priority. Limiting the construction/ development of marinas is related to the protection of valuable areas and has priority, but it also allows for the development of nautical tourism providing all precautionary measures are taken.

The development, redesign and renovation of existing marinas, berths and anchorages aimed at improving nautical tourism should be planned with some caution and should not cause any further adverse effects, such as the loss of natural habitats.

The construction of new marinas is possible provided the area meets the ecological criteria and the clean-marina principle (Johnson, 2005) is adhered to. This principle addresses the issue of collecting, storing and disposing of all types of waste produced by vessels and marina facilities.

Out of all nautical tourism ports in Croatia, marinas represent the most concentrated type of development in the littoral, and the numerous activities involved in marina development (e.g. interventions on the coast, dredging, draining of waste waters etc.) tend to significantly modify the environment.

Concentrating berths and anchorages in a smaller region will contribute to the better rationalisation of the coastal area. Where possible, floating docks will be able to accommodate a greater number of yachts per surface unit. Moreover, the existing infrastructure allows for higher safety and better solutions related to environmental protection.

This way the adverse impacts on the environment will be limited to a smaller number of locations, which means that fewer natural habitats will need to be sacrificed and that the quality of the sea and biodiversity will be affected to a smaller extent (Favro et al., 2010). The construction of new marinas has to be an exception, rather than a rule, and untouched, exceptionally beautiful islands and maritime zones have to be preserved.

Instead of such locations, it is recommended to consider locations in devastated bays and parts of the littoral where the construction of marinas and tourist capacities within the general recovery plan might have additional positive effects, such as the creation of new jobs for residents (Kovačić et al., 2011).

4.3. Protection from Pollution of the Open Sea

Pollution protection of the sea and the coast primarily refers to pollution resulting from the discharge of waste waters and waste from vessels. In general, pollution protection in ports (such as the Port of Rijeka, and special purpose ports, such as nautical tourism ports) is under the authority of the entity managing the port. Pollution on the open sea and during anchoring in uncontrolled anchorages and in harbours is within the authority of the harbour master's office. Although preventing and detecting such pollution is not simple and is almost impossible, it can be reduced by implementing a series of promotional measures (Zec et al., 2007):

- Developing awareness of the need for environmental protection (by distributing promotional leaflets and educating people about the consequences of pollution, methods of waste disposal, methods of reporting pollution incidents, etc.);
- Using means that will allow efficient action in case of pollution incidents (e.g. skimmers);
- Providing a sufficient number of containers for oily waters and waste, especially close to attractive destinations;
- Checking anchorages more frequently, consistently implementing the ban on discharging oily waters and waste into the sea and putting in place warning signs;
- Granting concessions for gathering waste in unmonitored coves and anchorages.

Most of the above activities are not business-oriented. However, some of them could be organised in such a way. This is an approach that should also be taken into account wherever possible.

5. INTEGRATED PLANNING NAUTICAL TOURISM DEVELOPMENT

Proper spatial planning is one of the most important pre-requisites to long-term and sustainable development in nautical tourism. Viewed broadly, space is a fundamental precondition to the arrival and stay of boaters, and at the same time, it is a development factor of nautical destinations. Because the construction of nautical tourism infrastructures is, by its nature, a long-term process, the integrated planning of spatial development is a primary condition for the successful performance of a nautical destination.

5.1. Model of Spatial Organisation of Nautical Tourism Ports

Spatial plans are the principal documents of nautical tourism development, as they direct and determine planning efforts in all economic branches and activities that take active participation in designing the nautical offering. The main task of spatial planning is to strike a balance between accommodation facilities, transport, communication and other services, while seeking to protect the attraction resources on which nautical tourism is based. Efficient spatial development management should help to boost the value and quality of the environment, enhance the rational usability of space for construction purposes, and development systems to protect biodiversity.

In devising spatial plans, it is essential to address issues regarding sustainable development, the protection of coastal and marine environments, and the development of the entire infrastructure (e.g. water supply, drainage and treatment of wastewaters, waste management, the use of alternative energy sources, etc.).

The specific natural and cultural features of a given area and locality should be used to determine, in conformity with legal regulations (Regulation on the Classification and Categorisation of Nautical Tourism Ports, "Official Gazette" Zagreb, no. 72/08 and the Law on Maritime Domain and Sea Ports, "Official Gazette" Zagreb, no. 158/03.), which type of nautical port will be capable of making optimal use of available resources, and they should determine the condition construction that is feasible and acceptable in respect of the key spatial attributes of the nautical destination. The basic determinants of proper spatial use involve (Favro and Kovačić, 2006):

- The formulation of a spatial plan of nautical tourism development – The plan should take into account not only the physical aspects of port development in nautical destinations, but also aspects relating to quality and logistics;
- The formulation of a Master Plan – This is a strategic document that also focuses on the targeted local development of nautical tourism in all tourism regions/destinations.

Master Plans need to be consistent with the strategic development of nautical tourism at the national level. Identifying and valorising existing nautical resources and specifying the nautical product and services that need improvement should be a component of any Master Plan. Importantly, a Master Plan should also specify the nautical infrastructure, accommodation facilities, logistics, and distribution channels required, and identify the key pricing principles and guidelines for devising a marketing strategy. An action plan for implementing a Master Plan, focuses on the sources of funding, local organisational structures, processes and the operatives is needed. Key elements in the development of nautical destinations involve collaboration among regional tourism associations and sharing know-how between regions.

5.2. Determining the Carrying Capacity of a Nautical Destination

The application of sustainable development entails defining the carrying capacity of a nautical destination. Carrying capacity is dependent upon a number of elements. It is a managerial decision made at the destination level following comprehensive and interdisciplinary research. The carrying capacity of nautical tourism is determined on the basis of a selected scenario of nautical development, taking into account the given limits of growth and development. Carrying capacity is a factor central to putting in place the concept of sustainable tourism development. Although a number of researchers have addressed this issue in the recent years, they have failed to come up with a singular technique of what would be the simplest way of determining a destination's carrying capacity. Recent studies have pointed to new problems that arise in measuring carrying capacity, in particular, in relation to planning locations for and constructing new nautical ports and determining their capacities. Nautical tourism and nautical ports represent a complex field requiring comprehensive, interdisciplinary research that must involve economists, sociologists, psychologists, technologists, technicians, spatial planners, biologists and ecologists, as well as professionals of other profiles depending upon the case at hand.

5.2.1. Conceptual and Contextual Definition of Carrying Capacity

In analysing tourism destination management issues, Cooper and colleagues argued that the concepts of sustainable development and carrying capacity will become central to the interests of tourism destination managers (Cooper et al., 1993, p.78). The concept of sustainable development represents a long-term approach that provides a destination with the opportunity of being competitive on the marketplace and meeting the requirements of nautical demand. There are two key factors that must be increasingly taken into consideration in defining the destination of the future: the environment and life styles.

The carrying capacity of a nautical destination represents the destination's ability to absorb boaters and to justify the construction and development of nautical ports, without degrading its total natural, built and socio-cultural environment to any significant extent. This refers to the presence boaters and their vessels, a factor impacting on the environment and residents. Initially, carrying capacities were identified in processes pertaining to developing and managing under-developed regions. Later, managers of recreational areas also began to apply the carrying capacity concept. Recreational carrying capacity can be defined as the amount of recreational use allowable in a given area, providing measures have been taken to ensure the quality of services and facilities, the environment and the recreational experience. Carrying capacity can also be defined as a manner of using space over a prolonged period and developing an area to a specific level without inflicting irreparable damage to the natural environment and without reducing the quality of experiences gained by tourists. Since the mid-1980s, approaches to understanding carrying capacity have developed from trying to identify an optimal number of users to working out complex methods involving resource management and the physical parameters of resources, as well as an analysis of tourist expectations and preferences.

5.2.2. Aspect of Accommodation Potential

Based on contextual analyses of carrying capacity stated in the literature (Mathieson and Wall, 1987; Klarić, 1994), the aspects of a nautical port's or marina's carrying capacity can be identified in terms of context. These include the physical, psychological, environmental, sociological and economic aspects of carrying capacity.

The *physical aspect* of carrying capacity refers to the amount of space available for the construction of a nautical port. It is necessary to determine the size and capacity of the port's sea area and land area to be used for accommodating vessels and to plan and manage development accordingly. Spatial plans impact greatly on this aspect of carrying capacity. In terms of a nautical destination, this refers to the size of the sea and land space being used for nautical purposes in a given destination. Considering that the interests of boaters today are varied and complex, focus should be placed on the capacity and size of facilities that can supplement the offering of a nautical port. The successful organisation and positioning of a nautical port offering is one of the elements examined in assessing physical capacity and the appeal of services provided at a given site.

The *psychological aspect* of carrying capacity is exceeded when there is a considerable decline in a boater's experience caused by the saturation of a destination. This aspect of carrying capacity can be identified by analysing the attitudes of target demand markets, and results linked to existing and expected trends. The opinion of the local population regarding nautical tourism development should also be investigated, because sustainable development emphasises the importance of taking into consideration the attitudes of residents and of planning development that is based on their preferences, rather than on economic considerations.

The *environmental aspect* of carrying capacity is exceeded when pollution and degradation have been reported or pose a threat. Such issues should be addressed through the need to maintain the integral eco-system in equilibrium. This is achieved by defining the point at which the ecosystem has not yet registered damage, establishing the acceptable level of noise, air and water pollution, and carrying out an Environmental Impact Assessment.

The *sociological aspect* of carrying capacity is derived from the idea that the entire local community should participate in the process of planning and sustaining nautical development. The objective is to define a level of development acceptable to the local population. From the standpoint of boaters, this means defining occupancy level for nautical ports that does not cause boater satisfaction to decline.

The *economic aspect* of carrying capacity implies the ability of developing nautical tourism and the activities that support it without exerting pressure on the other long-term economic activities profitable and acceptable to the local population.

5.3. Identifying Carrying Capacity

Problems arise in identifying the carrying capacity of a given destination because carrying capacity depends upon numerous interdependent factors that are subject to change over time (Kovačić et al., 2005). Planning nautical tourism development in a specific area (or in an established nautical destination) involves selecting sites for the construction of nautical ports and determining their size in terms of the number of boaters they can absorb and the number of new facilities the ports can accommodate. As the carrying capacity of nautical ports is not specifically discussed in the literature, this paper seeks to present certain assumptions and conclusions that have emerged as the results of research regarding the carrying capacity of other tourism destinations (e.g. hotels, beaches, etc.)

Carrying capacity depends on numerous factors that vary from one site to another, because of each site's specific attributes. An analysis of previous research and data collected shows that the factors that have substantial impact on a nautical destination's carrying capacity can be classified into two basic categories (Kovačić et al., 2007):

- Boater attributes;
- Attributes of a nautical destination.

The category of *boater attributes* includes all the vital characteristics of boaters, in particular, their socio-economic characteristics (age, sex, and income), their motivations and beliefs, expectations, ethnic group affiliation and their life style. Boaters differ in how they impact on a destination; the way they relate to the environment also differs based on their educational level and the cultural circle they belong to. This category also includes the level of use, i.e. the number of boaters staying in a nautical port and its surroundings at any one time and their length of stay.

To determine the number of vessels and boaters that can be allowed to stay in a nautical port without exceeding its carrying capacity threshold, it is necessary to define the maximum daily number of boaters, which is connected to the number of vessels a nautical port can absorb. Although the total annual number of boaters and the number of vessels and vessel lengths represent significant data, primary importance is given to the maximum daily load of a nautical port's aquatorium. Upon defining a nautical port's carrying capacity, it is necessary to determine the maximum acceptable (or permissible) number of boaters and their vessels that can be present at any one time; with regard to vessel size, this number is a variable. This is of special importance for marinas. The average length of stay of boaters in a nautical port is also important, as it relates a nautical port's carrying capacity to the maximum number of boaters that can stay at the port at any one time.

The attributes of a nautical destination and the local population describe:

- The features of the natural environment;
- Economic structure and development;
- Political structures and institutional characteristics;
- Social culture;
- The development of nautical tourism ports.

The features of the natural environment are exceptionally important in assessing carrying capacity. They are considered to be fundamental factors in planning nautical tourism development. Spatial use has a crucial effect on carrying capacity, and it must be regulated in spatial plans. The regions and individual sites for constructing nautical ports should be determined through functional spatial management. This is important for the islands, the development of which should be coupled to the continuous control and monitoring of the marine and coastal environment.

Political structure impacts on how a nautical offering is organised, as well as on the potential of a nautical port to absorb boaters. These features are linked to the ruling social system, the political openness of a country, and the safety and institutional organisation of a nautical port. Granting concessions may help to stimulate nautical port development, but it can also become a constraining factor, in particular, for marinas, considering that the duration of concessions in Croatia is usually 30 years.

Regional economic structure and development also impact on a nautical destination and its offering, as well as on the economic development of residents. This can also relate to the social structure of the population. A more developed society is more open to different cultures and other people - boaters. In less developed societies or societies with particular cultural features, social conditions may play a vital part in determining the level of carrying capacity. More advanced economic development should entail better infrastructure facilities, a crucial factor that can have a positive influence on nautical port construction.

The term "social structure" refers to the general demographic features of the local population, local culture, social organisation, labour issues, employment for women, moral and religious beliefs, the level of hygiene standards, the health of the population, language, traditions, indigenous customs, and the attitude of residents towards boaters.

The achieved level of nautical development has a bearing on the psychological, physical, environmental, sociological and economic aspects of carrying capacity. From a psychological aspect, residents are likely to be more receptive towards boaters in the later, rather than in the initial phase of nautical tourism development, because, with time, they will grow more open to boater arrivals. This effect is less manifested in advanced urban settings where residents are more willing to communicate with others. The development level of a nautical destination influences the physical aspect of carrying capacity with regard to the built receiving capacities and other services available to boaters. The physical aspect of space and natural resources does not affect carrying capacity regardless of the destination's level of development. As to the economic aspect of carrying capacity, the development of the economy (tourism included) will increase the potential to absorb. The environmental aspect of carrying capacity is variable. If it is disrupted, it will decline. Because the concept of carrying capacity takes nautical resources into account it is increasingly gaining recognition, especially now when the depletion of natural resources due to nautical tourism development is becoming visible at a destination level in Mediterranean countries.

The management of a nautical port can take action to increase the port's carrying capacity, primarily through efforts to reduce seasonality by improving its offering in terms of quality and quantity.

5.4. Development Scenarios

In designing a development policy for nautical tourism that focuses on sustainable development, numerous elements need to be analysed. A number of various alternatives are formulated, and each alternative is assessed in terms of how it leads to attaining the goals of nautical tourism development and achieving optimal economic benefits, while minimising adverse impacts to the environment and socio-cultural setting. In principle, there are several phases in determining carrying capacity (PPA/CRA, 1996; p. 14-32):

1. Collecting documentation and creating maps;
2. Analysing data;
3. Building nautical tourism development scenarios;
4. Identifying carrying capacity;
5. Implementation and monitoring.

The first phase defines the territorial boundaries of a nautical port; presents the basic features of the port and its development; underlines its appeal and attraction factors; analyses the relationship of nautical tourism, the economy and residents; assesses the state of the documentation; and gathers additional data as required. The analysis phase focuses on determining the design of the nautical port; defining its relation to the broader environment; presenting the prescribed constraints; assessing nautical resources, supply and demand; and proposing alternative solutions. In the third phase, alternative scenarios are constructed and analysed, and the best scenario is selected. To formulate carrying capacity in the fourth stage, a development model is designed, carrying capacity is calculated, and instructions are provided for its application. In the end, implementation takes place, which is followed up with continuous monitoring. Carrying capacity, however, is not an unchanging, absolute value; its value varies depending upon the objectives set for a specific area and upon the development cycle of the relevant nautical port. Carrying capacity must be consistent with the development scenarios of a given nautical port. Therefore, although certain aspects that determine carrying capacity may impose strong constraints, some shifts are possible depending upon the objectives of nautical tourism development in a destination. Development scenarios can be considered through four basic forms (Kovačić et al., 2007):

- Completely free development, with no constraints;
- Intensive nautical development, but with certain elements of control;
- Development of alternative or nautical tourism;
- Sustainable development of nautical tourism ports.

The study on nautical tourism development in the Republic of Croatia (Croatian Hydrographic Institute, 2006), together with the 2009-2019 Strategy of nautical tourism development in Croatia (Ministry of Sea, Traffic and Infrastructure, Ministry of Tourism. (2008), has confirmed the logical choice in developing nautical infrastructure that underlines steady and balanced development. This development involves an increase in the number of sea berths and dry berths from the present 16,913 to 31,000 in the future.

To ensure the optimal use of natural resources by nautical tourism ports, an assessment of the carrying capacity of a specific, potential location should become a part of planning and managing nautical tourism development.

5.4.1. The No-Constraints Scenario of Nautical Port Development

The scenario of free development with no constraints is considered acceptable, and, in practice, it means exceeding the limits of carrying capacity in all its aspects. This type of scenario may yield short-term but high profits for a nautical port, but it will have disastrous consequences for the environment. Development of this kind is a blind force due to the absence of any planning in building a nautical port. Typically, residents tend to offer resistance to this development scenario and, often, even the State may find it unacceptable, except in situations where there is only one goal – economic gain. Such a scenario needs to be analysed in the case of endeavours to implement it in:

- An area of developed nautical tourism;
- An underdeveloped area;
- Areas in which it has previously been applied, i.e. in the remediation of built locations.

5.4.2. The Intensive Development Scenario

Intensive development implies large-scale interventions in space undertaken to gain high profits. The State plays a central role in this kind of development and imposes various control mechanisms. This scenario takes carrying capacity partially into consideration, but it tends to portray carrying capacity values as being higher than they actually are. While on the one hand taking account of economic and political aspects, on the other hand it minimises the importance of socio-cultural carrying capacity. The opinions of residents are marginalised.

Calling for a middle-ground approach to relationships between boaters and residents, this scenario is offered as an alternative in all plans, except when dealing with highly vulnerable and valuable areas, where it is not acceptable under any conditions.

5.4.3. The Scenario of Development of Special-Interest Forms of Tourism – Nautical Tourism

The development scenario of special-interest tourism and, in particular, nautical tourism has evolved as a response to the concept of mass tourism. Typically, the concept is introduced in moderately and less developed countries, imposing limitations but neglecting the economic growth required. Nautical tourism is very important when it comes to implementing the concept of special-interest tourism. The lowest possible carrying-capacity values are presented, and while socio-cultural and environmental aspects are overstated, the economic and political aspect is understated. This type of scenario is taken into consideration in the case of highly vulnerable areas, areas rich in cultural and historical heritage, and areas in which the local population has a specific identity.

5.4.4. Sustainable Development of Nautical Tourism and Nautical Tourism Ports

The sustainable development scenario is positioned between maximum and minimum carrying capacity, that is, between scenarios of intensive and moderate nautical tourism development. The values of the relatively fixed components of carrying capacity (physical capacity, environmental capacity, resource capacity, demographic capacity) are established, as well as the range of values for the more elastic components (infrastructure, a local community's socio-cultural capacity). The economic and political complex, that is, the willingness of the State to encourage or discourage a project through legal regulations or direct investments, is vital in selecting and implementing a development option. The carrying capacity threshold at which a model of sustainable nautical tourism development will be set depends upon the specifics of a given area, and the demands and considerations of decision-makers at a local and national level. For example, limitations imposed on boater arrivals to prevent the intended carrying capacity from being exceeded will depend upon the nautical port's capacity, which determines the maximum number of vessels and boaters.

In Croatia, development plans, adopted at the national level, define the exploitation of space for nautical tourism ports as follows:

- The capacity of nautical centres with regard to commercial berths is limited to a maximum of 1,000 berths, while the minimum capacity is limited to 200 berths;
- The number of berths in nautical ports is determined in relation with marine-area use. Accordingly, nautical tourism ports with less than 100 berths will be regarded as ports in exclusive nautical centres that offer superior quality services.

5.4.5. The Optimal Carrying Capacity of Nautical Tourism Ports – a Systems Approach

In practice, different stakeholders will have different opinions regarding the acceptable level of use of a site for nautical purposes. Also, limitations exist to the size of a nautical port, and in particular, a marina; these limitations are dictated by the size and design of vessels (Koelbel, 1999). Another important point is that environmental damage to natural resources may occur even at a low level of use.

In the future, nautical tourism ports will be exposed to a series of influences that will surely change their current method of business operations. The main influence will come from the larger size of vessels (both of smaller and larger ones) that will decrease the security level in current nautical tourism ports. Attempts to accommodate the same number of vessels as before will often lead to mooring vessels in spots that are not fully adequate for their size. The same refers to ports under construction or that are planned to be built and in which it will be necessary to adopt the present standards to new values, especially those referring to the width of vessels and their distribution in groups. Moreover, other influences are expected which will require modifications to the technological organisation of nautical tourism ports (Cooper, 2010). In particular, these influences include new types of mobile and other technical equipment, pontoons and other.

In terms of environmental protection, it is necessary to distinguish other conditions to be fulfilled when building new nautical tourism ports in relation to the conditions fulfilled by the existing ports. When new ports are to be built, environmental protection measures will refer to protecting the environment from the consequences of performing the planned activities. Spatial protection will be manifested in the form of a demand to observe two main requirements (Zec et al., 2007):

- The principle of minimum spatial interventions;
- The principle of acceptable impacts on the environment.

The principle of minimum spatial interventions is self-explanatory and assumes taking up only the area that is necessary for performing a particular activity. Simultaneously, this principle assumes the use of space in such manner that it can be restored with minimum intervention to the state equal or similar to the original state. Accordingly, it may be expected that the construction of solid buildings will be limited to the necessary volume and emphasis will be placed on the use of facilities that can be removed easily and quickly. This idea can be primarily realised by building floating piers, both in new ports and in existing marinas with built breakwaters. If the recommended procedures are observed, such piers will fully satisfy safety requirements for people and vessels.

The principle of acceptable impacts on the environment assumes that no activity on the sea should significantly affect the living world in the immediate neighbourhood nor change the main properties of the marine environment. The acceptability of environmental impacts is presented in a study and is approved accordingly. Impacts include those resulting from construction and impacts resulting from the operation of marinas.

The effects of activities in nautical tourism ports (new and existing ones) should be viewed in terms of direct impact. This refers to preventing large-scale pollution caused by accidents or by regular activities. Successful pollution prevention requires adequate equipment and trained personnel. The current situation, however, shows that the level of organisation and training of the personnel in nautical tourism ports is limited where large-scale pollution is concerned (Emergency Plan for Accidental Marine Pollution in the Republic of Croatia, "Official Gazette" 8/97). If properly applied, the current system of pollution protection during regular activities may be considered as satisfactory. It is important to emphasize that raising the awareness of the users of nautical ports to environmental conservation helps to bring beneficial effects. These effects are evident in the augmented business competitiveness of ports that implement a higher level of environmental protection standards.

CONCLUSION

The construction of new nautical tourism ports, especially marinas, requires an integral approach to the management of the coastal area in harmony with sustainable development. When considering sustainable development as a goal and objective of coastal economy and ecosystem management, development priorities arise, where the protection of marine environment will be of primary importance, and the expansionist development of nautical tourism ports will be harmonised with ecological criteria. It is also necessary to encourage and guide users of coastal resources to apply modern technical and technological equipment and devices. Development should not be seen as merely of tool of equity capital. Instead, the location of marinas should be systematically planned and efforts made to train efficient marina managers.

Being a Mediterranean country with numerous islands, Croatia has many opportunities for the further development of nautical tourism. Thanks to scientists and experts in a variety of fields, nautical tourism development in Croatia has not exceeded its growth limits. However, in recent years, there has been mounting pressure and attempts to use some of the beautiful parts of the aquatorium and of the protected areas for developing nautical tourism. Nevertheless, awareness of the need to plan new locations has resulted in a development strategy that respects the growing demand for berths and defines the sustainable development of nautical tourism ports in Croatia as the most important development aim of the future. The importance of nautical tourism and its future development for Croatian economy is evident not only in the direct income-related benefits that it generates, but also in socio-cultural benefits, such as new jobs.

It is reasonable to conclude that Croatia will be able to take advantage of numerous opportunities, but will also need to addresses many challenges in the further development of this form of special-interest tourism.

REFERENCES

Adriatic Croatia International Club, ACI Marinas. Accessed in25/11/2011. www.aci-club.hr/, 25.11.2011.

Cooper, C., Fletcher, J., Gilbert, D. and Wanhill, S. (1993). *Tourism principles and practice*. Harlow: Pearson.

Cooper, W. (2010). *Yachts and yachting, being a treatise on building, sparing, canvassing, sailing and the general management of yachts*. Memphis, Tennessee: General Books.

Dulčić, A. (2002). *Nautical tourism and managing nautical tourism ports: Conceptual attributes, and characteristics of nautical tourism*. Split: Ekokon.

Duplančić, L. T., Ujević, T. Čala, M. and Viđak, I. (2000). Categorization and number of islands in the Republic of Croatia, *Period, biol. ,102(1)*,281-84.

Duplančić, L. T., Ujević, T. and Čala, M. (2004). Coastline lengths and areas of islands in the Croatian part of the Adriatic Sea determined from the topographic maps at the scale of 1:25.000, *Geoadria, 9,* 5-32.

Emergency Plan for Accidental Marine Pollution in the Republic of Croatia, "Official Gazette" 8/97.

Environment Protection Act, "Official Gazette" 82/94, 128/99.

Favro, S. and Kovačić, M. (2006). Physical plans in managing sea and coastal area. in *25th International Conference on Organizational Science Development, „Change management"*. (pp. 1049-1058). Portorož, Slovenia.

Favro, S., Kovačić, M and Gržetić, Z. (2010). Towards sustainable yachting in Croatian traditional island ports, *Environmental Engineering and Management Journal, 9(6)*, 787-794.

Favro, S. and Kovačić, M. (2010). *Nautical tourism and nautical tourism ports, Spatial features of the Croatian Adriatic, Selecting locations for nautical tourism ports*. Split: Branch of Matica hrvatska.

Gvozdanović, N. (1969). *Some live issues concerning nautical tourism (with special reference to nautical tourism in combination with fishing tourism)* Split: Institute of Economics of Split.

Croatian Hydrographic Institute and associates. (2006). *Study on the development of nautical tourism in the Republic of Croatia*: Split: Croatian Hydrographic Institute.

Johnson, L. 2005. Clean marinas, clean boat bottoms and nontoxic antifouling strategies. Accessed in 05/08/2011. http://www.icomia.com/library/ introduction.asp.

Klarić, Z. (1994). Determining carrying capacity in the Mediterranean, and its impact on understanding sustainable tourism development In: *Towards sustainable tourism development in Croatia. Proceedings International conference* (pp. 17-32). Zagreb: Institute for Tourism, Zagreb.

Koelbel, W. H. (1999). Boat design reflected in marine design. Accessed in 05/08/2011 http://www.icomia.com/library/introduction.asp).

Kos, L. and Dončević, L. (1970). *Status and development of nautical tourism in Yugoslavia, legal economic aspects, studies*, Zagreb: Institute of Economics of Zagreb.

Kovačić, M., Bošković, D., Dundović, Č. (2005). Nautical tourism development through integrated planning. *Pomorstvo, 21(1)*, 189-210.

Kovačić, M., Gržetić, Z. and Dundović, Č. (2006). Planning and selecting locations for nautical tourism ports in promoting sustainable development. Naše More 53(3-4), 118-124.

Kovačić, M., Gržetić, Z. and Bošković, D. (2011). Nautical Tourism in Fostering the Sustainable Development: A Case Study of Croatia's Coast and Island. *Tourismos: an International Multidisciplinary Journal of Tourism, 6(1)*, 221-232.

Kovačić, M. and Luković T. (2007). Spatial characteristics of planning and construction of nautical tourism ports, *GEOADRIA, 12(2)*, 131-147.

Law on Maritime Domain and Sea Ports, "Official Gazette", 158/ 2003.

Luck, M. (2005). Coastal and marine tourism: Origins, development and prospects. *4th Coastal and Marine Tourism Congress, Cesme, Turkey*.

Mathieson, A., and Wall, G. (1987). *Tourism: Economic, physical, and social impacts.* Harlow: Longman Scientific and Technical.

Ministry of Sea, Traffic and Infrastructure, Ministry of Tourism. (2008). *2009-2019 Development strategy of nautical tourism in the Republic of Croatia.* Zagreb: Ministry of the Sea, Transport and Infrastructure, Ministry of Tourism.

Riđanović, J. (2002). *Geography of the sea, Croatian geography.* Zagreb: Dr. Feletar.

Orams, M. (1999). *Marine tourism: Development, impacts and management.* London: Routledge.

PPA/CRA. (1996). *Guidelines in evaluating the carrying capacity of coastal areas in terms of tourism.* Split: Priority Actions Programme Regional Activity Centre.

Regulation on management and protection of coastal marine areas, "*Official Gazette*" 128/04.

Regulation on classification and categorisation of nautical tourism ports, "*Official Gazette*" 72/08.

Tourism Industry Law, "Official Gazette" 8/96, 19/96, and 76/98.

Turina, A. (1967). The Yugoslav Adriatic and yachting tourism, *Pomorstvo br. 9-10*.

Zec, D., Kovačić, M. and Favro, S. (2007). Importance of the safety of navigation and safety protection to nautical tourism. In *14th TIEMS Annual Conference - Disaster recovery and relief–Current and future approaches, June 5th-8th*. Trogir, Split: TIEMS.

In: New Trends Towards Mediterranean Tourism Sustainability   ISBN: 978-1-62257-627-2
Editors: L. M. Rosalino, A. Silva and A. Abreu   © 2012 Nova Science Publishers, Inc.

Chapter 6

INDICATORS FOR ASSESSING TOURISM SUSTAINABILITY IN PORTUGAL

António D. Abreu[1,] and Diogo Stilwell[2]*

[1]LETS-ISLA – Laboratório de Ecologia, Turismo e Sustentabilidade
Quinta do Bom Nome Estrada da Correia, Lisboa, Portugal
[2]Faculdade de Ciências da Universidade de Lisboa, Lisboa, Portugal

ABSTRACT

Tourism was considered for a long time a non-polluting industry, even being called "the industry without chimneys". However, as the world′s population increased and technological developments allowed for more frequent travels, tourism grew and began to generate significant impacts, whether social, environmental or economic. Sustainability is therefore a key factor in current and future tourism development and rather than an abstract concept, it must be measurable.

Considering that a truly sustainable tourism trade is an unrealistic objective for the foreseeable future, a more realistic target is monitoring the performance of tourism and its trends through sustainability indicators.

Being difficult to define the concept of indicators, they assume a priority role as instruments. Although they are uncertain and imperfect models of the reality and are made of compromises between various factors, such as relevance or scientific validity, they are still robust tools that promote sustainability.

Due to the current crisis, the Portuguese tourism sector is becoming increasingly important for the country's economic development. However, for proper development towards sustainability we need not only strategy and planning instruments, but more importantly instruments for monitoring and evaluating the progress towards the objectives.

In this chapter, we discuss the importance of a system of indicators of sustainable tourism adapted to the Portuguese reality. It is also proposed the GIST (Group of Tourism Sustainability Indicators) that aims to assess the state of the Portuguese touristic sector. This group is divided in six sub-themes: Qualification, Diversification, Economic Relevance, Seasonality, Environment and Impact in the Community. These sub-themes

---

* E-mail: antoniodabreu@netmadeira.com.

where based on the three pillars of sustainability (social, environmental and economic) and the strategic lines for development outlined by the Portuguese National Tourism Strategy.

INTRODUCTION

In the twentieth century, the movement of populations and the advances in transportation and communication technology have turned tourism into one of the largest industries on a global scale (Choi and Sirakaya, 2006). Touristic exports represent 30% of the total commercial services, and 6% of the world´s exports in this category; tourism appears in the fourth position preceded only by fuels, chemicals and automotive products (UNWTO, 2011).

For many developing countries Tourism represents one of the main sectors of the economy, creating jobs and income sources (UNWTO, 2010). Therefore, it is not surprising that, in recent years, many governments have focused in the advantages of a market with high growth rates and opportunities, concerning social and economic benefits (Jenkins, 2006).

Like many other sectors, the tourism industry was greatly affected by the 2009 recession, the deepest since the Great Depression (IMF, 2009; WTTC, 2009). Global GDP (Gross Domestic Product) declined 2.1%, being developed countries the ones who suffered the most (IMF, 2009). Within the tourism sector, many investments have been postponed or canceled, even in touristic destinations previously dynamic and in expansion (WTTC, 2009).

Research conducted by the World Travel and Tourism Council (WTTC) showed a recovery of the sector, with the contribution of tourism to the world GDP growing of 3.3% in 2010. This growth is expected to increase to 4.5% during 2011, adding three million new jobs to a total of 258 million (WTTC, 2011). Forecasts for 2020 indicate a growth increase of 4.4% per year, confirming the importance of this economic sector for employment (WTTC, 2009).

For a long time Tourism was considered, a non-polluting and clean business, the so-called "industry without chimneys" (Viegas, 2008). However, as the world's population increased and technological developments allowed for more frequent travels, tourism began to cause significant adverse social, environmental, cultural and economic impacts (Choi and Sirakaya, 2006; European Communities, 2006b; Cooper, 2008; Hardy and Beeton, 2011; Saarinen, 2006; Viegas, 2008). The unplanned growth of tourism has damaged the natural and socio-cultural environments of many touristic destinations, reducing its popularity in the eyes of the tourist (Farsari and Prastacos, 2001; Rebollo and Baidal, 2003 ; WWF-UK, 2002).

The tourism industry has the particularity of having as a commodity the concept of "touristic attraction"; this product should be formed by a set of elements in which the perception of nature, the variety of environments, landscapes and biodiversity, play an essential role. For this reason, tourism and environment should never be antagonistic elements (APA, 2007). Touristic destinations, especially the mature ones, are much in need of a change towards sustainability (Rebollo, 2004), not only because their socio-economic structure is very dependent on tourism (UNWTO, 2011), but also because a high intensity tourism leads to processes of environmental degradation that may reach inconceivable proportions for a society where quality of life has become increasingly important.

In recent years, new ways to develop tourism began to arise. "New" tourists seek as much as possible, new destinations with an intact environment and a greater integration of the local social and cultural characteristics. Destinations seek alternative ways of development that reduce the negative effects of tourism on the environment and try to integrate in a harmonious manner the needs of tourists and local people (SIET-MAC, 2005).

Being so dependent on external variables such as environment, culture, community and territory, touristic destinations are influenced by tourism itself, sometimes to the point that the specific site turns out to be less attractive for tourists. This phenomenon is known as the Butler sequence (Weaver and Lawton, 2002) in European Communities, 2006a).

Therefore, the tourism industry, being an activity of numerous interdependent sectors of the economy, has in sustainability the only option for future development (European Communities, 2006a; Hall, 2008; Ko, 2005; Rebollo, 2004; SIET-MAC, 2005).

The notion of sustainable tourism is a sequel of the concept of sustainable development introduced by the Brundtland Report in 1987 (Hardy and Beeton, 2011; Saarinen, 2006). Thus, the understanding of what is sustainable development is necessary to explain sustainable tourism.

With the economic, social and environmental dimensions as the pillars, this definition has been subject to many interpretations since its formulation. Since the concept of sustainable tourism did not deserve an explicit mention on the Brundtland Report, the result was a huge variety of uses of this concept in the context of tourism (Butler, 1999; Ko, 2001; Ko, 2005), including an ideology, a political slogan, a concept, a philosophy or even a product.

As tempting as it might seem, and although statistics may indicate so, an *ad infinitum* growth is not possible. Destinations should be seen and treated as finite and non-renewable sources (Butler, 1980).

In a broader context, sustainable tourism can be used to defend different views: by local traders to support the income from tourism, by different social classes to preserve the characteristics of their holidays or by the communities as a way to exclude non-locals (Mowforth and Munt, 2003).

Conceptually, sustainable tourism can be defined as:

- Tourism which is developed (environmentally and socially) in such a way and in such a scale that ensures its viability for an indefinite period of time, without degrading or changing the existent environment (human or physical) and without jeopardizing the development and well being of other activities and processes (Butler, 1999).

To Swarbrooke (2000) (in Cordeiro, 2008) it is a type of tourism economically viable, but that does not destroy the resources on which the activity in the future will depend, mainly the physical environment and social fabric of the local community.

Johnson (2002) (in European Communities, 2006a) rather than presenting a definition, highlighted a number of guidelines which sustainable tourism must meet, where all three dimensions of sustainability are represented. The Mohonk Agreement, in 2000, poses as criteria for sustainable tourism the minimization of ecological and socio-cultural impacts, including the promotion of economic benefits to local communities and host countries.

Simultaneously to the discussions on the concept of sustainable development, and even if it is evident the lack of consensus on the definition of "sustainable tourism", there is an overall understanding of the changes that must be carried out (European Communities, 2006a).

In recent years, a growing awareness of many national governments and local authorities to sustainability issues emerged (DCMS, 2005;MEI, 2007; Brazil Ministry of Tourism, 2007; Notarstefano, 2008; SIET-MAC, 2005). However, the mere acceptance of the concept of sustainable development does not mean that the same has been transposed and implemented in practice (Moniz 2006 in Cordeiro, 2008).

On the other hand, the key objective of sustainable tourism should not only consist in the creation of new touristic destinations considered sustainable. It is imperative to confront and propose solutions to the problems of existing touristic areas (Butler, 1998). The challenge is to make mass tourism destinations more balanced, rather than introducing new forms of small-scale tourism (Butler, 1999).

Authors cited above involved in the definition of sustainable tourism agree, in general with, two assumptions: firstly, the concern about the economic, social and environmental balance and secondly, the preservation of life quality for future generations. However, due to the existing ambiguity, almost all forms of tourism can be classified as sustainable. Hence, the main issue is how the sustainability of a destination can (and should) be monitored and evaluated (Butler, 1999).

In conclusion, the term sustainable tourism is not a type of tourism (such as rural tourism or ecotourism) but a different way to promote tourism (Cordeiro, 2008).

The term "*sustainable tourism*" should be used to refer to a state of tourism, and not a type of tourism. This is the concept followed in this chapter that proposes an index of sustainable tourism that can be used to assess trends in the sector, its actors and the contributions that they give to the overall development of the social, economic and environmental panorama.

TOURISM AND SUSTAINABILITY IN PORTUGAL

According to Beni (2002) the tourism sector will always be a national priority because of the ability it has, or will have, to contribute to the achievement of the objectives and goals of a national strategy. Given its important economic, social, environmental, political and cultural impacts, organized and planned tourism is an important tool to accelerate or complement the development of a country. Portugal is a proof of that.

Apart from the government of Salazar (1932-1968), the tourism in Portugal has been seen as an activity of great importance for the country (Cordeiro, 2008). All over the world, different national plans focused on tourism were produced (e.g. Australian Government, 2009; CHL 2002; Ministry of Tourism of Turkey, 2007). Obviously the goals of the different strategies vary greatly from one another, since they are dependent upon various factors connected with the economy, social context, level of development, human resources and market conditions. For example, while Brazil's strategy is highly focused on integrating social and labor supply in an attempt to reduce poverty and crime (Brazil Ministry of Tourism, 2007), the Spanish is focused on increasing domestic tourism and maintaining the country as a world's touristic power (Ministerio de Industria, Energía y Turismo de España, 2007).

In the last decade, more precisely from 1997 onwards, successive governments have set up several "strategies" for tourism in Portugal. Starting with the PAIET (*Intervention Action Plan for Tourism*) approved in 1997, but never executed, until the PENT (*National Strategic*

Plan for Tourism) in 2007. These programs have set 24 goals for tourism (Cunha, 2009). They were all different from each other, and could range from making tourism the highest national priority to focusing on specific touristic markets and/or clusters.

The PNDES (*National Plan for the Social and Economic Development*) identifies the cluster "Tourism/Leisure" as one of the most important activities of the country. Not only because of the existence of certain direct advantages, but also due to a certain multiplying and enhancing power to other related activities, that causes significant impacts at local and regional level (Cordeiro, 2008).

Today, tourism is considered a strategic sector for Portugal, not only because of its ability to create jobs and wealth, but because Portugal has clear competitive advantages as few other countries have (e.g. geographical position, climate, a strong culture or a cheaper lifestyle - MEI, 2007). There is political intent through the PENT to make Portugal one of the fastest growing destinations in Europe, through a development based in competitiveness and qualification of the offer, which will transform the sector into a growth engine of the national economy. Although the term sustainable tourism is not mentioned once in the PENT, the existence of a plan focused on the next lines of action in the sector is still commendable. As Swarbrooke (2000, in Cordeiro, 2008) pointed, one of the characteristics of sustainable tourism, to the detriment of non-sustainable tourism, is that the former is characterized by "planning before developing", and the second by "developing without planning".

As in most countries, Portugal has already recognized the benefits of tourism on the economy and the international image of the country. It is essential to have a well defined strategy, brand or market position so that there can be an edge over competition. And above all, a strategy that promotes sustainable tourism.

SUSTAINABILITY INDICATORS USED IN PORTUGAL

Considering that sustainable tourism is a truly unrealistic objective, Ko (2005) proposed that an appropriate approach might be to measure improvements in performance in terms of tourism sustainability.

The fundamental objective that supports the monitoring of sustainability is to improve the quality of management decisions (APA, 2007). It also serves as a way to divulge timely information about the sustainable actions of a particular geographic area (Ferreira, 2008). According to some authors, the need to monitor the efficiency and impacts of policies that are implemented will have an increasing demand over the years (Gallopín, 1996; Meadows, 1998). The use of indicators will fulfill this need.

Indicators are reflections of the reality based on imperfect models (Meadows, 1998), but they still facilitate the analysis and evaluation of the information collected (Hanai, 2009). Usually these indicators arise from values (we only measure what we value) and they create values (we value what we measure) (Meadows, 1998). It should also be noted that an environmental indicator becomes an indicator of sustainability (or unsustainability) with the addition of the variables time, limit or goal to achieve. With a time unit, sustainability indicators allow an objective analysis of current conditions and desirable situations and should be able to show trends over time, enabling stakeholders to reduce the possibility of inadvertently adopt bad decisions (Organización Mundial do Turismo, 2005*).*

There is no perfect indicator, only the best indicator available. Consequently, it is only possible to adopt attitudes and actions with appropriate and clear indicators that can actually display the paths and progress towards sustainable development (Hanai, 2009). The very process of developing sustainability indicators should contribute to a better understanding of what exactly is sustainable development (Van-Bellen, 2005).

The scientific community has the habit of distinguishing between "objective" and "subjective" indicators. Objective indicators measure the quantity, while subjective ones focus on quality. Meadows (1998) argued that all indicators are somewhat subjective, since the very choice of an indicator is based on a value. Therefore, the choice of what is important is inherently subjective.

The concept of indicators is difficult to define, since they represent uncertain models and are unable to portray reality perfectly (Gasparatos et al, 2008). Their selection is always subjective due to the large and complex information available and can lead to misunderstandings since they can be interpreted from different perspectives. However, these difficulties do not mean that indicators should not be used. It is essential to choose a small set of indicators that is, at the same time, significant enough to be understood (Meadows, 1998).

INDICATORS OF SUSTAINABLE TOURISM FOR PORTUGAL

Knowing that tourism can and should have indicators that show sustainability, does Portugal need a system of indicators for the country's leading industry? What is the most appropriate group of indicators to apply to the Portuguese reality, so that the environmental, social and economic dimensions are equally evaluated?

The diversity of cultures, values and traditions worldwide provides many different perspectives, each valid in its own particular context. It may be inappropriate the use of international indicators for judging values in local development. For this reason, the concept of international performance indicators for sustainable development is politically unacceptable (Dahl, 1997).

According to Valentin and Spangenberg (2000), each community is individual and must develop its individual set of indicators at a local level, which also represents an opportunity to increase the visibility of this individuality in the selection of indicators, and thus make them part of the local identity.

The National Sustainable Development Strategy (ENDS) (Mota, 2005) and the System of Indicators for Sustainable Development (SIDS) (APA, 2007) are two reference documents in Portugal. The first paper addresses the sectorial instruments available and proposes a set of indicators (environmental, economic, social and institutional). It also sets targets for 2015, such as a reduction by 10% of the ecological deficit. The SIDS consists of a set of 118 indicators (concerning all aspects of the Portuguese society), the sources of information used and the methodology applied, demonstrating also the country's situation at the date of publication.

Currently, the PENT is the document where all the strategic plans for the touristic sector are complied. However, the lack of an assessment or monitoring, the numbers achieved, what was the meaning of the evolution occurred or the lack of comparison between national and international examples are some of the critics made in relation to the national strategy for tourism, at the date of its approval. The need for statistical information obtained from monitoring programs, as well as an independent comparison of several global realities, are both key points when sustainability is the basis of a strategic planning. These points will not only allow remaking the targets and goals already set but it also makes it possible to learn from the mistakes of others. On the other hand, a *bottom-up* approach constituted of an active participation of different stakeholders, public and private, is considered essential in a modern tourism planning. Unfortunately it is another issue not observed in this document.

Although the Ministry of Economy and Innovation through the "*Lei de Bases do Turismo* (Decreto-lei Nº. 191/2009)", states that one of the general principles for sustainable tourism development is to ensure participation of all stakeholders in the definition of public policies, it is once again considered that there is a lack of participation in the PENT. Regional Tourism entities can provide the know-how when the potential, diversity and specificity of touristic destinations are concerned. Universities, companies, associations and research centers linked to the tourism sub-sectors can also be added to this group. Their counsel would certainly have been an important feedback during the preparation of the PENT.

As already mentioned, the use of structured, comprehensive and neutral indicators based on the principles of sustainability is a methodology that, when applied correctly, results in important compensations, ranging from the evaluation of the objectives of the National Plan to the analysis of future market trends.

Part of the structure of the PENT and its revision (PENT 2.0) is a series of indicators that seek to move beyond the rhetoric and show the evolution of some parameters. Virtually all the indicators are simple, meaning that they consist of an obvious correlation between the index and its metrics.

The PENT 2.0 (Turismo de Portugal, 2011) considers as main indicators: i) the number of guests and ii) the number of overnight stays by type of market. An indicator that measures total revenues by region is also assumed to be of great importance. It is clear that the three indicators considered most important in the national plan are indicators that fall within the economic dimension of tourism.

The characterization of European tourists by age, the contribution to employment and an evaluation of Lisbon as a touristic destination (in the form of inquiry) by foreign tourists are the only considered indicators that provide some information within the social dimension. Even though indirectly, some indicators in PENT may be relevant to an assessment of the environmental dimension (for example, through the pressure imposed on tourist destinations - evolution of overnight stays by region - or through the environmental impacts - air traffic growth), it can still be considered that there is no direct environmental indicator in the document.

It appears that almost all the indicators provided in the strategic plan and subsequent review are status indicators. They reflect the quality of tourism within a given range of space/time. This is suggestive of a very linear analysis, a linear relationship between income and expenditure.

The PENT believes that the tourism sector can be an engine of growth for the national economy and even for social development (MEI, 2007). This development must be based on qualification, competitiveness, environmental excellence, training resources and business modernization. The objectives are not only the aforementioned contribution to the economy but also a sustainable development of regions and a reduction of seasonality. To this end 11 strategic development lines were created (for example: Aerial accessibilities, promotion of events or urban and environmental quality), and with its implementation it should also have been created a policy of continuous improvement (which is essential an instrument directed towards sustainability), because only with a set of routine assessments it is possible to determine trends.

The PENT 2.0 was in a privileged position to present the evolution occurred in each of the development lines, however, only indicators related to economic aspects have been documented, where tourist profitability, dependence on the tourism markets and air traffic are the main components (Turismo de Portugal, 2011).

Once again the social and environmental dimensions are in the background when compared with the economic impacts and benefits. In a strategy that claims sustainability as the basis for development, this is clearly an error. Being a proposal with insufficient detail to make a diagnosis of the current situation, it will also be unable to foresee the coming years.

The gaps presented above reveal the importance of creating a group of indicators to assess the sustainability of the Portuguese tourism industry. A group where the three pillars of sustainability and the progresses made towards meeting the targets proposed in the PENT are evaluated.

GIST (GROUP INDICATORS FOR THE SUSTAINABLE TOURISM IN PORTUGAL)

The proposal of a set of indicators, that supports a system for monitoring the sustainability of tourism in Portugal (Figure 1), was based on the analysis of different existing systems of indicators in different realities, including the Portuguese. It was also considered the necessary feasibility regarding the availability of data on each of the areas referred to.

Figure 1. Map of Portugal in Europe.

**Table 1. GIST - Group Indicators for the Sustainable Tourism
in Portugal (Rev-Par - Revenue per Available room)**

	GIST	
	Green Key	
Qualification	Blue Flag	
	Tourism Schools	
	Dependence on International Markets	
Diversification	Aerial Acessibilities	
	Diversity in Accomodations	
	Tourism in the Economy	
Economic Relevance	Occupancy rates and Rev-Par	
	Shares in the International Panorama	
	Seasonality in Unemployment	
Seasonality	Seasonality Rates	
	Good Practices in the Hotel Trade	
Environment	Energy and Greenhouse Potential	
	ISO and EMAS	
	Employment in Tourism	
Impact on the community	Touristic Intensity	

As a result, it is proposed a set of 16 indicators organized into six sub-themes, where the three classic dimensions of sustainability are present. According to the criteria of Meadows (1998) the selection of indicators was guided by the: relevance to the specific problems of Portuguese tourism; availability of information, scientific validity; and simplicity of interpretation.

Six sub-themes were considered of particular importance to the development of a sustainable tourism strategy, particularly in Portugal: Qualification, Diversification, Economic Relevance, Seasonality, Environment, and Impact on the Community. This distinction has been based on the objectives, strategic development and implementation programs available in the PENT (MEI, 2007; Turismo de Portugal, 2011).

For each indicator, when possible, the latest data available was gathered. An attempt was made to collect data for the last 5 years (at least), so that it would be possible to make an interpretation of the key trends and developments. It was also decided to discuss the results of each indicator individually. This method makes the discussion easier and clearer.

To facilitate reading, a three-color scheme for the classification of individual indicators was used, as proposed in the work: "Sustainability Indicators in your pocket 2009" (DEFRA, 2009).

- There was a clear improvement. The data evolution is towards sustainability.
- The data is inconclusive. The evolution was not clear in any sense (negative or positive) or there isn't enough data for a safe conclusion.
- There was a deterioration of the data analyzed. The trend was negative and there is a tendency to depart from sustainability.

It is now presented the set of selected indicators and the correspondent tri-colored classification for Portugal. Each evaluation will be justified individually in the following pages (Table 1).

Green Key

The "Green Key" is part of the FEE (Foundation of Environmental Education) program and it's an eco-certification for environmental and sustainability issues. It aims to increase the perception of managers, staff and customers of touristic developments for their potential impact on the environment. Although the program was born in Denmark in 1994 it is now implemented in 17 countries, and recognizes the efforts made towards a sustainable tourism (ABAE, 2011). Green Key aims to achieve four objectives that include: environmental education of the people involved, reduction of the impact of infrastructures on the environment and a balanced economic management. Naturally is also serves as a marketing strategy to promote certification and award-winning facilities (ICS the Green Key, 2010). The implementation process begins with an application of the business in question followed by a process of documental and physical assessment. It should also be noted that the award is followed by follow-up evaluations to ensure that these quality levels are maintained.

Although each country develops its own rules, these are based on international standards set by the FEE (ICS the Green Key, 2010). The criteria for Portuguese hotels are divided into 11 thematic areas: environmental management, involvement of employees, customer information, water, hygiene and cleaning, waste, energy, food and beverages, indoor and outdoor environment, "outdoor" activities; and management (ABAE, 2011).

It was in 2007 that the first "Green Keys" were awarded to a total of 12 projects (Figure 2 and 3). In that year the regions of Algarve, Azores and Madeira were not represented. The Centro region has been the most distinguished and, most interestingly, the first awards to the Algarve occurred only in 2011. The large increase of projects in Madeira was a great contribution for the record verified in 2011.

While Spain does not have any information available on Green Key, Greece has only one award and Italy has 10. France is at the top, with 244 awards. In Portugal, several reasons may justify why the Centro is the most awarded region. The smaller, more sustainable and environmentally friendly tourism practiced in this region is surely one of the reasons.

With the globalization of markets and the consequent competitiveness increase, the presence of evidences that recognize the fulfillment of certain criteria related to sustainable practices is a factor of increasing importance in attracting new customers. Because of this, Green Key certification not only brings economic benefits to the business but it's also a symbol of an effort made towards minimizing the environmental and social impacts (the latter through a focus on environmental education, a factor which is exclusive of the "Green Key" - FEE, 2011a).

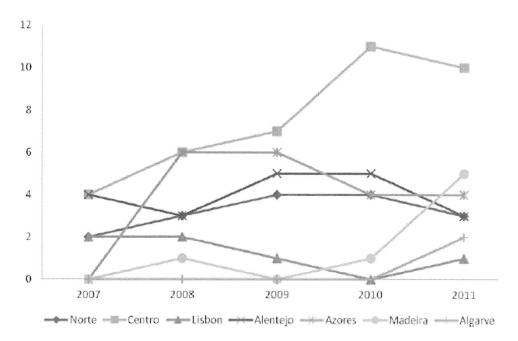

Source: ABAE – European Blue Flag Association.

Figure 2. Number of businesses with the "Green Key" by region.

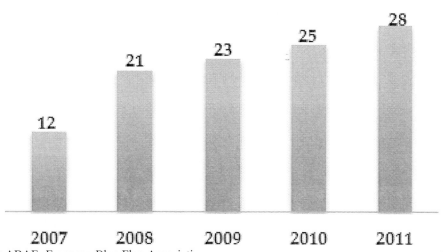

Source: ABAE- European Blue Flag Association.

Figure 3. Portuguese businesses with the "Green Key" award.

Blue Flag

Created on a European scale in 1987, this certification is the result of the initiative of FEE and the support of the European Commission. Due to its high prestige, this international award is a guarantee that a particular beach or marina offers a high water quality, infrastructure, security and management (FEE, 2007, 2011b). 3554 Blue Flags were hoisted worldwide in 2011.

After 25 years, Portugal now has 271 blue flags for beaches and 14 in marinas (www.abae.pt) (Figure 4 and 5). Portugal is the 6th country in the world with more blue flags, where almost 50% of designated beaches have this certification. Mira is the only beach in the world which will fly for the 25th consecutive year the Blue Flag.

Several studies show that the fact that a beach is certified has little influence in attracting tourists (McKenna et al, 2010 Nelson and Botterill, 2002). However, according to these authors there is a strong correlation between the criteria for a Blue Flag and the issues considered most important by tourists. Despite the skepticism around environmental awards and its potential to attract tourists, its added value as a tool for sustainable management is undoubted (Micallef and Williams, 2004).

The Blue Flag is therefore an important indicator when trying to ascertain the sustainability of the touristic sector, since beaches play an important touristic role, especially in Portugal where the product "Sun and Sea" is considered central in the national strategy (MEI, 2007).

The regions of Centro, Alentejo and Madeira hoisted fewer blue flags in 2011 compared to 2010. However, when compared with the beginning of the century all regions registered an increase in the number of beaches awarded (Figure 5).

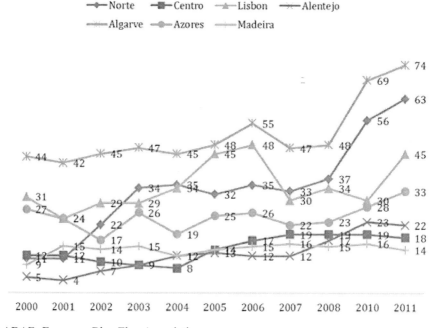

Source: ABAE- European Blue Flag Association.

Figure 4. Number of Blue Flag beaches by region.

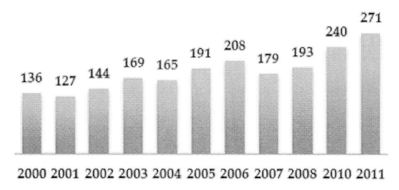

Source: ABAE – European Blue Flag Association.

Figure 5. National total of Blue Flags in Portuguese beaches.

Interestingly, the year 2007, dubbed the "best year ever" by *"Turismo de Portugal"* (*Turismo de Portugal*, I.P. is the central public authority responsible for promotion, enhancement and sustainability of Tourism activities.), was the one that had the least number of Blue Flag beaches in the last 6 years. This raises the question of the attractiveness effect of rewards for good environmental quality on international tourists. The quality of beaches and its management play an important role in the perception of the tourism impacts on the environment. A progress assessment of these aspects through environmental quality criteria represents an effective indicator of the effects of tourism in coastal areas.

Portugal has increased the number of blue beaches along the years; in 2000 136 were entitled to the Blue Flag and in 2011 the all time record was beaten with 271 beaches. This is particularly relevant when compared to Spain, that despite having 511 blue flag beaches, they had a decrease of 10 beaches since 2010 (ADEAC, 2011).

It can therefore be considered a positive development when 1 in 12 of the world's blue flags is in Portugal. Being directly linked with a better quality of bathing areas and indirectly with a healthy and sustainable Portuguese coastal environment, these awards may, therefore, turn Portugal more attractive to tourists.

Tourism Schools

The National Plan for Tourism states that Portugal should base its growth in the quality of touristic offer (among others factors) (MEI, 2007). The development and implementation of a policy for a specific education in tourism is essential, as it will enable an approach between the policies for the sector and their needs (Amoah, 1997). A high qualification in tourism gives the professionals the knowledge necessary to move from theory to practice and provides the labor market with professionals aware of the needs and expectations of the tourism industry.

Employment in the tourism sector is often seen as temporary, which results in poor investment in training and consequently a decrease in quality of service (MEI, 2007). It is therefore important to realize how the offer of high qualification for Tourism has evolved (Figure 6 and 7).

Portugal opened seven new schools specialized in teaching Tourism and Hospitality from the beginning of the century, a 70% increase in options for students of the sector.

Between the academic years of 2008 and 2010 some changes were noted in the influx of students. Schools in Faro, Portimão, Fundão, Setúbal and Santarém saw the number of students dropping between the two years, while 68.75% of schools had a positive trend in the number of subscribers (Figure 7).

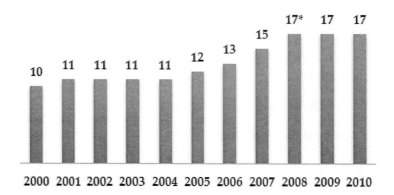

Source: Escolas do Turismo de Portugal.

Figure 6. National total of Schools of Tourism. * - The school of Óbidos was merged with the school of Oeste, but they were still recorded separately.

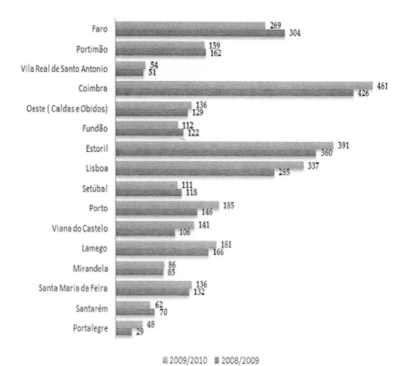

Source: "Relatório de Sustentabilidade do Turismo de Portugal (2008, 2009)".

Figure 7. Number of students in Portuguese tourism schools.

Despite the overall positive results, there isn't an equal distributed offer throughout the country. An example of this is the Alentejo region. There is no degree or learning program approved by the Tourism de Portugal in this region. This fact is even more serious if we consider that the PENT aims not only a growth of over 6% in the number of nights spent by foreigners, but aims primarily for an increase in the value of tourists. The University of Évora is the only establishment that has a degree in Tourism, but this was not recognized by "*Turismo de Portugal*" until April 2009 (Turismo de Portugal, 2009a). The large number of investments planned for the region makes the existent skilled labor in tourism insufficient for the market demand. The president of the Tourism Region of Évora, João Andrade Santos, ensures that the tourism plan designed for the Alentejo in 2002 failed, precisely, "due to lack of human resources" (taken from an interview in Diário de Notícias in 2007).

For a sustainable tourism industry it is important to have a qualification of labor and of all stakeholders in the sector since it will indirectly ensure better management of projects and resources, minimization of environmental impacts and greater attractiveness to tourists. Even with the serious gap when it comes to offering a cross-sectional distribution in the teaching of Tourism, the truth is that there has been an increase in the number of schools and an increase in the number of students enrolled. And for that, the overall picture can be considered a positive.

Dependence on International Markets

Effective planning, which includes a marketing strategy focused on diversification, can be used to rejuvenate and give a more sustainable future for the tourism product offered, the environment and development in general (Farsari and Prastacos, 2001).

A diversity of source markets is necessary to guarantee that the dependence on certain countries does not affect sustainability. The national plan has separated three groups of source markets according to their importance to the industry: Strategic markets - which should be subject of a major promotional effort (Portugal, United Kingdom, Spain, Germany and France); Markets with potential – where the aim is a significant absolute growth (USA, Brazil, Holland and Italy); and Markets of diversification - in which the objective is to increase market share (Switzerland, Russia, Canada and Poland) (MEI, 2007).

Portugal is highly dependent on the first group. For this reason the development of a broad portfolio of international markets that allows a high growth of revenue in the short, medium and long term is one of the strategic lines for Tourism (MEI, 2007).

The selection of these markets was based on its revenue potential, the prospects for the future, proximity to Portugal (less than 3 hours flight) and contribution to the reduction of seasonality. This classification was created in 2007, and it will therefore be interesting to see if the ranking remained stable or whether there were significant changes.

This indicator will consider the evolution of the main markets in terms of nights spent by tourists and revenue. With these two data it will be possible to assess the validity of the classification of the PENT and the evolution of the tourist markets diversification for Portugal (Figure 8).

There was no change in the rankings. UK, Germany, Spain, Holland and France remained the top five countries between 2005 and 2010. It is important to note the large decrease in overnight stays for tourists from the United Kingdom and Germany; there were breaks in 5 years of 25.5% and 13.3% respectively. This is surely related to the impact that the recession has had on the two largest economies in Europe. Also note the increase in the share of Brazil that has overtaken the USA and closed in with Italy in 2010. Being a country with tremendous growth and considering the cultural affinities with Portugal, its potential as a source market is growing every day.

Whereas a lower reliance on a small number of source markets is an objective of the Portuguese tourism sector, the increase in overnight stays by countries that are not part of the main markets is a positive result. Russia, Czech Republic and especially Poland (with a growth of almost 250% in 5 years) were among the main contributors to this progress.

Possibly more important than the number of tourist overnight stays are the revenues from international tourists. To walk the path to a tourism quality and not quantity (MEI, 2007) it's necessary to analyze the dependence of tourism in terms of revenue and the progress over the years (Figure 9).

When it comes to tourism revenue, the UK remains the country with the largest share, and despite the huge break it suffered since 2007 and the proximity of France (17.4%), it still ended 2010 with 18.3% of the share.

Spain ended 2010 with exactly the same share of 2005, 14.6%. On the other hand, Germany had a slight decrease, with 10.4% of the total revenues. Another important aspect that can be drawn from Figure 9 is the large increase of the "Other" category, especially Angola, which surpassed the USA (4.0%), Brazil (4.1%) and Netherlands (4.2%), ending 2010 as the fifth largest market in terms of revenue, with a share of 4.3%. As with overnight stays, there is a convergence of markets, indicating a wider range of markets.

Another topic of interest and that can contribute to a more effective marketing strategy in the various source markets is the ratio between revenue and overnights, since it allows assessing what nationality spends more money in tourism activities in Portugal (Figure 10).

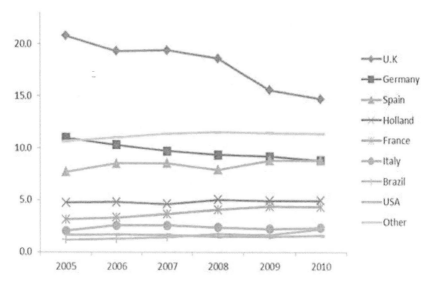

Source: "INE - Inquérito à Permanência de Hóspedes e Outros dados na Hotelaria".

Figure 8. Share of overnight stays in hotels (%), resorts, apartments, motels, inns and pensions, by country of residence (Thousands).

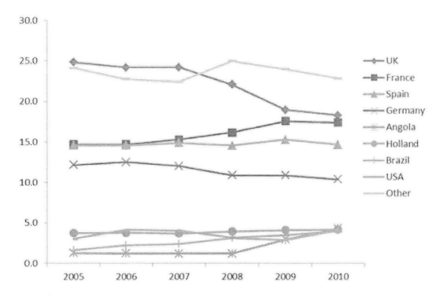

Source: Banco de Portugal last updated on 21/02/2011.

Figure 9. Share of tourism revenue (%) by country of residence.

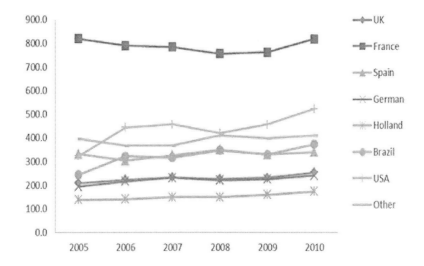

Figure 10. Revenue per night spent by country of residence (€/Overnight).

When relating the number of overnight stays with revenues, the rankings change dramatically. With over €800 per bed in 2010 France is biggest spender, with a large distance to the second place, the United States, with 521€. This discrepancy may be related to the large number of Portuguese immigrants in France. Although they are considered tourists and produce tourism revenues, they usually sleep in family homes or in a second house, and therefore are not considered for the overnight numbers.

UK and Germany, the two countries with the highest number of overnight stays, are in 5th and 6th place respectively with 253€ and 240€ per night. Brazil is another example of an outbound market with great potential despite the (still) small number of overnight stays per year.

The sustainability of tourism in its economic dimension involves a diversification of products and source markets. Only then may be endowed with greater flexibility in the face of external variables in the economies of countries. A greater balance in shares of tourism markets is therefore an asset that should be praised and promoted.

The data analysis showed a rise in the share of countries outside the top 5 ("other" category) in both overnight stays and revenues. This seems to indicate an evolution towards sustainability.

Data on revenue/overnights ratios are important information that can be used to create more effective marketing strategies. It allows for a refocusing of attention on countries that do demonstrate a potential for future tourism.

In short, although Portugal is still dependent of four major markets (UK, France, Spain, Germany), the evolution that is evident brings optimism about the coming years regarding this indicator.

Aerial Accessibility

The number of air travel with touristic purposes increased 33% between 1998 and 2005, so by that year one in every four tourists used the plane to travel (Demunter, 2008). There was also a 47% increase in short trips (1-3 nights) (Demunter, 2008) and an increase of 18% of travelers carried by low-cost high-growth travel companies (Dobruszkes, 2006; Turismo de Portugal, 2011).

"Enhancing the air accessibility of the touristic cities with the greatest potential in each market" (MEI, 2007). This is how the PENT demonstrates the importance of good air connections on the tourism industry.

Portugal, being located at a corner of Europe is more dependent on air transport when compared with its main competitors like Spain, France, Italy or Croatia. For this reason, the strengthening of air accessibilities will have a major impact on the growth of tourism in the short term.

In 2007, the National Plan stated that it was necessary an improvement of accessibilities through the creation or expansion of links, suggesting a total of 35 new routes spread among the different Portuguese airports. For the Lisbon airport it was suggested the creation of 13 regular routes, where nine of them were related to strategic markets: Berlin, Hamburg, Birmingham, Manchester, Leeds, Glasgow, Hannover, Dortmund and Liverpool. Four new routes were assigned to the other two groups: Helsinki, Gothenburg, Torino and Cracow.

This indicator seeks to analyze what resulted from this proposal. It's only addressed the results for the Lisbon airport (Figure 11). Yet one can easily adapt this instrument to other Portuguese airports.

According to data provided by ANA (ANA - Aeroportos de Portugal, SA, national company that manage Portuguese airport infrastructures) one can observe that there are 14 new connections since 2007. This is a positive evolution since it shows that Lisbon is a destination that is now connected to a greater number of international cities and therefore to a larger number of potential tourists.

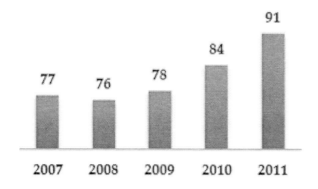

Source: ANA – Lisbon Airport Traffic Reports (2007, 2008, 2009, 2010, and 2011).

Figure 11. Number of direct routes to the Airport of Lisbon.

**Table 2. Priority routes according to the PENT and its existence
in the respective year**

		2007	2008	2009	2010	2011
Strategic Markets	Berlin	x	x	x	x	x
	Hamburg		x	x	x	x
	Birmingham	x	x			
	Manchester	x	x	x	x	x
	Leeds					
	Glasgow					
	Hannover					
	Dortmund					
	Liverpool		x	x	x	x
Secondary Markets	Helsínquia	x	x	x	x	x
	Gotemburg					
	Turim					
	Krakow	x				

Fonte: ANA – Lisbon Airport Traffic Reports (2007, 2008, 2009, 2010, 2011).

Interestingly after the publication of the PENT, there was a reduction in the number of routes. Some companies ceased to operate certain routes, as was the case of Air Nostrum that stopped operating Alicante or TAP that stopped the Clermont Ferrand route. However, more important than the number of routes *per se* is the analysis of the progress towards the compliance of the proposals of new routes made by the PENT (Table 2).

Despite the desire of PENT to act proactively in order to create conditions for the development of connections, the truth is that only two of the routes identified as priorities (Hamburg and Liverpool) were inaugurated after the publication of the document.

Twenty one new routes were created since 2007. Among those, it should be noted the opening of routes to cities in developing countries with great potential for tourism (as shown on the indicator of international markets), as Brasilia and Porto Alegre, in Brazil and Luanda, in Angola (this one not entirely new, but reinforced).

When analyzing traffic from the Barcelona airport (Table 3), which was compared with the Lisbon Airport in the PENT, we found that accessibilities to the main touristic markets are much more numerous.

Even taking into account the near extinction of some routes, such as Krakow and Glasgow, Barcelona Airport continues to offer a considerable number of flights to the cities considered a priority by the Portuguese strategy.

There are two main conclusions that can be drawn from the analysis of this indicator. Firstly, the Lisbon airport, the main supplier of tourists to Portugal, having received 6598 thousand passengers in 2009 (ANA, 2009), has increased the number of international routes, which is a positive factor that will certainly enable more tourists to visit our country. Despite this increase in routes, the objectives of the PENT, when it comes to tourist accessibility, are far from being met. Curiously, there has been no significant increase in this indicator after the publication of the plan.

Table 3. Number of flights to Barcelona from the cities considered priority in the PENT

	2008	2009	2010
Berlin	1324	1012	1001
Birmingham	273	143	43
Krakow	46	2	2
Dortmund	339	200	194
Glasgow	288	41	14
Gotemburg	88	3	105
Hamburg	647	292	292
Hannover	10	5	148
Helsínquia	563	547	529
Leeds	304	259	210
Liverpool	656	617	482
Manchester	432	455	310
Turim	663	453	269

Source: ANEA - Aeropuertos Españoles y Navegación Aérea.

Secondly, the airport of Barcelona is much more connected with major international centers than the Lisbon airport. It is understood that there is a difference between these two cities. Barcelona is a city larger than Lisbon and Spain has a tourist industry much stronger than Portugal. However, it is undeniable that the large number of connections from Barcelona steals tourists from Portugal.

The term accessibility is a constant in the PENT and it is clear the need for an improvement and expansion of air routes. It is a fact that the number of routes has increased over the past 5 years. However, there was no progress toward achieving the objectives. The PENT review in 2011 also made no mention to the progress made in this area, referring only that there was an increase in the number of routes. In light of what was presented it is considered that there is not enough data to conclude that the evolution has been clearly positive or negative for the sustainability of tourism in Portugal.

Diversity in Accommodation

A key factor in tourism is the accommodation capacity of the various establishments, as it reflects the offer, expressed in number of beds available (APA, 1999). The requalification of the multi-segmented hotel accommodations, targeting different demands in order to maximize the different features of various types of tourism is another of the PENT proposals (MEI, 2007). Taking these two important factors (the increase in offer and the requalification of accommodations) into account and knowing that the supply of a wide range of diverse experiences is one of the objectives of the PENT, it is very important that all regions of the country have an accommodation capacity that can meet the market demands.

A progressive diversification of tourism throughout the various regions not only induces positive impacts by reducing the intensity of tourism in popular destinations, such as the Algarve and Madeira, but also allows an increase in the impact of tourism on the local economy.

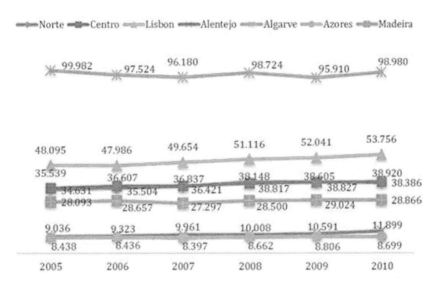

Figure 12. Accommodation capacity by NUTSII (Nº beds). Fonte: "INE – Inquérito à Permanência de Hóspedes e Outros dados na Hotelaria".

In Portugal, the number of beds has been increasing since 2005 (Figure 12). The Algarve region was the only one that showed a lower number of beds in 2010, when compared to 2005 (1002 beds less).

There was also a trend in the Azores, Madeira and the Centro regions, which had negative variations of -1.2%, -0.5% and -1.3% respectively between 2009 and 2010 (Figure 12). This decrease is possibly associated with the closure of some businesses due to the economic recession of 2009.

Sustainability also involves the development and structuring of a multi-product supply on all regions (Figure 13-19).

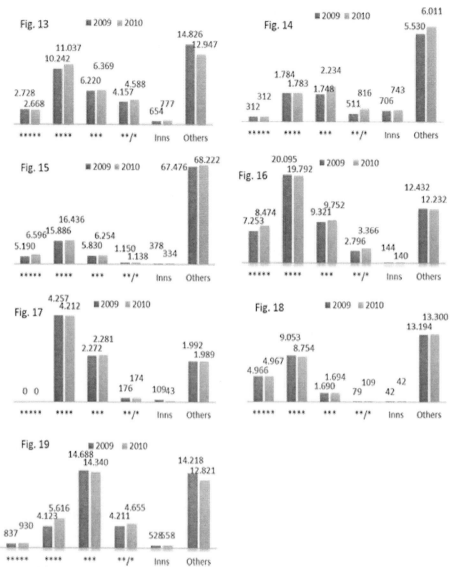

Source: "Inquérito à Permanência de Hóspedes e Outros dados na Hotelaria 2010 and 2009".

Figures 13. (Norte), 14 (Alentejo), 15 (Algarve), 16 (Lisboa), 17 (Azores), 18 (MAdeira) and 19 (Centro) - Total of beds by type of housing and NUTS II (Hotels of 5, 4, 3 ,2/1 stars and Inns; Others: Apartment hotels, motels, pensions, apartments).

In 2009, the survey was redesigned, allowing not only to breakdown data by type of establishment, but also by the respective categories (INE, 2009). Therefore, information on the number of beds in different types of accommodation is only available for the years 2009 and 2010. Fortunately these data still allows the drawing of some conclusions. In 2010 there were 2011 active hotels, 23 more than the previous year. The number of hotels increased significantly: 90 more than in 2009, representing an increase of 13.2% (INE, 2010).

When it comes to the number of beds, there was an increase of 2.1% from 2009 to 2010, being hotels the major contributors to this growth, with 53.4% of available beds. According to the data in Figures 13-19, there was an increase in the supply of beds in institutions with different typologies. We also observed that the Algarve and Madeira, have plenty of beds in the category called "other" which includes, for example apartment-hotels and pensions. The regions of Norte, Centro and Lisbon are the ones with a better balance between the different categories. Also note that the beds in 5-star hotels increased in the most important regions (Algarve, Madeira and Lisbon), while the Azores still has no 5 stars bed.

According to the PENT, the target for Portugal should be to grow in quality and not quantity of tourists. It was defined as a target an annual growth higher than 5% in the number of international tourists (MEI, 2007). This goal was then refocused for more realistic numbers with the recession. That objective is now between 5.7% and 3.6% growth of overnight stays of foreigners by 2015 (Turismo de Portugal, 2011).

To achieve the set goals there is a need for beds, but one must take into account that there has been a decrease in the rate-of-occupancy and Rev-Par in the different regions of the country (no region in 2009 had values above 60%). It is important to create poles of attraction for international tourists, because only thus can one stimulate demand, which in turn will increase occupancy rates and make it necessary to increase the number of beds.

It would be unsustainable the investment in new hotels and creation of more beds at a time when demand and tourist revenues are declining. Portugal must wager an increase of its attractions and a more diverse market, covering all regions of the country. The Portuguese Tourism must grow as a whole and not supported by 2 or 3 regions. For all these reasons it is considered that this indicator has positive data because the growth in supply of beds is not too aggressive when compared with the current occupancy rates. Although based on still preliminary data, the diversity of housing has increased not only with regard to the supply of various qualities, but also within a national perspective of requalification.

Tourism in the Economy

Tourism is one of the main sectors of the Portuguese economy. In recent years, international tourism receipts exceeded 600 billion Euros. In fact, Portugal has had revenues in excess of 6 billion over the past 5 years (UNWTO, 2010).

Because the PENT states that tourism should have an even higher importance in the economy due to strong growth prospects, it was proposed a target of 15% contribution to the GDP by the sector (MEI, 2007).

Unfortunately the global economic downturn, exacerbated by uncertainties surrounding the H1N1 virus, turned 2008 and 2009 into two of the toughest years for the sector. Despite this dramatic change in world affairs, the review of the National Plan (Turismo de Portugal, 2011) did not provide any assessment of what were the numbers achieved and how they evolved.

Tourism revenue is clearly the biggest impact of the industry in a country. Whereas Portugal is no exception, it is essential to include an indicator to analyze this evolution.

According to the INE, the internal tourism consumption is the consumption in tourism made by residents and non-residents when traveling outside their usual environment for leisure, business and/or others and that does not give rise to any remuneration in the destination. It also includes the costs incurred by other entities on behalf of those visitors. In turn, tourism revenue is understood as the total expenditure made by a visitor, including recipes for, and during his trip and stay at a destination (CST, 2009).

It appears that tourism revenues have a large weight in the national economy, with 4.2% of GDP in 2009. Although still a considerable percentage, the share of tourism receipts in GDP has been declining: it was 4.7% in 2000 and 4.2% in 2009 (Figure 20).

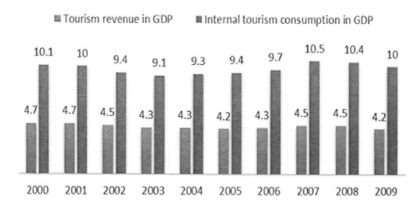

Source: "INE – Conta Satélite do Turismo".

Figure 20. Share of Tourism revenue and internal tourism consumption in the Portuguese GDP (%).

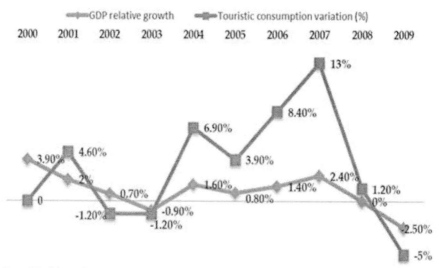

Source: Data World Bank; "INE - Conta Satélite do Turismo".

Figure 21. GDP relative growth and Touristic consumption variation (%).

Internal consumption presented in 2009 a similar percentage to that of the beginning of the century. Despite a decrease between 2000 and 2004 and a very positive development by 2007 (10.5%), the values decreased again in the last three years to 10.1% in 2009.

The period between 2003 and 2007 was very positive for the Portuguese tourism industry, with a record growth reaching double figures (13% in 2007 – Figure 21). It was also during this period that the growth of tourism consumption was higher than the economy.

Tourism industry, due to its highly dependence of external factors, decreased at a faster pace than the economy, notably in 2009 with values of -2.5% and -5% for the economy and tourism consumption, respectively (Figure 21).

As already mentioned, the global recession had a major impact on the values analyzed by this indicator. Being the main cause of the observed declines in tourism revenue, the recession led to an influence decrease of the tourism sector in the economy. Despite the growth prospects of the direct contribution to GDP (2.6% by 2021 according to the WTTC), due to the negative results recorded in the last three years, it is considered that the evolution of this indicator is not positive.

Occupancy Rates and Rev-Par

An indicator that measures the occupancy rates and the Rev-Par[1] can be approached in different ways. On one hand, occupancy rates reflect not only the increase in the number of overnight stays, but above all, the relationship between supply (number of rooms available) and demand (needs of the market). The hotel occupancy rate allows us to assess the extent to which tourism fits the demands.

A decrease in the number of tourists intending to stay or a disproportionate increase in the number of rooms compared to the market needs, are the two reasons which directly can best explain a low occupancy.

Continuing the trend of previous years, the regions with the highest occupancy rates were Madeira, Lisbon and the Algarve (Figure 22). The year 2001 was the best year of the decade for all regions, with the exception of Lisbon, where 2007 was better. Although 2007 was a positive year concerning room occupation, in general there is a negative trend in occupancy rates in most regions.

Note that only the Norte region had a positive trend between 2008 and 2009. It is important to highlight that in just eight years the overall rate declined by 11.1% (Figure 22).

The Rev-Par is measured representing the ratio between the income of the room and the number of rooms available (Turismo de Portugal, 2009b). The total for the country in 2009, while greater than 2006, had a decrease of 4.5 Euros compared the previous year, representing a reduction of 12.2% (Figure 23).

All regions contributed to this negative trend, with the most significant declines occurring in the region of Madeira and Lisbon (-17.6% and -15.1%, respectively). Interestingly, these two regions, together with the Algarve, are the ones with the highest values of the Rev-Par, as has been the case in previous years.

The evolution of Rev-Par and the occupancy rate has not gone according to the claims of PENT. There is a negative trend in values. The low occupancy rates result in low levels of Rev-Par. A stagnation of tourist arrivals leads to a decrease in demand, which may be related to the low occupancy rates.

---

[1] Rev-Par is an acronym in Portuguese for Revenue Per Available room. It is a widely used index in the hotel industry to evaluate and compare the revenue of hotels.

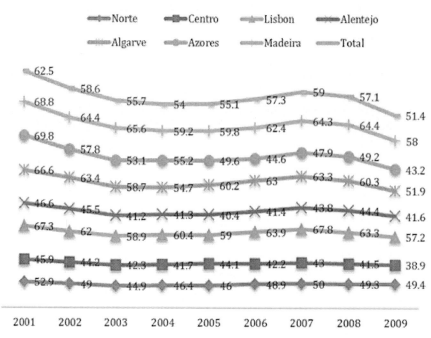

Source: "Turismo de Portugal".

Figure 22. Room-occupancy rates in hotel establishments, resorts and apartments by NUTS II (%).

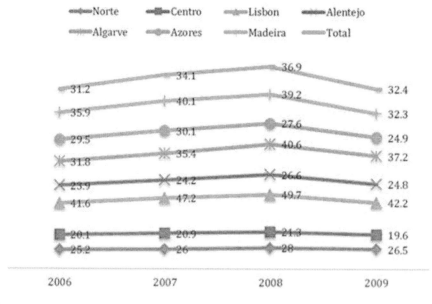

Figure 23. Revenue per Room (Rev-Par) in hotel establishments by NUTS II (euros). Fonte: *INE*.

Between 2006 and 2009 there was a 3.5% increase in accommodation capacity in hotels and similar establishments at national level (Turismo de Portugal, 2009b) This increase, if not accompanied by an increase in demand, leads to a deficit that will ultimately result in a decrease in occupancy rate and Rev-Par.

A sustainable tourism can't be evaluated only on the environmental and social impacts. Without the economic dimension the concept of sustainability does not make sense.

The Portuguese tourism did not have a positive development of this indicator. The figures (Fig 22 and 23) show an almost general decline of revenues and occupancy rates since 2008. There may be several reasons for this decrease, but it's crucial that this negative trend must be corrected.

Shares in the International Panorama

Total visitor spending on accommodation, food, local transportation, entertainment and shopping, are a major pillar in local economies of many destinations, creating revenue, jobs and opportunities for development. In 2010 more than 80 countries had revenues estimated at over one billion dollars.

International tourism receipts count as exports and includes daily transactions generated by a daily visitor as well as those who stay (UNWTO, 2011).

To understand the situation in Portugal and what developments occurred in the international scene, it is important to have a global contextualization.

The global international tourism revenues saw a decrease of 5.7% in 2009 (UNWTO, 2009). Of all the regions of the world, Europe, whose tourism sector is the largest and most mature, was the one that suffered the most with the crisis (UNWTO, 2010). In just three years, from 2008 to 2010, there was a decrease of more than 6% (Figure 24).

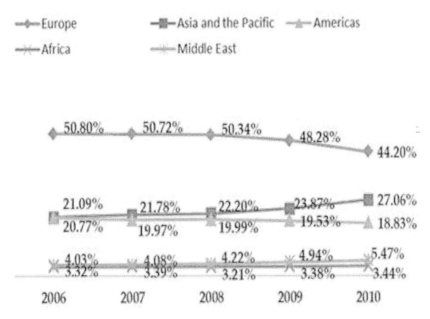

Source: UNTWO.

Figure 24. Share of international tourism revenues by world region (%).

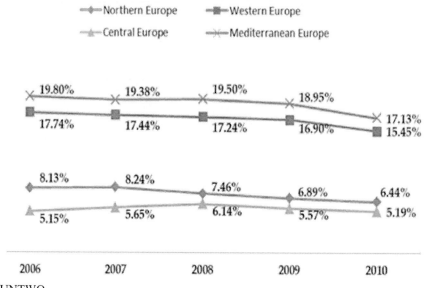

Source: UNTWO

Figure 25. Share of international touristic revenues by European region (%).

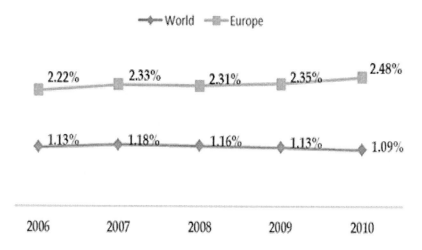

Source: UNWTO.

Figure 26. Share of Portugal in the international tourism receipts (%).

In contrast, Asia, where some of the most important and emerging economies, like India and China, are located, has increased its share of international revenues consistently.

It was in January 2010 that a series of 19 months of negative growth for Europe ended, both in arrivals and tourism receipts. This recovery is more evident when it comes to volume (arrivals), rather than profit (income). This situation is typical of periods after economic recessions, as competitors become more balanced and providers make an effort to contain prices. Tourists on their part, have a tendency to travel to places closer to home and for shorter periods (UNWTO, 2011).

Within Europe, only the countries of Central Europe have had slight positive results in the last 5 years. The region where Portugal is included was the most outlined, when it comes to tourism revenue, with a decrease of more than 2% (Figure 25).

As already mentioned, Europe is losing the race with other world regions, including Asia (Figure 26). However, Portugal has endured with a relatively constant share of income, and there even has been an increase in 2010. This increase can be related more with a decrease in performance of other countries like Spain or France, than with a real growth of the Portuguese tourism revenue. Nevertheless, the truth is that it is still a positive result.

In a global scenario, where Portugal competes with more countries than just the Europeans, the share has decreased, encompassing a similar situation to most countries of this continent. For this indicator, Portugal does not show negative results, but the developments are very slight and it cannot be said that it is undoubtedly positive.

Seasonality in Unemployment

The tourism industry can have a negative impact on the quality of life of local communities. However, the influx of tourists can also catalyze the local economy, including the labor market (Eurostat, 2009).

Seasonality is not just a problem affecting revenues and tourist arrivals. The increase and decrease of unemployment in the tourism sector, with jobs often temporary, is also an impact derived from tourism intensity fluctuations throughout the year. It is therefore an important indicator for a good assessment of social and economic sustainability of the sector (Daniel, 2010). The category "Accommodation, restaurants and similar" was part of the top five economic activities with the highest potential for employment during 2010, representing about 62% of all offers obtained (IEFP, 2010). Because it is an activity with a considerable weight on employment in Portugal, it is essential that tourism walk a sustainable path, supported by a number of factors, including a balanced seasonality in both tourist arrivals and job creation.

In the last three years, the monthly evolution of registered unemployment in the regions (NUTS II) shows periods of greater or lesser volume of unemployed people registered in Job Centres (Figures 27-29).

These periods of higher or lower unemployment, can be matched according to the seasonal nature of much of the structural activities of the country's tourism sector: the periods of lower unemployment coincide with the warmer months (June to August), where, in general, markedly seasonal activities occupy a greater number of people. This is verifiable in a more blatant way in the Algarve region, where in the summer months unemployment falls substantially (Figures 27-29).

Regardless of the growth rates of unemployment in recent years, it is important to realize the unemployment trends in the tourism sector from a perspective of seasonality (Figure 30).

The first conclusion one draws from figure 30 is the large increase in unemployment after the hottest months of the year. With the exception of 2010 (4.07%), all other years had growth rates above 5% in September/October. It is still observable a decrease in the unemployment rate in the spring months, which can be interpreted as a preparation for the high season by the hotels and restaurants establishments.

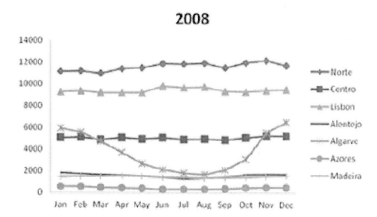

Figure 27.

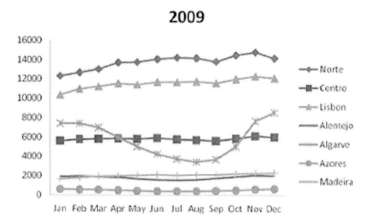

Figure 28.

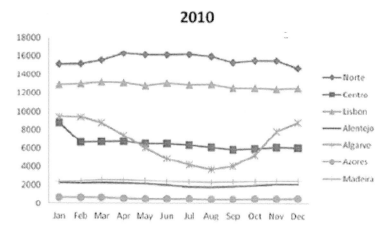

Figure 29.

Source: "Instituto do Emprego e Formação Profissional (IEFP)".

Figures 27, 28 and 29. Monthly evolution of unemployment in hotels, restaurants and similar, recorded by region in 2008, 2009 and 2010 respectively (situation at the end of the month).

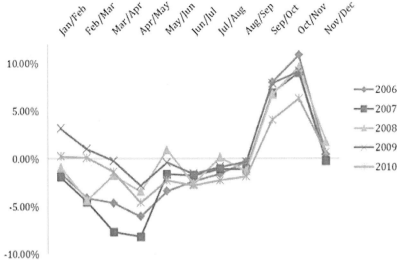

Source: "Instituto do Emprego e Formação Profissional (IEFP)".

Figure 30. Monthly evolution on the growth rate of unemployment in hotels, restaurants and similar.

The detected trends show that, with the exception of 2006, 2010 was the year which saw the largest drop in unemployment in May to June (-2.28%) showing positive results. In general, these results are encouraging, and there is optimism that the poor 2009 figures have been overtaken and that the next year will bring a maintenance of this improvement.

Of course, tourism is not the only factor affecting the results for unemployment. The economic situation of the country (and the world by that matter) also shapes these figures. You can however say that 2010 was better than the previous year regarding the association between unemployment and seasonality. Despite the positive results, it is considered that there isn't robustness enough to suggest that these improvements are clearly positive developments. It will take another year like this for this conclusion to be reached.

Seasonality Rates

Portuguese tourism, despite being an important sector for the economy, it's greatly affected by a high seasonality (MEI, 2007). Seasonality is a common problem among mature tourist destinations, but it still is poorly understood and difficult to resolve.

Portugal owes some of its tourist popularity to the good weather affecting its territory, especially during the summer months. There is, however, an awareness that there is a need for greater diversification of supply and increased air accessibilities to reduce this dependence.

Seasonality has been regarded as one of the biggest problems of tourism, as it causes imbalances, not only economic but also environmental, due to an high pressure on sewage systems, water supplies, energy consumption, pollution and stress derived from automobile congestion (APA, 2007).

A model for managing seasonality with focus on innovation, diversification and qualification of human resources allied with the development in each region of a set of products for lessening the effects of seasonality, are the proposals in the revision of the PENT (Turismo de Portugal, 2011).

According to the Sustainability Report of 2008, the seasonal evolution of the rate is calculated by the percentage of overnight stays in July and August, considering the total overnight stays in hotels (Turismo de Portugal, 2008). This equation will demonstrate the evolution of the importance of the summer months in the Portuguese tourism (Figure 31).

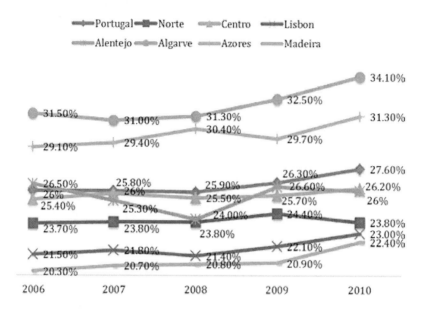

Source: "INE –Estatísticas do Turismo".

Figure 31. Seasonality rates by region NUTSII (%).

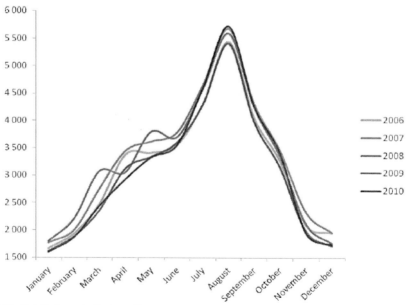

Source: "INE- Estatísticas do Turismo".

Figure 32. Nights spent in hotel establishments by month (%).

The data from recent years show that the seasonal rate has risen in almost all regions, being the Norte and Alentejo the only exceptions with a decrease of 0.6% and 0.4% between 2009 and 2010, respectively. The Algarve in turn was the region with the largest increase (2.6% between 2006 and 2010). This increase in the regions leads to an increase in the national seasonality rate, particularly over the last five years where there has been an increase of more than 1%.

Despite the efforts that have been made to mitigate this seasonality, the truth is that the motivations "Sun and Sea" still remain dominant in the tourism demand; it is still in the warmer months that the country sees a higher increase in tourist arrivals.

As already shown by the rate of seasonality, the weight of the hottest months of the year is increasing (the rate of seasonality in 2010 was 27.6%). It is clear that in Portugal there are two "peaks" of tourist activity: at Easter and, especially, in the summer months (Figure 32).

Figure 32 confirms that the objectives of the national plan, indicating a reduction of seasonality, are not being achieved.

It can be argued that there hasn't been sufficient time since the publication of the PENT (2007) to new strategies can have an effect and it's also important to realize that, given the characteristics of the country, seasonality will continue to always be very marked in tourism and should always be taken into account in the development of studies in this area. However, it is a fact that an increase in seasonality leads the Portuguese tourism sector further away for sustainability.

Good Practices in the Hotel Trade

Good practices among hotel businesses promotes a better environmental, social and even economic performance. When one aims for sustainability it is essential to combine good environmental management of enterprises with a good performance in terms of social responsibility.

It is of great importance the dissemination of good practices by the hotel sector, as well as the awareness among entrepreneurs to the benefits of reduced environmental impacts generated by the activity, whether in terms of management (cost reduction) or market positioning (marketing strategy) (Seguro, 2006).

Besides the civic importance, the contribution to environmental sustainability from hotel and tourism entrepreneurs increases the competitiveness of their business in the face of guests that are increasingly demanding about the impact of these investments in the ecosystems.

Agenda 21 identifies ten priority areas (e.g. Public awareness, monitoring of processes and planning for the sustainable development (WTTC, 1993). Yet, the three surveys analyzed focused primarily on three areas: water management, energy and waste (Figure 33). Thus the indicator will be developed focusing only these three aspects.

The use of energy-saving light bulbs was the category with the highest percentage of positive responses, with 95% in 2008. The decrease between 2008 and 2009 is not enough to cause concern.

When it comes to water management there are positive developments in some aspects. For example, 78.80% of the hotels don't collect used towels and sheets unless if asked by the client, enabling for a larger reduction in water consumption for washing clothes.

The use of lower quality water for irrigation and washing, despite not being a general measure, together with the use of wastes for composting and the use of solar energy had an increase in positive responses. These are, however, very low percentages that show the need of an increase of awareness by the managers of various hotels.

The use of low-consumption toilets and of automatic light sensors had the largest decrease with 19.1% and 15.7%, respectively. These are values that demonstrate a non-sustainable future, if maintained.

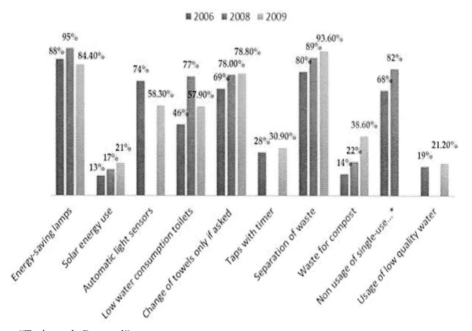

Source: "Turismo de Portugal".

Figure 33. Results of surveys made to hotels on environmental impact and social responsibility.
Percentages represent the amount of hotels that apply the category.
(* Non-usage of single-use or disposable products, except when required by law).

Recycling, in turn, is a practice already widespread in our country. Thus, it is not surprising that positive numbers were observed here (93.6% in 2009). Within the same area, it is also notable a growing concern to avoid the use of disposable or single use products, except when required by law.

In short, a growing acceptance by hotel establishments of measures that reduce their ecological footprint is essential in the path to a sustainable development. With the results of the three surveys it is clear that the vast majority of hotel enterprises are more focused on the rational use of energy (light bulbs) than in the efficient use of water (such as the use of lower quality water).

If we consider that Portugal is in the Mediterranean region, characterized by a water shortage aggravated during the summer months (which are also the busiest in terms of tourism), this is incomprehensible.

Aiming sustainability, we can say that this indicator had a positive evolution when comparing the results of the three surveys and the efforts made in the development of greater awareness through the publication of documents/guidelines for good environmental practices in the sector (AHRESP, 2011).

It is, however, crucial a tighter focus on raising awareness to reduce and manage the use of water, a resource that will be increasingly valuable.

Energy and Greenhouse Potential

Emissions of greenhouse gases, notably carbon dioxide, and the total energy consumption are two important indicators of the tourism impact on the environment. Unfortunately neither is mentioned in the national plan nor in its revision, showing some neglection on the environmental dimension of sustainability.

Figure 34 shows the growth rate of energy consumption (measured in gigajoules) in three sectors of the economy where tourism is more representative: accommodation, restaurants and travel agencies. These three areas are all compiled in the category "Tourism".

The data provided by the INE showed that the travel agencies sector was the only one of the three analyzed that showed negative growth rates. On the other hand, accommodation and restaurants rates have reached 9.63% and 6.8% growths, respectively.

Due to the results of these three sectors, tourism also has rates of energy consumption progressively larger. This trend would be expected. However, when comparing with the total consumption of the Portuguese economy (which has had negative growth rates since 2006), it appears that the results are not positive, which is possibly caused by a low efficiency and excessive consumption by the Tourism industry.

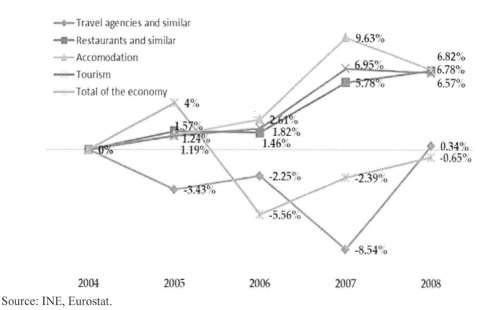

Source: INE, Eurostat.

Figure 34. Growth rates of total energy consumption in Portugal.

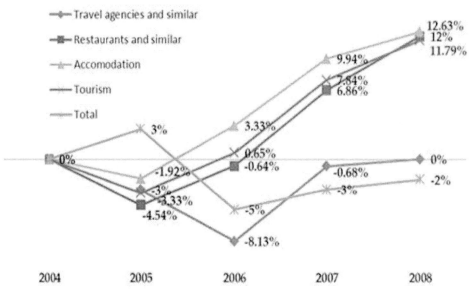

Source: INE, Eurostat.

Figure 35. Growth rates of the potential for greenhouse emission in Portugal.

The potential for greenhouse effect is an indicator that calculates the tons of carbon dioxide equivalent emissions in the various sectors of the economy. This indicator was based on a methodological document, the Manual for Air Emission Accounts (Eurostat, 2009).

The potential for greenhouse gas emissions showed a very similar pattern to what was registered for energy consumption, although growth rates are much higher. Again tourism doesn't have an evolution similar to the economy (Figure 35).

These results show a negative trend in the tourism sector when compared to the Portuguese economy. This may be related to low energy efficiency, lack of good management practices or over consumption. Whatever the cause, the truth is that a national strategy, which states concern about the sustainability of the industry, should take into account environmental impacts such as those analyzed in this indicator.

In short, both energy consumption and potential for greenhouse effect show growth rates that are negative for the goal of sustainability.

EMAS and ISO in Tourism

Green washing is, today, a practice more common than one would like. This concept is used when one can observe a business spending a significantly greater investment of time and money to advertise environmentally friendly practices, instead of actually using these resources to improve environmental practices.

It is, in essence, the use of public relations (including marketing) to deceptively promote the perception that the company's policies or products are environmentally sound (Lyon, 2011). For this reason it is important that consumers can distinguish between truly sustainable and "green-washers."

The lack of methods to promote sustainable management and to regulate the "green messages" in tourism has led to a large increase in voluntary certifications, codes of conduct and awards (Font, 2002). A certification is presented as an essential strategy to maintain and promote sustainable and economically interesting tourism.

In fact, with the globalization of markets and the growth of competition, the need and capacity to submit a proof of the fulfillment of specific requirements assumes an increasingly important role.

EMAS and ISO certification (14001 and 9001) are the two main environmental management tools that have been applied by a growing number of organizations, both national and international (APA, 2007). They allow a company: to demonstrate the organization's performance on the control and management of emissions, waste and wastewater; to optimized resource management strategy; to minimize the risk of environmental liability; to promote environmental awareness among its employees; and to improve their image with customers, partners and the general public (APCER, 2011; TUV, 2011).

Table 4. Touristic Businesses in Portugal with an EMAS certification and the correspondent time of renewal

Company	Date of certification
HTA – Terceira Mar Hotel	06-09-2010
HTA – Hotéis, Turismo e Animação dos Açores	05-10-2008
Melo, Baptista and Mota – Aparthotel do Mirante	25-11-2008
Aparthotel Mira Villas	11-08-2010
Imoareia – Investimentos Turísticos	29-11-2010

Source: European Comission – Environment.

Effective management of business activities environmental aspects including environmental protection, pollution prevention and legal compliance of the socio-economic needs, are some of the criteria evaluated by these certifications (SGS, 2011). It is therefore interesting to see how progress has been made on the number of touristic establishments with certifications that promote sustainability, such as EMAS and ISO.

For this indicator, contact was established with companies that are qualified to award these two certifications according to the Portuguese Institute of Certification (IPAC). The intention was to obtain data on the number of certified companies in the tourism sector and the date of certification (to be possible to perceive the evolution).

Although APCER, TUV, BV and LRQA granted a response to this request, unfortunately there is no database on certifications of this kind at a national level and the information kindly provided didn't include the dates requested. This made it impossible to analyze the progress made in the last 10 years.

Data showed that the number of companies certified with EMAS is a very small percentage of the total number in the sector (see Table 4).

Regarding ISO 14001 and 9001, despite its recognized importance for the promotion and development of tourism products, there is no national database that compiles statistics on these labels. SIDS in its environmental management and social responsibility indicator, counts the number of annual certifications under ISO 14001 (it should be noted that ISO 9001 is not considered) and EMAS. It would be very useful if there was an organized database that would allow the adaptation of this indicator to the tourism sector.

Despite the increase in the voluntary implementation of these instruments (in 2005 there were 499 companies certified to ISO 14001 and 19 with EMAS (APA, 2007), in the tourism sector it is not known how the evolution has been made, which is a relevant fact since this is an indicator that is so important to sustainability.

Employment in Tourism

Job creation is one of the biggest impacts of tourism on the local community (Tsaur et al., 2006), and it's even considered by many experts as a key indicator for assessing the sustainability of the sector (Miller, 2001).

Nationally, tourism has a truly strategic importance for the Portuguese economy, because of its ability to create wealth and employment. One of the objectives of the National Plan is to promote tourism so that it contributes positively to the economic development in order to represent 15% of national employment in 2015 (MEI, 2007).

The percentage of the tourism sector on the total employment in the country has been increasing over the years, but it is still too early to say whether the proposed targets are likely to be achieved (Figure 36).

With the exception of 2002, employability in the tourism sector has risen steadily in recent years. Although it is clear the positive development of employment related to tourism, it is appropriate to understand what is the relation with the evolution of the total number of jobs in the Portuguese economy. This comparison allows us to contextualize the data on figure 36 (see Figure 37).

In recent years, tourism activities have contributed positively to job creation, since they have shown higher growth rates than the overall economy, except in 2002.

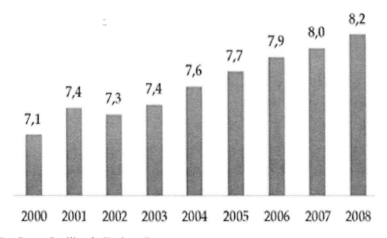

Source: "INE – Conta Satélite do Turismo".

Figure 36. Employability of the tourism sector in relation to the total of the economy (%).

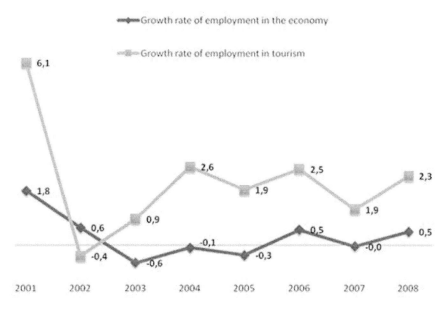

Source: "INE- Conta Satélite do Turismo".

Figure 37. Growth rate of employment in tourism and the economy (%).

Employment in tourism showed, since 2003, a more favorable evolution than in the overall economy (2.3% in 2008 compared to 0.5% of the economy). Therefore, the impact of tourism on employability has been very positive between 2001 and 2008, bringing some confidence for positive results in the following years. There are even predictions of a 1.8% increase in the direct contribution of tourism to employment in the year 2021 (WTTC, 2011).

Touristic Intensity

Tourism is an activity of strategic importance to Portugal, not only from an economic perspective, but also as a social and environmental dimension (MEI, 2007). Regardless of all the positive impacts that tourism can bring to a community, such as employment, income and international image, it can also generate economic, social and environmental imbalances. These impacts can, in the long-term, compromise the potential for generation of well-being and sustainable development.

According to the European Union's document *Environment and Tourism in the Context of Sustainable Development* (1993), touristic intensity is calculated by the ratio between the number of overnight stays (thousands) along the reference year in hotels and similar establishments (including campsites and youth hostels) and the number of residents (hundreds). According to this methodology:

- Sustainable Tourism: Touristic intensity <1.1
- Borderline Sustainable Tourism: 1.1 <Touristic intensity <1.5
- Unsustainable Tourism: 1.5 >Touristic intensity

The indicator "Touristic intensity" assesses the pressure intensity from tourists that stayed in the country. The country's overall value of 0.42 in 2010 was less than in 2007 and 2008 and it can be considered sustainable since it's below the limit (1.1).

However, when you focused on a regional analysis, such as shown in Figure 38, it is obvious that the limit of sustainability in some regions, particularly in the region of Madeira and the Algarve, was exceeded (with values greater than 2.0 and 3.4, respectively). High above the sustainable limit cited in the literature (1.6).

All other regions remained with fairly constant values over the past years. The "unsustainable" regions were the ones that had a bigger change; these values can be explained with the large decrease in tourist arrivals due to the international economic recession.

Nationally, it can be stated that the touristic intensity is not a point of concern since the limit of sustainability is at a comfortable distance. Unfortunately, two of the most important touristic regions of Portugal, Madeira and the Algarve, have values that in some years were more than twice the threshold of sustainability. The evolution over the years shows a decrease in these two regions. The reasons for this decline are easily explained and it can be predicted a recovery for the "normal" values with the passing of the economic crisis. Diversification for Portuguese tourism, through new products in different regions is a strategy that must be followed if we want to move towards a sustainable development of the sector (MEI, 2007).

For these reasons, the assessment of this indicator needs more time to fully understand the consequences of the economic crisis and the strategies of the national plan.

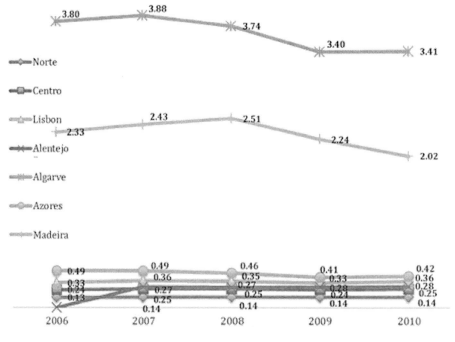

Source: "INE- Instituto Nacional de Estatística".

Figure 38. Touristic intensity by region, NUTS II.

CONCLUSION

Tourism is an important economic activity in most countries of the world and Portugal is no exception. Despite the major revenue and employment it provides, in recent years the social, environmental and economic impacts (positive and negative) have greatly increased.. We must therefore have some capacity to assess the impacts of these trends and variations in a sustainability perspective.

In recent years Portugal has focused its investment efforts on its great touristic potential. The investment in the tourism industry has been increasing, and in 2011, 10.5% of the total capital investment of the country went to tourism. This high percentage, which is above the world average (8.27%) or that of huge tourism power nations such as Spain (5.4%), France (3.03%) or the United Kingdom (3.88%), shows the effort that Portugal is doing to promote and develop the tourism (WTTC, 2011).

According to the WTTC, Portugal is well placed in the world rankings (always above the world average) regarding tourism contribution to national GDP or employability, but the expectations of future real growth place Portugal below the world average, which is symptomatic of a strategy or efficacy problem.

The importance of tourism in the Portuguese reality does not allow the stagnation in a state of lack of procedures to oversee the identification and management of economic, environmental and social development in the tourism sector. Hence, the proposal for a set of indicators as a system for the evaluation of touristic sustainability in Portugal is crucial.

Even taking into account the vagueness of the sustainable tourism concept and the discussion regarding the best methodology for its evaluation and monitoring, it is important to obtain some preliminary indicators that can be put into practice. This way, knowing that no group of indicators is perfect, since it implies trade-offs between the relevance of the indicator, the scientific validity of available data, measurement capability, ease of understanding and accessibility to its costs and time, it is nevertheless important to start this creative process.

The system proposed here consists of indicators referenced in other works of its kind and with applicability to the Portuguese reality. However, there was, in many cases, a lack of information on aspects that certainly would be important indicators, as is the case of water use in the tourism sector or the number of international tourist arrivals.

Tourism is an activity that aggregates several environmental, social and economic descriptors. For this reason, it has every advantage in having its characteristic activities measured by a composite index. This index will have its main vectors constituted by sustainability indicators as the ones showed above. Through its dissemination and discussion, this index, together with the measurement of sectorial performances, could provide an incentive for more sustainable practices as a means of promotion and dissemination of the most abiding.

REFERENCES

ABAE (2011). *Guia de Interpretação e Explicação do Programa "Chave Verde"*Lisboa: Associação Bandeira Azul da Europa.

ADEAC (2011). *Comunicado de prensa Bandera Azul 2011 en España.* Asociación de Educación Ambiental y del Consumidor.. Portal, 7.

AHRESP (2011). *Guia de boas práticas ambientais no sector Horeca.* Lisboa: Associação da Hotelaria Restauração e Similares de Portugal.

ANA, (2009). Aeroportos de Portugal. Relatório anual de tráfego. Lisboa: ANA - Aeroportos.

APA, (1999). *Relatório do estado do ambiente.* Lisboa: Agencia Portuguesa do Ambiente.

APA, (2007). *SIDS –sistema de Indicadores de Desenvolvimento Sustentável.* Lisboa: Agencia Portuguesa do Ambiente.

APCER,(2011). APCER - The certification´s brand. http://www.apcer.pt/intro/ index.html.

Mohonk Agreement (2000). *Proposal for an international certification program for sustainable tourism and ecotourism.* (I. for P. S. with support from the F. Foundation, Ed.) (pp. 97-100). New York: Mohonk Mountain House.

Amoah, V. A. (1997). Tourism education: policy versus practice. *International journal of Contemporary Hospitality Managment,* 5-12.

Australian Government (2009). National long-term tourism strategy. Canberra: Department of Resources and Tourism. Beni, M. C. (2002). *Análise estrutural do turismo.* 7ªed. Ed. São Paulo: SENAC.

Brazil Ministry of Tourism (2007). *Brazil - National Tourism Plan 2007-2010 - A journey Towards Inclusion.* Brasilia: Brazil Ministry of Tourism.

Butler, R. W. (1980). The concept of a tourist area cycle of evolution: Implications for managment of resources. *The Canadian Geographer/Le Géographe canadien,* 24(1), 5-12.

Butler, R. W. (1998). Sustainable tourism - Looking backwards in order to progress. In C. M. Hall M. and A. A. Lew (Eds.), *Sustainable tourism : A geographical perspective* (pp. 25-34). Harlow: Longmsan.

Butler, R. W. (1999). Sustainable tourism : A state of the art review. *Tourism Geographies,* 1(1), 7-25.

CHL, (2002). Tanzania Tourism Master Plan Strategy and Actions. Components. Dublin: CHL Consulting Group.

CST, (2009). Conta satélite do turismo. O turismo na Economia. Indicadores de actividade turística e económica em Portugal 2000-2009. Lisboa: Instituto Nacional de Estatística.

Choi, H., and Sirakaya, E. (2006). Sustainability indicators for managing community tourism. *Tourism Management, 27(6),* 1274-1289.

Cooper, C. (2008). Tourism: principles and practice. Harlow: Pearson Education.

Cordeiro, I. J. D. (2008). *Instrumentos de avaliação da sustentabilidade do turismo: Uma análise critica.* Ms Thesis. Lisboa: Universidade Nova de Lisboa.

Cunha, L. (2009). Turismo: "Coragem para agir". Lisboa: Universidade Lusófona.

DCMS, (2005). *National sustainable tourism indicators.* London: Department for Culture Media and Sport.

DEFRA, (2009).. *Sustainable development indicators in your pocket 2009.* London: Department for Environment Food and Rural Affairs.

Dahl, A. L. (1997). The big picture: comprehensive approaches. In B. Moldan and E. Bilharz (Eds.), *Sustainability Indicators: report of the project on indicators of sustainable development* (69-83). Chichester: John Wiley and Sons.

Daniel, A. C. M. (2010). Caracterização do sector turístico em Portugal. *Review literature and arts of the Americas, VIII*, 255-276.

Demunter, C. (2008). Are recent evolutions in tourism compatible with sustainable development? *Statistics in focus, 1/2005*, 1-7.

Dobruszkes, F. (2006). An analysis of European low-cost airlines and their networks. *Journal of Transport Geography*, 14(4), 249-264.

European Communities, (2006a). *Methodological work on measuring the sustainable development of tourism. Part 1: Technical report*. Luxembourg: European Communities.

European Communities (2006b). *Methodological work on measuring the sustainable development of tourism. Part 2: Manual on sustainable development indicators*. Luxembourg: European Communities.

Eurostat, E. C. (2009). *Manual for Air Emissions Accounts 2009*. Luxembourg: European Communities.

FEE, (2007).. *The blue flag - Eco-label for beaches and marinas*. Copenhagen: The Foundation for Environmental Education.

FEE, (2011a). *The Green Key FAQ*. The Foundation for Environmental Education. Accessed online: http://www.green-key.org/.

FEE, (2011b). *Blue Flag Beach Criteria*. Copenhagen: The Foundation for Environmental Education.

Farsari, Y., and Prastacos, P. (2001). Sustainable tourism indicators for Mediterranean established destinations. *Tourism today*, 1-27.

Ferreira, M. P. (2008). Análise dos modelos de indicadores no contexto do desenvolvimento sustentável. *Revista Electronica de Ciencias Sociais Aplicadas, 3(1)*, 17.

Font, X. (2002). Environmental certification in tourism and hospitality: progress , process and prospects. *Tourism Managment, 23*, 197-205.

Gallopín, G. C. (1996). Environmental and sustainability indicators and the concept of situational indicators. A systems approach. *Environmental Modeling and Assessment, 1(3)*, 101-117.

Gasparatos, A, Elharam, M. and Horner, M. (2008). A critical review of reductionist approaches for assessing the progress towards sustainability. *Environmental Impact Assessment Review, 28(4-5)*, 286-311.

Hall, C. M. (2008). Tourism planning: policies, *processes and relationships*. Harlow: Prentice Hall.

Hanai, F. Y. (2009). *Sistema de indicadores de sustentabilidade: uma aplicação ao contexto de desenvolvimento do turismo na região de Bueno Brandão, Estado de Minas Gerais, Brasil*. PhD Thesis. São Carlos: Universidade de São Paulo.

Hardy, A. L., and Beeton, R. J. S. (2011). Sustainable tourism or maintainable tourism: Managing resources for more than average outcomes. *Journal of Sustainable Tourism, 9(3)*, 168-192.

ICS The Green Key, (2010). *International Baseline Criteria for the Green Key. Baseline*. Vol. 6. Copenhagen: The Foundation for Environmental Education.

IEFP (2010). *Estatisticas de Emprego Mensais*. Lisboa: Instituto do Emprego e Formação Profissional.

IMF, (2009). *World Economic Outlook: Crisis and Recovery, April 2009*. Washington, DC: International Monetary Fund.

INE, (2009). *Estatísticas do Turismo 2009*. Lisboa: Instituto Nacional de Estatistica.

INE, (2010). *Estatísticas do Turismo 2010*. Lisboa: Instituto Nacional de Estatistica.

Jenkins, C. L. (2006). Tourism development: Policy, planning and implementation issues in developing countries. Department of Geography occasional paper #20. Waterloo: University of Waterloo.

Ko, J. (2001). Assessing progress of tourism sustainability. *Annals of Tourism Research, 28(3)*, 817-820.

Ko, T. (2005). Development of a tourism sustainability assessment procedure: a conceptual approach. *Tourism Management, 26(3)*, 431–445.

Lyon, T. P. (2011). Greenwash: Corporate environmental disclosure under threat of audit. *Journal of Economics and Managment Strategy, 20(1)*, 3-41.

MEI, (2007). Plano Estratégico Nacional do Turismo (PENT). Lisboa: Ministério da Economia e Inovação..

McKenna, J., , Williams, A. T. and Cooper, J.A. G. (2010). Blue flag or red herring: Do beach awards encourage the public to visit beaches? *Tourism Management, 32(3)*, 576–588.

Meadows, D. (1998). *Indicators and information systems for sustainable*. Lynedoch: Sustainability Institute .

Micallef, A. and Williams, A. (2004). Application of a novel approach to beach classification in the Maltese Islands. *Ocean and Coastal Management, 47(5-6)*, 225-242.

Miller, G. (2001). The development of indicators for sustainable tourism: results of a Delphi survey of tourism researchers. *Tourism Management, 22(4)*, 351-362.

Ministerio de Industria, Energía y Turismo de España (2007). *Turismo 2020- Plan del Turismo Español Horizonte 2020*. Madrid: Ministerio de Industria, Energía y Turismo de España.

Ministry of Tourism of Turkey (2007). *Tourism strategy of Turkey - 2023*. Culture. Ankara: Ministry of Tourism of Turkey.

Mota, I. A. (2005). *Estratégia nacional para o desenvolvimento sustentável, ENDS. Economia*. Lisboa: Ministério do Ambiente e do Ordenamento do Território.

Mowforth, M., and Munt, I. (2003). *Tourism and sustainability: New tourism in the third world*. London: Routledge.

Nelson, C., and Botterill, D. (2002). Evaluating the contribution of beach quality awards to the local tourism industry in Wales — the Green Coast Award. *Ocean and Coastal Management, 45*, 157-170.

Notarstefano, C. (2008). European sustainable tourism: context, concepts and guidelines for action. *International Journal of Sustainable Economy, 1(1)*, 44.

Organización Mundial do Turismo (2005). *Indicators de desarrollo sostenible*. Madrid: Organización Mundial do Turismo.

Rebollo, J. F. V. (2004). Indicadores de sostenibilidad para destinos maduros: balance y propuestas de aplicación. Oral presentation in the Organización Mundial de Turismo conference *"Creando Estructuras para la Investigación y la Educación en Política Turística y Gestión de Destinos"*, Madrid, 2-3 july..

Rebollo, J. F. V., and Baidal, J. A. I. (2003). Measuring sustainability in a mass tourist destination: Pressures, perceptions and policy responses in Torrevieja, Spain. *Journal of Sustainable Tourism, 11(2-3)*, 181-203.

SGS,(2011). SGS in Portugal. Société Générale de Surveillance. Accessed online: http://www.pt.sgs.com/.

Saarinen, J. (2006). Traditions of sustainability in tourism studies. *Annals of Tourism Research, 33(4)*, 1121-1140.

Seguro, P. (2006). Boas práticas ambientais nos establecimentos hoteleiros.FALTA O RESTO DA REFERªENCIA

SIET-MAC (2005*). Sistema de indicadores de sustentabilidade do turismo da macaronésia 2000-2005*. Funchal: Direcção Regional de Estatística da Madeira.

TUV (2011). TÜV Rheinland Portugal. Accessed online: http://www.tuv.pt/.

Tsaur, S., Lin, Y., and Lin, J. (2006). Evaluating ecotourism sustainability from the integrated perspective of resource, community and tourism. *Tourism Management, 27(4)*, 640-653.

Turismo de Portugal (2008). *Relatório de Sustentabilidade*. Lisboa: Turismo de Portugal.

Turismo de Portugal (2009a). *Listagem de cursos e escolas reconhecidos ou homologados pelo Turismo de Portugal, I.P* Lisboa: Turismo de Portugal.

Turismo de Portugal (2009b). *Anuário das estatísticas do turismo*. Lisboa: Turismo de Portugal.

Turismo de Portugal (2011). Plano Estratégico Nacional do Turismo - Propostas para revisão no horizonte 2015 – versão 2.0. Lisboa: Turismo de Portugal.

UNWTO (2009). *Tourism highlights 2009*. Madrid: World Tourism Organization UNWTO.

UNWTO, (2010). *Tourism Highlights 2010*. Madrid: World Tourism Organization UNWTO.

UNWTO, (2011). *Tourism Highlights 2011*. Madrid: World Tourism Organization UNWTO.

Valentin, A., and Spangenberg, J. H. (2000). A guide to community sustainability indicators. *Environmental Impact Assessment Review, 20*, 381-392.

Van-Bellen, H. M. (2005). *Indicadores de sustentabilidade: uma análise comparativa*. Rio de Janeiro: FGV Editora.

Viegas, M. M. A. (2008). Práticas ambientais no sector Hoteleiro do algarve. *dosAlgarves, 17*, 31-37.

WTTC (2009). *Progress and priorities 2009-10. Environment* London: World Travel and Tourism Council. .

WTTC (2011). *Travel and tourism economic impact 2011 - PORTUGAL*. London: World Travel and Tourism Council.

WTTC (1993). *Agenda 21 - Para a indústria de viagens e turismo*. London: World Travel and Tourism Council.

WWF-UK,(2002). *Holiday Footprinting*. Surrey: WWF.

Weaver, D., and Lawton, L. (2002). *Tourism management*. John Wiley and Sons: Pacific Book House.

INDEX

D

T

TAP, 137
target, 4, 8, 12, 19, 65, 70, 109, 119, 141
techniques, 41, 49, 71, 95
technological developments, 119, 120
technologies, 17, 24
technology, 37, 76, 120
temperature, 28
territorial, 37, 100, 112
territory, 16, 33, 35, 37, 39, 41, 50, 56, 57, 69, 70,
    81, 97, 121, 149
terrorism, 98
Thailand, 27
threats, 91, 98, 101
time periods, 68
total energy, 153
total revenue, 2, 16, 97, 125, 134
trade, 98, 119, 159
traditions, 37, 83, 111, 124
training, 21, 115, 125, 131
transactions, 99, 145
transformation, 99
transport, 4, 39, 65, 107, 136
transportation, 21, 120, 145
treatment, 37, 73, 107
tropical rainforests, 2
Turkey, 17, 117, 122, 162
turtle, 90
Type I error, 86

U

unemployment rate, 147
UNESCO, 17, 37, 47
United Kingdom (UK), 2, 29, 58, 59, 60, 61, 64, 66,
    120, 133, 134, 135, 136, 159, 163
United Nations (UN), 17, 31, 101
United States (USA), 3, 5, 20, 30, 77, 80, 93, 97,
    133, 134, 135universities, 37
urban, 34, 37, 39, 41, 42, 45, 51, 52, 62, 64, 65, 69,
    80, 82, 83, 85, 90, 91, 102, 111, 126
urban areas, 45, 80, 82, 83, 85, 91
urban settlement, 102
urbanization, 66, 82
USDA, 70

V

valuation, 75, 93, 94
variables, 85, 86, 87, 88, 89, 121, 123, 136
variations, 139, 159
vegetation, 68
vehicles, 99
vessels, 4, 5, 10, 18, 22, 96, 97, 98, 99, 100, 105,
    106, 108, 109, 110, 114, 115
vision, 4, 5, 57, 75

W

Wales, 162
Washington, 27, 53, 77, 78, 162
waste, 23, 101, 105, 106, 107, 128, 151, 155
waste disposal, 106
waste management, 107
waste water, 101, 106
wastewater, 62, 64, 71, 73, 76, 155
water, viii, 17, 21, 49, 55, 56, 57, 62, 64, 65, 68, 70,
    71, 72, 73, 75, 76, 77, 96, 97, 100, 101, 102, 103,
    104, 107, 109, 128, 130, 149, 151, 152, 153, 159
water quality, 130
water resources, 55, 68, 71, 75, 76
water supplies, 149
waterways, 96
wealth, 19, 123, 156
web, 41, 46
well-being, 6, 34, 41, 157
wellness, 22
wetlands, 15
whales, 5, 8, 9, 12, 13, 14, 15, 18, 26, 27, 28, 29, 31
whale-watching, 1, 2, 3, 4, 5, 6, 7, 8, 9, 10, 12, 15,
    16, 17, 18, 19, 20, 21, 22, 23, 24, 25, 26, 27, 30
wildlife, vii, 1, 2, 28, 80, 82, 92
working conditions, 20
World Bank, 31, 142

Y

yield, vii, 113
Yugoslavia, 117